Pale Girl SPEAKS

A Year Uncovered

HILLARY FOGELSON

D1052884

SEAL PRESS

PALE GIRL SPEAKS
A Year Uncovered

Copyright © 2012 by Hillary Fogelson

Published by
Seal Press
A Member of the Perseus Books Group
1700 Fourth Street
Berkeley, California

All rights reserved. No part of this book may be reproduced or transmitted in any form without written permission from the publisher, except by reviewers who may quote brief excerpts in connection with a review.

Library of Congress Cataloging-in-Publication Data

Fogelson, Hillary.
Pale girl speaks : a memoir / Hillary Fogelson.
p. cm.
ISBN 978-1-58005-444-7
1. Fogelson, Hillary. 2. Fogelson, Hillary—Health. 3.
Melanoma—Patients—California—Biography. 4.
Skin—Cancer—Patients—California—Biography. 5. Cancer—Psychological aspects—Case studies. 6. Cancer—Patients—Family relationships—Case studies. I. Title.
RC280.M37F64 2012
616.99'4770092—dc23
[B]
2012003840

10 9 8 7 6 5 4 3 2 1

Cover and interior design by Domini Dragoone
Printed in the United States of America
Distributed by Publishers Group West

For Dr. Bach, Randy,
and Sherry

Contents

Introduction

_____

I always thought I was adopted. Strangely, there were no Polaroids of my birth. My supposed hospital baby picture looks more like an Asian boy than anything else, and by the age of thirteen, I shamelessly towered over my mother by a solid five inches. Her brown hair and olive complexion just barely reached the bottom of my white, white chin. The evidence was overwhelming . . .

And so I often dreamed of what my *real* parents were like. I wondered who gave me my carrot orange hair and translucent skin. I questioned why they gave me up, and I always hoped they were looking for me. Because, of course, I was looking for them. I remember tailing red-haired women in the supermarket, hoping they might turn around and recognize me as their long-lost loved one. I imagined tearful reunions and heart-wrenching goodbyes. It was all very dramatic. The stories became more and more elaborate over the years.

I eventually drew family trees and lined the branches with people who looked just like me. Every member could have easily been mistaken for an albino, or an anemic, or, as it turns out, someone with melanoma. But back then, they were beautiful—at least, they were to me.

And so I played out this fantasy, month after month, year after year, right up until I turned fourteen. At fourteen, my fine features finally made their way into a face so closely resembling my father's, it was scary: high forehead; pronounced brow; small, pursed mouth; and the inevitable short, short upper lip—a family trademark. By fifteen I could pull my hair back and image how my father must have looked at the very same age. Kinda eerie.

And so I guess it all should have been clear back then. It was in the cards for me: a lackluster complexion mixed with years of glaring abuse. I should have seen it coming. And yet I sat, passive and unaware, wonderfully oblivious to the obnoxious endgame. Life slowly burned and poisoned me as I sat idly by, twiddling my thumbs and sucking down gin and tonics. Ah, to be young. To be clueless.

To be . . . free.

And So It Began

I have two hours before my mother arrives from Ohio for a visit. Two hours before her rental car peeks its turquoise nose around the bend of my Hollywood Hills street. Two hours and counting before she trots up my front steps, throws open my front door, and spots something she needs to clean. I've been having hot flashes all morning as I scrub toilets and wash molding. Hot flashes, flashbacks, backaches. And I can't stop sweating. My mind is flooded with the memory of my mother spotting a ball of pubic hair in the corner of my New York apartment bathroom and using it as a point of reference for the rest of her Big Apple visit—"Honey, my filet is about the same size as that hairball of yours . . . " Shit, one hour fifty-eight minutes. Okay okay *okay* . . . left to do: a list.

1. Wash windows around front door (both inside and out)
2. Sweep stairs leading to front door (want her to have a debris-free walk to house)
3. Swiffer hardwood floors
4. Mop hardwood floors (if time permits)

5. Arrange fresh flowers in guest bedroom
6. Final Swiffer of floors (to be done two minutes before
she arrives)
7. Shower (I smell)

Shit. Fuck. Deep breath and . . . go.

The mother figure is en route, on her way, gettin' kinda close. Okay, most of the "to do" list is complete, with the exception of sweeping the outside stairs, but I can't be held accountable for the untidiness of nature. I guess I could use that argument for the accumulation of hairballs and dust, along with the collection of some undeterminable substance in all my outdoor votives. Anyway, the house is as good as it gets—oh, that makes me think of Helen Hunt. I love her.

Ring, ring.

Shit. Mom is lost. She is most definitely lost . . . I'm coming, I'm coming. Jesuschrist, already. (That's right—"Jesuschrist": one word. A statement, really. The end-all, be-all, and "enough said" of curse words. Usages range from the perfect expletive when one stubs one's toe to the necessary precursor of the much-loved statement "[ ], can't you see I'm trying to sleep?" And in my house growing up, it was the word of choice. "Jesuschrist" has power. Even more so than "fuck" or "shit" or even, dare I whisper it, "shut up." Our house would not have been the same without my father using the famed word at least five times between the time he got home from work and bedtime.)

Ring, ring.

I'm coming. I'm coming.

Me: Hello, Mom?
Other: No, is Hillary there?
Me: Yeah, this is Hillary.
Other: Oh, hello, it's Dr. Bach.

Me:

Other: . . . your dermatologist.

Me: Of course, sorry, I didn't recognize your voice.

Dr. Bach: I didn't recognize yours either. I'm actually away from the office, but I wanted to give you a call. I got the pathology back from the mole I biopsied from your stomach two weeks ago—

Me: Oh yeah, I forgot about that—

Dr. Bach: I wanted to call you right away because the mole is malignant.

Me: What . . . what do you mean?

Dr. Bach: It's a malignant melanoma.

Me: Like, skin cancer? Melanoma? Is that the bad one?

Dr. Bach: Well, yes, it's the most serious form of skin cancer. I'm sure you have a lot of questions. I'm actually on vacation, but I went ahead and called the surgical oncologist I recommend to my cancer patients and made an appointment for you for tomorrow morning for a consultation. I would like you to have surgery as soon as possible. The surgeon's secretary thought he might be able to squeeze you in Monday morning.

Me: Um . . .

Dr. Bach: I know this is a lot to try and take in. I'm so sorry. I really am. I want you to know that we caught this early and your odds of a full recovery are very good. Do you have any questions you might want to ask me now?

Me: Um, no—I'm sorry. I just need a second. Um, you want me to meet with a surgeon tomorrow?

Dr. Bach: That's right. It's best to move quickly. I don't want to scare you, but—I recommend surgery as soon as possible.

Me: . . . and so I have surgery to remove what? I thought you removed the mole when you biopsied it.

Dr. Bach: I didn't get it all, and depending on the size and depth of the mole, there must be a margin of skin excised around the mole in order to guarantee all the cancer cells have been removed. You have to understand that melanoma can spread very quickly once it has penetrated the dermis, because—

Me: But *my* mole didn't, right? Mine didn't, um, go into my dermis.

Dr. Bach: Yes, it did, but we still caught it early—

Me: Uh-huh, but spread where?

Dr. Bach: . . . to your lymph nodes.

Me:

Dr. Bach: Dr. Gregory will be better able to answer all your questions. I'm going to connect you to the surgeon's receptionist. He'll tell you everything you need to know about tomorrow.

Me: Okay . . . yeah, ok.

Dr. Bach: I'll talk with you soon.

Click.

Ring, ring.

Other: John Wayne Cancer Institute.

Me:

Other: Hel-lo?

Me: Uh, yes, um, my dermatologist told me to call. I think I have an appointment set up for tomorrow—

Other: Which doctor?

Me: Oh, I don't know. My dermatologist scheduled the appointment and—

Other: Name?

Me: Bach. Jovanka Bach.

Other: I don't see any appointment here for a Jovanka.

Me: No, I thought you wanted my dermatologist's name.

Other: What's your name?

Me: Hillary.

Other: I'm going to need your last name.

Me: I'm sorry. Fogelson. *F* as in "Frank," *o-g-e—*

Other: I've got you down with Dr. Gregory for tomorrow morning at ten forty-five. You know where St. John's Hospital is?

Me: Yes.

Other: Come in the main entrance and take the west elevators to the cancer institute on the third fl—*ring, ring.* John Wayne Cancer Institu— *Click.*

I can't stop gripping the phone. For the first time in my life, my brain and fingers aren't cooperating. Maybe I'll just walk around a little bit, holding the phone. Or maybe I'll sit right here where I am. Yeah, sitting is good. No, I need to stand. Standing might help. Okay okay okay. Breathe in, then out. I'm dizzy. My lips are numb, and my heart is pounding out of my chest cavity. I'm having a heart attack. I may very well be having a heart attack. Great—"Woman with 'good' chance of recovery dies of heart attack upon hearing melanoma diagnosis, phone in hand . . . " I am sweating. My face is really sweating. No, I'm crying. I am crying the biggest and fastest tears ever. I've never seen tears like these tears. I'm Alice in Wonderland, drowning in a pool of tears. I could win some award, maybe, for these tears. I should get a picture of these bad boys. I need to cry for just a second . . . okay, no, wait . . . okay. Call husband. That's easy, since I'm still holding the phone.

Me: Is Adam there?

Adam's assistant: I think he's down the hall in Jim's office . . . oh, wait, here he is.

Adam: Hey, babe, what's up?

Me: Um . . .

Adam: Are you crying? Tell me what's wrong. What happened? Are you okay?

Me: I just talked to Dr. Bach . . . she says . . . she says that that mole she biopsied, the one on my stomach, is melanoma and I need surgery immediately . . . I—

Adam: What? What do you mean?

Me: The mole. The mole she removed a couple of weeks ago. It was malignant. The mole was malignant. Cancer. Dr. Bach said "cancer."

Adam: I'm coming home.

Me: No, no don't.

Adam: I'm leaving right now. I'll be home in—

Me: No, wait. You don't need to come home . . . oh, shit, it's the other line. It's probably Mom. I'm sure she's lost. Hold on—hi, Mom?

Mom: Honey, did you say a right on Hollywood Boulevard, because I—

Me: No, a left. Left *then* an immediate right. Just keep heading uphill. If you're going downhill, you're going the wrong way.

Mom: Left *then* right. Oh, okay. Are you okay, honey? You sound weird, sweetie.

Me: Mom, I have Adam on the other line. I'll see you when you get here. Adam? . . . Hello? . . . Shit.

He's on his way. She's on her way. The whole fucking world is on their way to my house, and I have cancer. I have cancer I have cancer I have cancer. I need to say it one more time. I have cancer. I feel like Chevy Chase before he jumps into the swimming pool with Christy Brinkley. This is crazy this is crazy this is crazy. Okay. I'm just going to sit here in my den with my dog at my feet—licking my feet—and wait . . . it's that word that's bothering me so much. The one Dr. Bach used. The one . . . ya know, the "c"-word. When I think of "that word," an old person springs to mind, with yellow skin, hollowed-out eyes, brown teeth, and a cough that sounds sick enough to hack up several pieces of lung. But that's not me. That's not even *close* to me. I'm young and healthy. I use whitening strips regularly, and my skin, albeit pale, has a rosy undertone. And yes, I admit I have the occasional nervous cough, but nothing deep or hacking or mucus-producing.

"That word" always seemed fairly easy to say when I'd used it in stories about other people. Stories about *older* people. It used to slip out, flow freely, along with a whole slew of nouns and adjectives. It was just another word. It's just another word when you're talking about someone else. But now, I don't have . . . that word. I just can't.

It's so weird. I'm sitting here on my couch and everything around me looks the same as always. Same coffee table, same TV, same light coming through the same French doors hitting the Berber carpet in the same old way, yet I feel like everything is so completely different. I am completely different. I feel like a completely different person than I did ten minutes ago. Shit. Fuck. Motherfucker. I am totally freaking myself out right now. I need to breathe. Need to focus on my breath. In . . . two, three, four . . . out . . . two, three, four. Okay, now I'm really light-headed.

Mom is right outside the front door. I can hear her panting, her body ready and in wait. A bundle of raw nerves set to burst the moment her size 5½ feet hit my recently swiffered hardwood floors. A modern-day June Cleaver on speed. Carol Brady with a perverted sense of humor and a southern drawl. She's passive-aggressive in the way all great mothers are: She can compliment and criticize all in the same breath. She's often distracted, walking into rooms and then immediately forgetting what she wanted to get in the first place. She can remember neither movie titles nor actors' names, and yet she insists on asking if I've seen "*that* movie. You *know*, the one with *that* actor. You know who I'm talking about; he has a *brother* who was in that movie that you just saw." I have never seen her drink a hot cup of coffee or finish putting on her mascara in any place other than the car. She makes the world's best carrot cake, assuming she hasn't left out some vital ingredient—like sugar. She can clean a house like no other. And she is a giver, through and through. The kind of mother I aspire to be. She is selfless. She would do anything for all of her children. And she has given everything, all of herself, for all of these years, to all three of us . . . and she is currently jumping up and down, desperately trying to peek in the upper panes of my front door, her coarse, dyed blond hair floating in and out of frame. I hate to let her in. I hate to let her into my world right now, into my "new" life, this new existence. I'll just pretend I've gone out . . . *knock . . . knock . . . knock, knock, knock, KNOCKKNOCK.* Okay. Be strong and smile . . .

Me: Hey, sorry, I didn't hear the door. I was—

Mom: Hi, honey. Your garden looks beauti—oh, the house smells so good. You've been slaving away on your hands and knees all morning, haven't you?

Me: No, not really. I—

Mom: Are these the new chairs you were waiting for? They must have cost a fortune. The leather is so soft. Oh, the life you lead. Your father and I sat on egg crates in our first house. I hope you realize how lucky you are to—

Me: Yeah, Mom, I know—

Mom: So many people never get to live like this. Never in their whole life. You are so fortunate.

Me: Yeah, well . . . let me take your bags. I have you set up in this room here. I cleared—

Mom: I think I hear . . . is that Adam? He's home for lunch? He's so lucky he has time to do that. Your father worked so hard, he never had time for a lunch break.

Me: I remember. Hey, honey . . .

Adam: It's going to be okay. Shh-shh-shh. I'm not going to let anything happen to . . . I'm . . .

Me: It's okay . . . I'm okay.

Adam: Honey, you're shaking.

Mom: What's going—

Me: Mom, why don't we all go sit down in the kitchen . . .

I told her. I told her everything. Everything I know. Which isn't much. The few tidbits of disturbing information. The unfinished CliffsNotes version. I kept it short and precise and told her I was going to be okay, even though I'm not so sure myself. I did my damnedest to hide my fear and calm the sudden twitch that had started in my upper eyelid. I told her everything a child never wants to have to tell a parent. And at first she was strong. And then . . . well . . . she wasn't.

What Dreams May Come

I'm on the beach right now. I'm lying on a black towel. I see cigarette butts and beer cans mixed in with the sand, like a bag of Chex Mix. It is so freakin' hot. I look up at the sky and it's too bright to see anything. I shade my face with my hand, but it's too bright. I am blinded. I reach over to grab sunscreen, and I can't find it. The bottle is gone. I'm searching frantically for the sunscreen, and I can feel the heat of the sun scorching my skin. Sunscreen . . . I need my sunscreen . . . I roll from one side to the other, looking for it. I feel like a piece of bacon frying in the microwave . . . I am a piece of bacon. I can smell myself cooking, bubbling and cracking under the heat of the giant light. I look to my right and see that the people next to me have turned into sausage links and they are frying in the sun, too . . . *beep, beep* . . . *beep, beep* . . . what the . . . Jesuschrist . . .

The Sweet Smell of . . . Hospitals

I am standing in the elevator with my mom, Adam, and a man who appears to be older than God. He looks like he was run over by a Mack truck, scraped up off the cement, and then propped up in the elevator like some discarded Muppet. I've just decided: I don't want to get old.

What is that smell? The air is thick with it, whatever it is. A disturbing combination of solvents, bodily fluids, and "old." For the love of all things holy, get me out of here. I want to jump out of my skin. I want to jump out of my skin, scramble to the nearest exit, and run like bloody hell as fast and as far as I can go. I hate hospitals. There's something so unsettling about them. Maybe it's that they remind me that sickness is out there, just waiting for me to "catch" it. Hospitals are full of all the things I spend time trying desperately to forget. Sickness. Old age. Death. The air is so stale. Stagnant. I breathe in, deep, my lungs stretching for oxygen, but instead I end up with a mouthful of carbon dioxide and a musty fart.

Me: Hi, is this the sign-in for Dr. Gregory?
Receptionist: Yes. Oh, but the patient needs to sign in for him- or herself.

Me: Oh . . . um . . . wait . . . I *am* the patient.

Receptionist: *You* are the patient?

Me: Right.

Receptionist: *You* are.

Me: *I* am.

Receptionist: Okay, then. Sorry. I mean, sorry for the mix-up.

Me: Not a problem. *It's not like I'm in a particularly vulnerable state right now or anything. It's not like I have cancer or anything . . . asshole.*

The real question: How cold can a patient room get? Hospitals must have thermostats that read 80 70 60 50 room temperature. I may very well lose toes on this visit. I have to fill out a medical-history report that the nurse just gave me. Let's see . . . this is not so bad. This packet is only . . . um . . . uh . . . twenty-five pages front . . . and . . . back. I'm so glad they didn't have me strip just yet, since it's going to take the better part of a year to fill out this motherfucker. Oh, wait, I'm already in my fucking birthday suit with a hospital gown the size of a . . . *Name? Address? Insurance info? Past surgical procedures? Family medical history?* . . . yada yada yada . . . *Miscellaneous complaints?* Complaints about what? Life? Love? Chest size? What? I'm just writing "too many to list."

Waiting. The waiting is killing us all. Mom, Adam, and I are still in this ten-by-ten-foot hospital room . . . waiting. Waiting for what? No one really knows. We've been making jokes to pass the time. Mom joked that on the prescription-medicine portion of my packet I should list all the drugs my grandmother takes, just for shits and giggles. (Aspirin, Gleevec, Fenesin, Ipratropium Bromide, Mucosil-20, Nuprin, Valium, Vicodin, Vioxx . . .)

Knock. knock.

The Doc: Hi. I'm Dr. Gregory. Nice to meet you.

Me: Nice to meet you.

This man, my surgeon, the person who will be removing skin from my stomach, looks like he's just stumbled out of a fraternity party, bought a pack of smokes at 7-Eleven, forgotten where he was supposed to go next, and wound up at a hospital (not knowing how or when he'd changed into a pair of scrubs). His hair is pulled back into a messy ponytail. His belly is big and is hanging over his pants, making the waist fold over onto itself. His teeth are large and yellow, coffee-stained from years of late-night study sessions. His handshake is crushing. But . . . his smile and voice are warm and instantly inviting, and his eyes sparkle. I can't help but immediately fall in love with him.

The Doc: So, let's get a look at you. Okay . . . uh-huh . . . lymph nodes under your arms feel normal. Let's check your neck . . . okay . . . everything feels normal here. Now, if you could just lie on your back, I'm going to . . .

Me: Whoa.

The Doc: . . . check the nodes in your groin.

Adam: I bet you say that to all the ladies.

The Doc: Those feel good too. So, let me tell you what's going to happen during the surgery, and then you can ask questions. Based on the depth and width of your melanoma, I will be removing an elliptical-shaped portion of skin approximately three and a half inches long, two inches wide. The skin above and below the incision will then be pulled together so you will have a single-line scar. I will remove tissue down to the layer of fat. You will have several layers of stitches. We will biopsy, *blah blah blah* . . . clear margins. We should receive the pathology, *blah blah* . . . *blah blah blah*. I don't think I need to remove *blah blah blah*, but I want to *blah blah* before making a *blah*. Lastly, you have an option when it comes to *blah blah blah blah blah blah blah blah blah. Blah blah.* You decide. So, what do you want to know?

Me: *Why am I so scared?*

Doc: Hillary?

Me: Huh? Um . . . yeah, could you repeat that last part?

Doc: What, the incision part?

Me: No, after that. Something about—

Doc: The scar?

Me: No. I got that. At the end.

Doc: The layer-of-fat part?

Me: No. At the very end. Something about having to decide something.

Doc: Right. Whether you want general anesthesia or local plus a sedative.

Me: What's the downside to the local and sedative?

Doc: Well, technically, with the local, you're awake during the procedure, so—

Me: General. I want the general. I don't want to experience a fucking—I mean, a second—of this thing.

Doc: What I was going to say was that while you are theoretically awake, you won't remember anything.

Me: Nothing?

Doc: Nothing.

Mom: Will she have less nausea with the local versus the general?

Me: *My mother only asked that question so she could use the word "nausea." "Nausea," "effeminate," "annual" (meaning, a yearbook)—to me, these words are like nails on a chalkboard and they are some of her favorites. They roll off my mother's southern tongue like water off a duck's back—"Looking at his high school annual, the effeminate teen felt a wave of nausea." Just kill me now.*

Doc: With a local and sedative, she shouldn't have any nausea.

Mom: Honey, no nausea. That sounds—

Me: Mom, the melanoma hasn't affected my hearing. Okay, I'll go with the local.

Doc: Great. So, any other questions right now?

Adam: Um . . .

Mom: Uh . . .

Me:

Doc: Well, I guess I'll see you bright and early on Monday. The nurse will go over our pain-management packet with you and she'll explain all the aftercare for the incision. Okay, well, it was nice to meet all of you, and I'll see you Monday.

Me: Thank you.

Mom: Did he seem effeminate to you?

Operation "Cancer Removal"

I just want this fucking thing out of me . . . couldn't sleep last night. Kept feeling my stomach. Touching it. The spot. The "bad" spot. I don't feel sick. I don't look sick. Well, no sicker than usual. I don't act sick . . . no sicker than usual.

I'm in my sweats, just like the nurse suggested. She said no makeup, but I'm wearing mascara. I mean, really. Who are they kidding . . . "News Flash: Woman dies on operating table. Investigators looking into possible mascara contamination." She said no deodorant, so, on top of everything else, I can smell like ass when I get out of surgery. And no hair products (just to add to the overall freakishness of the event). I love my life.

Me: Ok, babe. We're off.

Adam: I love you. Just remember, it's all going to be okay.

Me: Yeah, I know.

Adam: You do know, right?

Me: Yeah . . . here. You better get one last look at "the cancer."

Adam: I kissed the spot for good luck. Remember, I'll be there when you wake up, okay? And you're sure you don't need me to come with you, right?

Me: Yeah. I'll be fine. *I'm scared. I've never been so scared in my life. Can't you see that?* I'm fine. I'll be fine. I love you.

It may seem strange that Adam isn't coming with me to the hospital. I do have cancer, after all. I mean, my mother, my mother-in-law, and my father-in-law are coming, for fuck's sake. Not my husband. He can't come. Not really. "I have to finish a TV spot for *Fast & Furious.*" That's what he said, but that's not what he meant. What he meant was he's too scared, it's too hard, just too much. Adam doesn't like to do anything he isn't good at, and hospitals, he ain't good at. An overachiever since birth, he doesn't like to do or try unless he's sure to conquer. He wasn't a normal child, not normal in the least, according to the above-mentioned in-laws. At fourteen months, with neither a word nor a step under his belt, he had his parents convinced he was developmentally "challenged." Little did they know he was biding his time, waiting for that perfect moment to make his move. So one day, from the back seat of the Fogelson family truckster, a sixteen-month-old Adam asked—clear as day—"May I have a cookie, please?" He had waited sixteen long months, patiently sucking his thumb and toes, until he had the vocabulary for a beautifully constructed sentence.

So I understand why he can't be here with me today. Why it's too hard for him to sit next to me without the right words. There are no right words. And I don't blame him for not coming. For not wanting to see me this way. Vulnerable. Scared. No deodorant. He loves me more than anything in the world. This I know. This I see. I feel it always. He wants to make me happy. He wants to say something to make me better. To right all the wrongs. And he can't. Not today. Men can be so strong when things are good and easy, but they just fall apart when things get tough or bad or . . . anything. Women are the amazing ones. When the goin' gets tough, we get tougher. If our boyfriends or husbands or lovers are sick, we'll tend to their wounds, cook them dinner, feed their pets, take out their trash, wash and wax their cars, and still find the strength to just be there for them, with them—and listen. I really don't blame Adam for not coming with me to the hospital. I just . . . wish . . . he would.

Crunch time.

So, the gang's all here: me, Mom, Ma-in-Law, Pa-in-Law. We're all crammed into this tiny pre-op room (which, by the way, smells a lot like the inside of Adam's loafers), trying to pretend like we always meet here, on Mondays, at 7:00 AM, to have . . . melanoma surgery. Some cold somethin'-somethin' is being pumped into my arm to keep me hydrated or somethin'. I haven't really been paying attention. Just chatting. The gang's been talking about everything under the sun except the impending event. We've covered . . .

The Weather:

Mom: I'm surprised how hot it was this morning.

Ma-in-Law: The valley has been unbearable the last few days.

Pa-in-Law: It *has* been hot. I don't ever remember it being quite so hot.

The News:

Ma-in-Law: Did you see that story last night on . . . what was it, Channel 4, maybe, warning about mercury levels in certain types of fish?

Mom: Yes. Can you believe that? They're now saying we have to limit our weekly tuna intake to, what was it, two servings a week?

Me: But who eats tuna more than twice a week anyway?

Friends:

Me: Did you happen to catch *Friends* last night?

Ma-in-Law: No. Why?

Me: Oh my God, it was so funny. It was the one where we see how they all became friends in the first place. It takes place in the '80s, and . . . well, if you didn't see it, it'll take too long to go into the whole thing, but . . . it was so fucking funny. The Don Johnson outfits, Monica was really fat, Rachel pre–nose job—funny shit.

It feels like a huge pink elephant is sitting on my chest and no one wants to acknowledge it's there or ask it to leave. We're keeping the banter going full speed ahead for fear of the silence, but as the clock ticks down, I feel the room getting heavier; the elephant's circus act is drawing to a close, and it's just sitting there. Staring at me. Dead weight on my sternum. Maybe if we ignore it, it will go away. Maybe.

Nurse #1: So, what have we got here? Let's see. Okay . . . you're having a melanoma removed from your . . . upper abdomen and . . . uh . . . a couple of lymph nodes removed from under your left armpit. Correct?

Me: No. Well, actually, I never heard if Dr. Gregory felt it was necessary to remove the nodes. Can you check on that?

Nurse #1: Well, it's written right here in your chart. "Lymph node dissection."

Me: I understand that, but I'd feel better if you just confirmed it with the doctor.

Nurse #1: He wrote it right here.

Me: May*be,* but I'd still like for you to confirm it.

Nurse #1: Fine. I guess I'll have to go track him down, then.

Me: That would be great. Thanks. *Kiss my ass.*

Nurse #2: So, how are we doing today?

Me: *She doesn't really want me to answer that, does she?* You don't really want me to answer that, do you?

Nurse #2: It's not so bad. Everything will be over before you know it.

Me: I know it. *And it's not over.*

Nurse #2: So, let's see . . . we're removing a—

Me: You know, another nurse was just in here, and we went over everything.

Nurse #2: Oh, really? Who was in here?

Me: I didn't catch her name.

Nurse #2: Blond or brunette?

Me: Blondish brown.

Nurse #2: Huh. Was her hair short? Kind of pulled back behind her ears?

Me: I don't know. I wasn't really paying attention to her hair.

Nurse #2: Well, no big deal. We can just go over a few things—

Me: Actually, I was wondering if I could get a pen to circle the melanoma. It was biopsied, and I have so many moles that have been removed on my stomach, I just want to make sure he excises the correct place. Don't want a mix-up.

Mom: Remember that story of the guy who went in to have a leg amputated and they cut off the wrong one?

Nurse #2: I'm sure the doctor knows exactly which mole he's supposed to remove.

Me: I would just feel better if I circled it.

Nurse #2: I can't let you do that. It's against hospital policy.

Me: What? Why?

Nurse #2: The lines you draw could get confused with the lines Dr. Gregory draws to make his incision.

Me: *That's comforting. My surgeon is going to confuse my half-assed circle with his precision markings. That makes me feel so much better . . .* You know what? I'll take full responsibility if something bad happens. Just give me your pen.

Nurse #2: I can't do that.

Me: Does anyone have a pen? Mom, you must have one in your purse.

Mom: I must . . . have one in here . . . I don't . . . see one.

Me: Linda? Ted? Anyone?

Ma-in-Law: I had one in here . . . yesterday. No . . . I must have taken it . . .

Pa-in-Law: I didn't bring in my organizer.

This is FUCKING GREAT. I'M ABOUT TO HAVE A CHUNK OF CANCEROUS SKIN REMOVED FROM MY STOMACH, AND NO ONE, NOT ONE SINGLE FUCKING PERSON IN THIS ENTIRE FUCKING HOSPITAL, HAS (OR WILL GIVE ME) A PEN. A PEN TO MAKE SURE THE "CORRECT" CHUNK OF CANCEROUS SKIN IS REMOVED FROM MY STOMACH! I almost can't believe this is my life. I almost can't believe at twenty-five years old I have to beg for a pen from a nurse who is taking directions from a surgeon who is about to rid me of cancer—hopefully rid me of cancer.

Nurse #1: So, I talked to the doctor, and, in fact, you are not having lymph nodes removed.

Me: Could I borrow your pen for a quick second?

Nurse #1: You're not going to circle anything, are you?

Me: No. *Yeah, yeah, yeah.*

Nurse #1: All I have is a pencil. So, they're ready for you. I'm going to wheel you up to surgery. She should be done in about an hour. There is a nice waiting area on the first floor, by the elevators. Also, downstairs, next to the entrance, there is a great place to get some coffee. They have the best blended mochas down there . . . okay, we're off.

Me: Could you guys just follow me out to the elevator? Everything's going to be fine. Right?

Mom: Piece of cake.

Me: I love you.

Mom, Ma-in-Law, Pa-in-Law: I love . . . we love you—

Elevators look so different when you're strapped to a gurney, staring up at its ceiling . . . reddish-brown stain in the upper-right corner, a rip just off-center to the left, a small hole, possibly made by a pencil, in lower left, a thick yellow substance peeking out of lower-right corner . . . my heart feels like it's going to leap out of my chest. Deep breaths. Breathe from my diaphragm. In . . . two, three, four . . . out . . . two, three, four.

Shit, I'm freaking out. Motherfucker sisboomba. Shit-damn fuck-a-damn fuck-a-damn-damn. Some motherfucker just fucked my man. I'll fuck . . . the hills are alive with the sound of music with . . . what . . . shit . . . two roads diverged in a yellow wood and sorry I could not travel both and be one traveler long I stood and looked down one as far as I could to where it bent in the undergrowth . . . something something something . . . I took the road less traveled by and that has made all the difference. It was many and many a year ago, in a kingdom by the sea, that a maiden there lived whom you may know by the name of Annabel Lee. And something she did with no other something something than to love and be loved by me. Focus. Focus, Goddamn it. There is nothing to be afraid of. There is nothing to—I pledge allegiance . . .

Guy in Scrubs: I'm your anesthesiologist, and I'll be administering your drugs.

Me: Hi. *Thank God for the drugs.* Make sure you use enough. I'm pretty tall, so I might need more than most people—

Anesthesiologist: You'll just have to trust I know what I'm doing. Would you like me to turn on some music?

Me: Yeah.

Anesthesiologist: What station would you like?

Me: Um, 106.7 would be great, but if you need something a little more mellow to work—

Anesthesiologist: KROQ it is. Okay. So, now I'm giving you the sedative. You will start to feel . . .

Light. Bright light. Fluorescent light flickering above. A head. It's a face. An Adam face. Blue eyes. Tan skin. A warm hand holding my hand. Other faces sprinkled around my bed. Mom. That's my mom. Hi, Mom. A ponytail. Doc, saying something about me. I love my doc . . .

Orange. No apple. Apple juice from a box. It's a tricky little striped straw. I feel Adam next to me. And a nurse. A different one. Nurse #3. Hee hee. Funny . . . to . . . me.

Me: Thank you, Nurse #3. For the juice.

Adam: You did great. It's all over . . . walk around a little. I can . . . home.

Me: Ok. I'm ready. Home now.

Adam: Soon.

How did I get in the car? It's bright outside. Cars drive fast. Just rest my eyes. My lids. Just my lids. Heavy lids . . .

My own bed. Cool sheets. Soooooooo cozy in my bed. Good night.

Me: Mom. Mom? Mmooom. Adaaaaaaaaaaaaam? Could somebody bring me some water, please?

Mom: You're up. How ya doin'?

Me: What time is it?

Mom: I think it's around four.

Me: I can't believe I slept that long. So, did you talk to Dr. Gregory? How did everything go?

Mom: He said the surgery went fine and he'll call with the pathology as soon as he gets it.

Me: I want to look at it—

Mom: Well, you won't be able to see anything, because it's all bandaged up. Here, let me help you . . . don't—

Me: I got it. Huh, the bandage looks a little . . . low.

Mom: What do you mean?

Me: Low. It looks low. Where the gauze is. The melanoma was *just* below my breast, and the bandage is, like, an inch below my breast.

Mom: I'm sure it just looks that way because of how you're lying.

Me: I know where the fucking spot was. You don't think I paid attention to where the fucking cancer was on my stomach? He removed the wrong fucking chunk of skin! Goddamn it motherfucker! I knew I should have circled it. Why wouldn't they let me? I don't understand—

Adam: What's wrong? What happened?

Me: They removed the wrong place!

Adam: What are you talking about?

Me: Look. Look where the bandage is. The melanoma was much higher. You know. You saw where it was.

Adam: Honey, that looks like the right place to me . . .

Me: You're just saying that. I can tell from your eyes you think it's wrong, too.

Adam: I don't know what you're talking about. Call Dr. Gregory If you're so sure it's wrong. I can't wait to hear this conversation.

Me: Fuck you. Mom, hand me the phone. Give me that sheet with Gregory's number on it . . . hello? Is Dr. Gregory available? . . . could you please have him call Hillary Fogelson as soon as possible . . . yeah . . . regarding a melanoma surgery he performed this morning.

So now we wait. How could this have happened? I'm not just being paranoid or crazy or losing my mind, even though I feel like I am. I feel nauseous. And not from the anesthesia. It's a helpless, hopeless, this-can't-be-happening kind of nausea. Juice. When did I drink apple juice? Apple juice and stomach acid swirling around, working their way up . . . *this bandage is not in the right—*

Ring.

Me: Hello? Hi. Yeah, sorry to bother you. I know that is going to sound slightly crazy, but I think you may have removed the wrong spot.

Dr. Gregory: Why would you think that?

Me: Because I just looked at where the bandage is, and it looks lower than it should. My melanoma was *just* below my breast, and it looks like—

Dr. Gregory: It looks lower because, remember, we took out an elliptical-shaped section of skin. When we sew you back up, we pull and stretch the top of the ellipse to meet the bottom of the ellipse. That's why it might seem like there is a larger space between the bottom of your breast and the incision. It's why you're going to have a sensation of tightness until the skin stretches out. I've been doing this a long time. You're going to have to trust that I removed the correct thing.

Me: It's not that I don't trust you. I just . . . thank you for explaining it to me.

Dr. Gregory: Not a problem. I'll see you next week.

Me: Thanks again. And I really do trust you . . . I . . . just. I don't know. I freaked out. I'm better now. See you next week. *I'm an idiot.*

Dr. Gregory: Take it easy. Try to get some rest.

Me: Yeah, okay. Thanks. Sorry. See you soon.
Click.

Adam: Feel better?

Me: Yeah. Much. *It is low, though.*

God, I hate this. I hate this feeling. I'm supposed to be proactive, right? That's what the *Today* show and *20/20* and *48 Hours* keep telling me. The horror stories—doctors amputating the wrong limb, contaminated blood, organs mismatched—it all leads me to the same disturbing, insecure place of distrust. I'm trying the best I can to navigate this new world full of new terminology, and yet I feel totally ignorant and alone and confused. Tripping over myself and looking like an ass—so much for grace under fire. I can't help but wonder if this is how everyone feels. This can't be new territory.

Let the Healing Begin

Hardly slept last night. Hate sleeping on my back. How do people do it? I feel so . . . exposed. So . . . out there. I've been in bed all morning, watching TV. I've never really watched morning television past the *Today* show. I feel like an explorer who is hoping earth doesn't actually turn out to be flat. From what I've had to sit through thus far, I already wish I had fallen off the edge of the world. Mom has been cleaning all morning. The vacuum started around 7:00 AM, and since then I've heard the faint whisper of a Swiffer, a spray bottle, and something that sounds a hell of a lot like a chain saw. What the fuck is she doing down there? With a good, solid four hours under her belt, she may well have built a screened-in porch off our living room.

Mom: Knock, knock. Are you awake? Your father's on the phone.

Me: What are you doing down there?

Mom: Just trying to get up some of the dog hair. I'll come get the phone when you're done.

Me: Hey, Dad.

He's scared. I know he's scared because it's 11:00 AM, and it's the second time today we've talked. And my dad's not much of a talker. Not much of a talker at all. Not when it comes to these kinds of things. Not these kinds of talks. The stock market, he can do. What the market's doing, why, wherefore, bull, bear, and all the rest of it—*that,* he can handle. He can quote you Hemingway or lyrics to Neil Young songs, spout off the rules of fencing, or tell you the perfect condition for growing tomatoes—but sickness, he doesn't do. Matters of the heart, he keeps to himself. Under lock and key. And so he is awkward and stiff. Often formal and curt, even with his children. *Especially* with his children. But I have accepted all this long ago. I have stopped wishing he were different. I have given up on things changing. I have shifted my expectations so as not to be disappointed, and just enough to sometimes be pleasantly surprised. See, he's a man's man. A hunter-gatherer man. A "provider," an Orvis-catalog, Eddie-Bauer, fly-fishing, never-been-sick-a-day-in-his-life kind of man. A tender-heart-with-a-tough-J. Peterman-canvas-covering type of man. *That's* my dad.

Dad: How are you feeling?

Me: Uh, pretty good. Same as an hour ago.

Dad: Good. You'll bounce back quickly. You're tough. I know you. You won't let this slow you down.

Me: Yeah . . . well . . . I'll try not to.

Dad: Get some rest, and I'll check on you later.

Me: Okay. Thanks for calling. Bye. *I love you.*

Sometimes "I love you" is so hard to get out. Sometimes, with certain people, the phrase gets stuck somewhere between the tongue and soft palate. And then it gets swallowed down. Along with everything else.

Baby Steps

Today's a big day. I'm out of my sweats and into real clothes . . . well, sort of. I'm not in formal wear or anything, but I put on a pair of underwear. So that's good. That's progress. Still no bra, though. I've got a while before that happens. Tomorrow I hope to take a shower. I don't really smell; it's just that I'd like a chance to shave my armpits before my pit hair is long enough to French braid.

Oh, and I've made a decision. I'm not taking any more Vicodin. That shit is good. And addicting. Not that I have an addictive personality. I mean, I smoked on and off for ten years, but then I was able to quit. I had a brief addiction to laxatives, but that was typical college shit. I used to drink a little too much. Nothing crazy. A couple drinks in the afternoon. A couple more at night. I've picked my cuticles since I quit sucking my thumb.

Yeah, I'd better lay off the pain pills. They are good, though. They do help take the edge off. And help me relax. And sleep . . . yeah, I'm not taking any more Vicodin . . . unless I really, really, really need to. Really.

Bad Day

Me: Hello?

Other: Hi, sweetie, it's Kim. I didn't expect you to answer.

Me: Oh . . . well . . . I did. What's going on?

Kim: How are you? How do you feel?

Me: Oh, you heard . . . yeah, I'm doing pretty good. Still a little sore, but nothing too serious.

Kim: It's sooooooo good to hear your voice. You sound so healthy, so strong.

Me: Yeah, well, thanks. I feel good . . . considering. What's up with you? How's the play going? I was really bummed I had to drop out, but there's no way I would have been able to perform by Thursday.

Kim: Everything's fine. There have been a couple of blow-ups, but nothing, you know, major. I'm just so happy to hear you're doing well. The cast has been asking about you.

Me: Tell everyone I say hi.

Kim: I will. Definitely . . . anyway, I should let you go, get your rest. We're all thinking of you.

Me: Thanks. I'll call you next week. Take care.

Kim: Yeah, you too. Bye, sweetie.

Okay. That was fucking weird. I'm not dying, people. That was depressing. I'm fine. I'm going to be fine.

Ring, ring.

Me: Hello?

Other: Hi, it's Clara.

Me: Hey, what's up?

Clara: Oh, not much. What's up with you?

Me: Well—

Clara: Did you hear that Ronny is getting married? Can you believe that? I always thought he would end up with someone younger. She's *six* years older than him, you know. Do you think you'll get invited to the wedding?

Me: I doubt it. Ronny and I don't really—

Clara: God, I hope I'm invited. Do you think I'll be invited?

Me: I really don't know.

Clara: How are you feeling, by the way?

Me: Oh. Fine. Sore, but making progress. I just assumed you didn't know.

Clara: No, Tess told me. You must be relieved.

Me: Why?

Clara: You know, that it was only skin cancer. So many people in my family have had a skin cancer removed, and—

Me: They had melanoma?

Clara: Yes, I think. Well, actually, I'm not sure. I think my aunt had basal . . . is that the same thing?

Me: Well, no, not really. Basal and squamous rarely spread to other parts of the body. Melanoma, on the other—

Clara: I'm just glad you're okay.

Me: Yeah. *Whatever.* Oh, I think my mom's calling me. I've gotta go. I'll call you later. Bye.

Clara: Call me . . .

Okay. *That* was fucking weird, too. What an ass . . . That's it. No more. I'm not going to answer—

Ring.

Me: Hello? *Cancer Survivor's Network, may I help you?*

Other: Is this Carrot Top?

Me: Yeah, it's me, Grandpa.

Papaw: Does anyone else call you that?

Me: No, just—

Papaw: How ya' doin', babe?

Me: Pretty good, actually.

Papaw: Your dad called us yesterde' and tol' us. You know your great-grandmother, Hassie, had skin troubles.

Me: Oh, really? Did she have melanoma, because I didn't think there was any family history. My oncologist was asking—

Papaw: No, hon. Not melanomas, but she did have somethin' removed from her face this one time.

Me: Was it basal or squamous cell skin cancer?

Papaw: Hon, I don't really know. But you know who else . . . 'member Charlie, who used to come into your parents' store when you was a kid?

Me: Oh, yeah. With the scarf around his neck because of the throat cancer. That guy?

Papaw: You know he had skin problems.

Me: Huh . . . I never knew he had melanoma, too.

Papaw: His wasn't melanoma. It was somethin' else.

Me: Oh . . . well . . . um . . . actually, Papaw, I'm getting kind of tired. So, tell Mamaw I love her. I'll call you guys in a couple of days.

Papaw: Take care. Bye, hon.

So, what he really said was that he *hasn't known* one *fucking person in his whole life who* ever *had melanoma.* Wow. That was a great conversation! I feel soooooooo much better. Too bad I didn't talk to him earlier. Maybe I would have killed myself by now. No more phone calls for me. Whoever wants to talk to me is gonna have to come to my house and sit in front of my cancerous ass and insult me face-to-face. I'm just having a bad day. I'm pissed off, feeling sorry for myself, I don't know. I just want everything to go back to how it was before. I liked it all better before. Why are people such assholes? I feel like everyone I've talked to in the last couple of days has been speaking to me through one side of their mouth because a big fucking foot is sticking out the other side. It's like Debra Winger in *Terms of Endearment:* "It's okay to talk about 'the cancer.'" My problem is, no one seems to know diddly squat about melanoma, so I end up defending my illness. "People die from melanoma, ya know." "Melanoma spreads throughout the body faster than any other cancer." "Melanoma is the number one cancer among women twenty-five to twenty-nine." "Second to lung cancer, melanoma is the fastest-growing cancer in the world." "If not caught early, melanoma is almost always fatal." "Melanoma doesn't respond to traditional chemotherapy or radiation."

Yeah, that's right. I've been doing some online research. So *fuck you!*

Sorry. Like I said, bad day.

Heads Up . . . Checkup

I'm back on the third floor. The "Cancer Floor." In the last five minutes I've watched four people get off the elevator, glance at the enormous JOHN WAYNE CANCER INSTITUTE sign, and sheepishly slink back into the elevator like they're afraid to breathe the air up here. Terrified they might come down with a bad case of breast or prostate cancer. It's been going around lately, ya know. I'd love to have a bodysuit made to look like I'm covered in oozing boils and, just as some unsuspecting fool is sliding back into the elevator, spray a horrible hacking cough on them. Yeah, that would be funny—fucking hilarious.

Dr. Gregory: Hello there. So, are you still convinced I removed the wrong place?

Me: No, uh, sorry about that. Momentary lapse of judgment—the cancer made me do it.

Dr. Gregory: Not a problem. Not a problem. So, let's get a look at this thing . . . uh-huh . . . healing nicely. Stitches look good. You can just let this tape come off on its own.

Me: Yeah, I'm not in any rush to pull that off.

Dr. Gregory: And you heard the pathology came back. Clean margins all around. So . . . how are you doing?

Me: Just a little sore, but nothing major.

Dr. Gregory: No, I mean, how are you doing dealing with all of this? It's a lot to absorb in a couple of days.

Me: Overall, I think I'm handling things pretty well. I have my moments, but—

Dr. Gregory: I want to say something to you. And I'm only going to say it once.

Me: Wow, that sounded so . . . theatrical.

Dr. Gregory: You're not going to like it.

Me: O-kay?

Dr. Gregory: I want you to know it's okay to be scared. It's okay to be angry. It's okay to feel . . . whatever it is you are feeling. Just don't act like you're fine when you're not, because everything will catch up with you. It always does. I've seen it happen a thousand times. Men are usually the worst offenders. They come in here after surgery, all ready to put everything behind them, deal with nothing that has happened, ready to forget they ever had cancer. Most of them end up having a nervous breakdown within a couple of months. You've got to deal with your emotions. Deal with them now. You'll have to sooner or later. All this "stuff" isn't going to just go away. Trust me on that. You're very witty—you know that. You use your humor to cover how you feel. So, just know . . . I'm on to you.

Me:

Dr. Gregory: That's it. That's what I wanted to say.

Me:

Dr. Gregory: Do you have any questions for me?

Me: No, I don't think so.

Dr. Gregory: Then I will see you in a couple of weeks. You can head on into the lab now, and Howard will take your blood. Call me if you have questions or concerns. And remember, you need to talk to someone about how you feel. I don't care who, but you need someone you can confide in.

Me: Yeah, okay.

Dr. Gregory: Take care of yourself.

Me: Yeah, okay, you too.

Mom: How'd it go?

Me: Fine.

Mom: What did he say?

Me: Nothing.

On My Own

Mom's going back to Ohio today. She'd stay longer if I asked her to. She'd . . . do anything if I asked her to. It's the asking that's hanging me up. I mean, I'll be okay without her. I have Adam. And the dog. They're all I need . . . yeah, I'm gonna be fine. And she needs to get back anyway . . . I don't need her to . . .

Mom: . . . stay? I can, you know. Your father is fine. He can take care of himself. You—

Me: I'm fine. Totally fine.

Mom: Just don't do too much. You work too hard.

Me: What are you taking about? I've been lying in bed for the last week.

Mom: Just don't push yourself. You've had so much to deal with—

Me: *Mom,* really. Fly safe, okay?

Mom: I just wish you didn't have to go through all this. It's so hard to see you in pain.

Me: Don't—

Mom: I wish I could go through it for you.

Me: Yeah, I know you do. I love you. Thank you . . . for everything.

Mom: I love you so much. You're so strong. Bye, sweetie.

I've got a lump in my throat and it's killing me. It's that lump that keeps all the sadness from coming up, from spewing out, spilling onto the sidewalk, down the street and onto . . . everything. It's *that* lump. The lump of all lumps that has ever been created. The lump that I hate. If I could swallow it down I would, but I'm choking on it. And I can't breathe . . . and I can't stand up . . . and I can't . . . hold . . . it . . . down . . . anymore. So . . . I'm . . . not . . . anymore . . . I'm . . . not . . .

It feels good to let go. Let the tears run down my cheeks in a thick, hot stream, drip off my chin and onto my favorite worn-out NYU tee. I stick out my tongue and try to redirect the salty stream into my mouth so I can taste everything. Everything I've been trying to keep down. My eyes feel sticky, and I can tell my mascara is starting to give under pressure. Drip, drip, drip. I reach my neck high and to the left just in time to catch my mom's taillights disappear around the corner. She's gone. She's really gone. So . . . now what? I guess I could just sit here, wet and pathetic, and wait for Adam to get home. Yeah, that sounds like a good idea. He'll definitely want to see me like this—everything dripping.

Nice Talkin' to Ya

Me: Hello?

Dad: How are you feeling?

Me: Hi, Dad. Good. I'm feeling good.

Dad: Good.

Me: How are you?

Dad: Good.

Me: Good.

Dad: Do you want to talk to Mom?

Me: Sure.

My Savior, My Dermatologist

I know that guy sitting over there. From somewhere. It is driving me fucking insane. Think. Focus. Okay, he looks to be about my age. Did I go to school with him? Did I go out with this guy? I haven't slept with him—at least, I don't think that's how I know him. High school. I'm fairly sure I went to high school with him, but what the hell is his name? A, b, c Craig, d, e, f, g Greg Garry, h, i, j Jerry Jim Josh, k, l, m Mike *Mike* Mitch, no, n, o . . . shit. He's looking at me. Yeah, he knows me, but he can't figure out from where. I can't believe he doesn't remember me. I'm unforgettable . . . what the fuck is his name? And he's with a girl. I definitely don't know her. A girlfriend? He looks kinda gay. I don't remember him looking so gay in high school. A recent development. Huh . . .

Nurse: Hillary, you ready?
Me: Yeah.
Nurse: And what are you here for today?
Me: I think Dr. Bach is just doing a follow-up.

Nurse: Let's see here . . . what does your chart say? You had a melanoma removed.

Me: Yeah.

Nurse: So, why does Dr. Bach want to see you? You had the mole *removed,* right?

Me: Rrriiiight. *Déjà vu.*

Nurse: I'm sorry. I just don't know much about melanoma. I assumed—

Me: What?

Nurse: That once it was removed, that was it.

Me: No, it's not like basal or squamous cell. Melanoma is more like, um, breast cancer or . . . lymphoma. It has the potential to, uh, spread very quickly throughout the body, so—

Nurse: You know, I had a lump in my breast once. Scared me to death. They did a needle biopsy. I was flipping out. Thinking about having cancer and everything. I just started thinking about my future and my family and how my life would suddenly be so different if it turned out to be cancer.

Me: What happened?

Nurse: Turned out to be nothing, thank God. Just a fibrous cyst.

Me: Oh. Lucky.

Nurse: Dr. Bach should be with you—

Dr. Bach: Hi. How did everything go?

Me: *Theeere she is. Ms. Ameeeerica. Dr. Bach, my hero . . . a no-nonsense kinda woman. A down-to-business-in-no-time-flat kinda gal. In nearly a decade of visits, I've learned close to nothing about her personal life. I've heard neither hide nor hair of a spouse, of children, of trips she's taken, or of things she's proud of. I've gathered tidbits from discussions of dermatology conferences she's been to, heard about the occasional skin cancer screening she has participated in, but that's it. It's like she exists only within these walls. Like she's visible only when confined to this office. If Dr. Bach removed a mole in the forest and no one was around to read the pathology . . .*

Pretty good. *Dr. Gregory is great.*

Dr. Bach: I've sent a lot of patients to him . . . so, I want to do another full-body check, make sure there isn't anything else we should biopsy right now.

Me: Whoa, sorry . . . your hands are cold.

Dr. Bach: Did Dr. Gregory go over everything with you? Did he discuss the genetic factor in all this?

Me: No, not really. I mean, I told him no one else in my family has ever had melanoma—

Dr. Bach: Well, everyone in your family needs to start going to a dermatologist for regular skin checks. Because you're so young, you were probably genetically predisposed, which means—

Me: No one in my family is as fair as me, though.

Dr. Bach: I just think it would be a good idea. Also, did Dr. Gregory talk to you about birth control pills?

Me: No.

Dr. Bach: How long have you been on them?

Me: About ten years.

Dr. Bach: There have been a lot of recent studies looking at the relationship between melanoma and estrogen. Nothing is definitive at this point, but I would discuss other birth-control options with your gynecologist.

Me: Like what, condoms? *Adam, honey, I have something to tell you.*

Dr. Bach: You might want to investigate the new IUDs. Particularly the copper one.

Me: What does IUD stand for?

Dr. Bach: Intrauterine Device.

Me: *Intra, meaning "in"? As in, "in my uterus"? In it? As in, "not out"?*

Dr. Bach: I would ask about it . . . well, I see a couple more places I'd like to biopsy, but nothing that can't wait a week or two. Give you a little break. I'll tell Julia to schedule you for two weeks.

Me: Okay. And, you know . . . I wanted to say . . . thank you. Thank you. *I wish I could come up with something better to say. Something more meaningful. More emotional. Something more. Something better. I just don't know what it would be.*

Dr. Bach: It's my job . . . and you're welcome.

Wow, that was like out of a movie. "It's my job," the doctor says matter-of-factly, leaving the patient feeling foolish for trying to express her innermost feelings. Then, just as the doctor reaches for the door, she turns, slowly, purposefully, and with a warm smile adds, "And you're welcome." Exit doctor. Close-up on patient, who is left feeling awestruck from being in the presence of such a remarkable lady. Cut to—

I wonder if Fred's still in the waiting room. *Fred*—that's it. That's his name. Fred Freddie Fred-man. The Mayor of Fredville.

Fred: Hillary? It's me, Fred. From Thousand Oaks.

Me: Hey, I didn't even see you.

Fred: And this is my girlfriend, Melanie.

Me: Hi, nice to meet you. *He's gay, right? Your boyfriend's gay?*

Fred: We were about to head out. Let's chat on the elevator.

Me: So, what have you been up to?

Fred: Melanie and I are just finishing up law school. And we have a place together in Westwood. What's up with you? Weren't you dating some teacher or something? He was a lot older than you, I think. I don't remember the whole story.

Me: I married him. We've been together eight years now.

Fred: Oh. Great!

Melanie: Have you been going to Dr. Bach long? This was my first time with her.

Me: Yeah, I've been seeing her about . . . nine years. I started seeing her in ninth grade. Yeah, I guess it was ninth. I got a pimple and freaked out, and so my mom found Dr. Bach. I never really thought about it before, but I guess it's kinda weird that I've kept coming once a year. Dr. Bach always said I should have a full-body check at least once a year and . . . for some reason, I listened. She's amazing, isn't she?

Melanie: Well, I don't know. She's a little dry.

Me: She just likes to get down to business. She's an extraordinary doctor, though.

Melanie: I was actually thinking of looking around for someone else.

Me: Well, you won't find anyone more thorough. That I can guarantee.

Melanie: Huh. You really trust her?

Me: Yeah. With my life.

Melanie: That's saying a lot.

Me: *I know I'm going to regret saying this.* Yeah, well, she actually found a melanoma on me, pointed it out, thought it needed to be biopsied. So, yes, I really do trust her.

Fred:

Melanie:

Me:

Melanie: Wow, so . . . how's the cancer going?

Me: The cancer's . . . going good. *Yeah, it's going great. Couldn't be better. Love the cancer. Love it! You should get it. It's fabulous, just fabulous! I don't know who's the bigger idiot, me or her. Wonder how long it will take the rumor mill to start up. I'm sure by tomorrow evening I will be dying from inoperable testicular cancer, according to my high school gossip committee . . . I need a drink. Or a Vicodin. Whichever.*

Fred: P3—this is us. It was so great seeing you. Here, give me a big hug. Hope to see you soon. Take care of yourself, okay?

Melanie: So nice to meet you.

Me: Yeah, you too. *I will remember it always.*

As I search through my purse for my keys (going deep past the three tubes of sunscreen and cherry Chapstick), I can't help but wonder what would have happened if I hadn't been seeing Dr. Bach. How long would I have waited? How big and deep would I have let the cancer grow before I smartened up? It's not like I even knew what I was supposed to be looking for. It's not like the mole was holding a little red flag, waving and flapping CANCER. It's not like I'd grown a third nipple or had a little baby club foot sticking out from my chest! It was a small, dark, unassuming spot, as far as I could tell. A speck of dark chocolate. A chocolate kiss strategically placed under my breast. A mole. A nevus. A dot. Why was I still seeing Dr. Bach after all these years? That's the fucking million-dollar question. I really don't know.

Habit.

Loyalty.

Fate.

Sun Protection Factor

I've got to find a way to cut back on my morning routine. It's fucking killing me.

7:30: Wake up (standard procedure).

7:35–7:37: Pee and check moles for any signs of change.

7:37–8:15: Green tea, vitamins, high-fiber (low-tasting) cereal—*yummy*.

8:15–8:45: Strip down and check for any new moles (moles formed in last twenty-four hours).

8:45–9:15: Shower and recheck existing moles for a: *a*symmetry; b: irregular *b*order; c: variation in *c*olor; d: *d*iameter larger than a pencil eraser's.

9:15–9:30: Dry off and re-recheck for any new moles since last check (refer back to 8:15–8:45).

9:30–9:40: Check for swollen lymph nodes (which, of course, I wouldn't be able to distinguish from an aggravated sweat gland, angry mosquito bite, or infected pimple).

9:40–10:00: Apply sunscreen (to every crack and crevasse).

10:00–10:30: Apply SPF makeup over sunscreen.

10:30–10:50: Pick out long-sleeved shirt and pants that don't look too freak-ish to wear in the middle of the hottest part of the summer.

10:50–11:00: Find hat that doesn't make me look like a deck umbrella.

11:15: *Start my day with a smile.* (Fuck this. I'm ready for lunch already.)

I soon hope to create a morning routine that blends seamlessly into an evening routine, thus avoiding the need for sunscreen.

And So It Begins

Ring ring ring ring ring.

Mom: Hello?

Me: Hey, it's me. How'd it go at the dermatologist?

Mom: Oh, fine. The doctor said I looked good. He didn't see anything he thought needed to come off. I pointed out a couple places for him to look at, but he said they're just age spots. He took one place off your father's back but said it was nothing to worry about. He said if it's anything it could be basal cell, but nothing serious . . . I wish he could do something about all the age spots on my hands. I have the hands of an eighty-year-old.

Me: Why don't you try a bleaching cream?

Mom: Oh, honey, I've tried all that stuff. None of it works.

Me: You never use any of it long enough.

Mom: Who has the time?

Me: Well, if you want them to go away—when did the doctor expect the pathology report back on Dad's mole?

Mom: I don't know. Honey, do you remember when the path— . . . your father thinks he said it would be in on Monday.

Me: Good.

Mom: Do you want to say hi to your father?

Me: Uh . . . um . . . sure. Hey, Dad.

Dad: How are you feeling?

Me: Pretty good.

Dad: Good.

Me: *Here we go again . . .*

Dad: You sound tired.

Me: It was just a long day . . . I saw my ophthalmologist this morning and my gynecologist this afternoon. I'm just ready to be done with all this stuff. Apparently, you can get melanoma almost . . . anywhere. I don't know. I'm just—

Dad: It must be frustrating for someone like you, who is so driven and task-oriented, to have to deal with something you have no control over.

Me: Yeah . . . exactly. *Yeah, exactly.*

Dad: Well, I just wish you didn't—

Me: I know. I know. I'm okay, though.

Dad: Well, call if you need anything.

Me: I will.

Dad: Take care.

Me: I love you, Dad.

Dad: You too.

Me: Bye. *That was . . . I don't know what that was. It felt . . . easier. He seemed . . . different.*

Life Goes On

Can't wait for tomorrow. I have a date with a girlfriend. We're going to lunch and a movie. She said I could pick the film (cancer-survivor perk) . . . Can't believe I'm going to venture out into the big, bad, sunny world and enjoy a day with someone who doesn't have an "MD" following her name. I can't wait! I may actually wear a bra tomorrow.

Mellary

This is it. I'm back. Back in the real world. You know, just sittin' eatin' chattin', waitin' for the movie to start. Violet is a fucking gossip machine. From the concession-stand line to the first preview, she has covered all the new relationship stories: recent breakups (high school friends and celebrities), who's fucking whom, who fucked over whom, and who's just plain fucked, why, and if they deserve it. All the important things in life. I get such joy in hearing about others' misfortunes. She can turn the worst story—with the goriest details—into a masterpiece. She knows about everything that is happening, with everyone, all the time. She knows it before it happens . . . or it happens because she knows it. I never tell her anything I don't want repeated at least a thousand times to anyone and everything. Yeah . . . she sure can tell 'em . . . she sure can. Wonder what she has said about me lately. Wonder what spin she put on my story of late. Wonder if she has found a way to turn my ordeal into a one-liner . . . or if she secretly refers to me as Hillary-noma or Mellary? Yeah . . . yeah, that's not all that funny.

Violet: . . . stuck *in* her ass, and the cop—

Me: Shut up, it's starting . . . *This is nice. Nice and normal. Just me, some overly salted buttery popcorn, and a movie. Yeah, this is real nice. I'm normal again. I love feeling normal again. Yeah, this is great. Just hangin' out like a normal person. I mean, not* normal *normal, but as normal as I'd like to be . . . This popcorn tastes kinda stale. There's too much salt on it. It's kinda' making me nauseous . . . too much butter . . . It's hot in here. I'm sweating . . . my palms are sweating . . . I can't see! I can't see anything! . . . Whoa, what happened? . . . I think I just blacked out or something . . . fuck, that was so weird. Okay. Okay. I'm okay. Breathe deep . . . my heart's racing . . . I'm having a heart attack . . . I can't feel my fingers . . . or my feet . . . I can't breathe . . . I'm gonna throw up . . . or pass out . . . or . . .* I've gotta get out of—

Violet: Wait, what's . . . wrong? You are really fucking pale.

Me: I'm shaking.

Violet: You're shaking—

Me: I'm . . . just . . . gonna . . . lie down here in the hall.

Violet: What do you want me to do? Do you need a doctor?

Me: No, I just need to rest here.

Violet: Where's your purse? I'm calling your doctor . . . do you have his number?

Me: Look in my PalmPilot under "Braun." *B-r-a . . .*

Theater Manager: Should I call an ambulance?

Me: No, no. I just need a second.

Violet: Hello? I need to speak with Dr. Braun—

Me: *Oh God, don't let me die. I don't want to die. Not like this. Not with my cheek pressed to smelly, sticky movie-theater carpet, popcorn between my teeth, with a wide-eyed, pimply-faced, teenage theater manager whispering sweet nothings in my ear.*

Theater Manager: You look good. Real good. Just hold on.

Violet: —it's an emergency. I'm with one of his patients, Hillary

Fogelson, and she just blacked out and . . . Okay . . . hello, are you the doctor? Yeah, I'm with Hillary Fogelson and we were watching a movie and I think she may have blacked out. And now she's lying on the floor, she's shaking, she's really pale . . . I don't know . . . Okay . . . he says I need to elevate your legs, get them higher than your head . . . Okay . . . yeah, what else? . . . and move her legs? . . . like how? Oh . . . Okay . . . I'm supposed to move your legs as if you were on a bike . . .

Me:

Violet: Is this doing anything? Is this helping?

Me:

Violet: She's not saying anything, doctor. Her eyes are really glazed, and—

Me: Yeah, I think it's helping.

Violet: Oh, wait. She says it's helping . . . Okay . . . keep doing this . . . for how long? . . . Okay, I'll call you back if she gets any worse.

Me: I'm not shaking as much. My heart . . . is slowing . . . down.

Violet: I'm supposed to keep your legs up. Five minutes up, then five minutes down.

Me: You can stop now.

Violet: No, he said—

Me: Quit with the legs. Seriously, I'm starting to feel better . . . that was fucking scary . . . I don't know what happened. I was watching the movie, and then all of a sudden I realized I had missed part of it. Lost track or something . . . that was crazy . . . I think I can stand up now.

Violet: Just wait a second. Get up slowly. You scared the shit out of me. Thought you were dying there, for a minute.

Me: Yeah . . . me too.

Now What?

Yesterday wasn't one of my finer moments. I'm just relieved the horrid event happened with someone discreet (I'm royally fucked, by the way). And I'm still not sure what happened, either. I'd be convinced I had a brain metastasis if it weren't for the fact that I had a brain scan right before my surgery. They checked my melon real good. Lungs, too. Evidently, those are the melanoma metastases' hot spots. Melanoma knows all the best places—summers in the brain, winters in the lungs.

Doc Hollywood

Another day, another waiting room. But this is not your typical, run-of-the-mill, cheaply furnished, fluorescent-lit, disinfectant-smelling waiting room. There are no jumping-dolphin photos hanging on the wall. No silk-flower arrangements or indeterminable buzzing sounds. No one next to me hacking on their own saliva or snotting into a wrinkled hankie. This is a Berber-carpeted, Ming-vase, tropical-fish-tank kinda place. This is not a place for sick people—this is my internist's waiting room. Doctor to the stars. Doctor to the athletes. Doctor to almost anyone who has lots and lots (and lots) of money . . . And the "Doc," "Doc Hollywood," the man himself, is, as one might expect, a little snotty, a tad arrogant, and a whole lotta smart. And I mean really smucking fart. I shit you not.

> **Dr. Braun:** Okay. Tell me exactly what happened. Step by step.
>
> **Me:** So, my friend Violet called and invited me to the movies. I said sure, because I thought it might be nice to—
>
> **Dr. Braun:** Just tell me the part where you started to feel funny.
>
> **Me:** Oh, okay. So, I'm sitting in the theater and—

Dr. Braun: Was it hot in the theater?

Me: Not particularly. Anyway, I was sitting there and I started to feel—

Dr. Braun: Where in the row were you sitting? Middle, end . . . ?

Me: Um, a few seats from the end—

Dr. Braun: Toward the back of the theater?

Me: Yeah, and—

Dr. Braun: Had the movie started?

Me: Well, yeah. It was a couple minutes in, and—

Dr. Braun: Had you just eaten a big meal?

Me: Not really. I had an omelet.

Dr. Braun: Uh-huh . . . and?

Me: Do you . . . need to know what I had *in* the omelet?

Dr. Braun: Not unless you feel it's important to the event.

Me: I guess I'm a little fuzzy on what *is* important to the event. *I was finally wearing a bra—is* that *detail of any consequence?*

Dr. Braun: I just want to make sure I have all the pieces to the puzzle. So, you were sitting in the theater, movie had just started, and you felt . . .

Me: I noticed my heart was pounding really fast and my palms were sweating. And then I think I may have blacked out for a second—I don't know.

Dr. Braun: Sounds like you had an anxiety attack.

Me: What?

Dr. Braun: It was anxiety.

Me: A panic attack? No, no, no. This was something . . . my sister has panic attacks . . . this wasn't . . . no, no, this was something else.

Dr. Braun: You had all the classic symptoms: racing heart, sweaty palms, shaking. When you started to feel all these things, I bet you jumped up out of your seat—

Me: Well, yeah, I didn't particularly want to die in the movie theater.

Dr. Braun: And you felt like you were going to die. It was a panic attack.

Me: But I passed out. You don't pass out during panic attacks.

Dr. Braun: Some people do. And you have really low blood pressure to begin with. You were sitting, so all the blood pooled in your legs, you passed out, your body released all these chemicals, including adrenaline. The surge of adrenaline then caused the shaking afterward.

Me: No. That doesn't sound like what happened.

Dr. Braun: Have you given any thought to seeing a therapist?

Me: Uh . . . no . . . not lately.

Dr. Braun: You should consider it. Ask your hospital to recommend someone. They might even have a therapist who works exclusively with cancer patients.

Me: Wait, wait, wait. What does one have to do with the other? The melanoma thing is almost over. I mean, on the whole, I've been feeling—

Dr. Braun: Your body has been under a lot of stress lately. Maybe more than you realize. I can prescribe an antianxiety drug for when you're feeling especially anxious—

Me: *I'm feeling especially anxious.*

Dr. Braun: —but these attacks usually get worse before they get better.

Me: Great. Gives me something to look forward to.

Dr. Braun: You know, a therapist might be able to show you some breathing techniques to help you get through the attacks. You should really think about seeing someone . . . and try not to worry about having another attack. That'll only make things worse. I'll have the nurse give you a prescription for Paxil. See if it helps. Take care. And call me if you have any questions. And tell your husband and in-laws I say hello.

Me: Yeah, I will. *I'm not worried about having another panic attack . . . if I have another one, I'll know what it is, and just wait it out . . . I'll just take deep breaths and not let it upset me . . . yeah, okay . . . I mean, it wasn't that bad . . . it was scary, yes, but only because I didn't know what was happening . . . now I will . . . good . . . great . . . yeah, it's kinda hot in here . . . feels stuffy*

. . . making me dizzy . . . and it's hard to breathe . . . oh . . . okay . . . stay
calm . . . I know what this is . . . just relax . . . deep breaths . . . it's o-kay . . .
SHIT MOTHERFUCKER I'M GONNA DIE!

Nurse: Okey-dokey. I've got the—are you okay? You're so pale, sweetie.

Me: I've gotta . . . stand up for a second. I—

Nurse: Sweetie, can I get you some juice?

Me: No, no. I just . . . I just got dizzy for a second . . . I'm okay . . .
I'll be okay. *I think.*

I'm standing at the front desk, auctioning off my firstborn, and I've
had a mental breakthrough. Breakout. Break-in, actually. Something has
fucking broken through. Melanoma doesn't give you time to heal. The
healing is not written into the melanoma proposal. There's no chapter
entitled "Healing Time." There's no blurb. Or even a "Time for Healing"
footnote. And I mean, it doesn't give your *mind* time to heal. At least, it
hasn't given *my* mind time to heal. To take it all in, make sense of it, accept the change, and then move on . . . I was lucky—I had surgery, and
that's it. No chemotherapy ('cause it doesn't really work), no radiation
(refer back to chemo), no nothing but a load of sunscreen, a good-luck pat
on the back, and a "let's keep our fingers crossed that we got it all." With
other cancers you get the benefit of time. As your body is recovering from
some horrible treatment or other, your mind is adjusting to the change.
The life change. The "cancer" change . . .

I need more time. I've got things to figure out and no time to figure
'em. I've gotta slow down. I've just gotta . . . or else . . . I don't know what.

DINNER:

Adam: Oh, I forgot to ask: how did everything go at the doctor's?

Me: Fine.

Adam: Well, what did he say?

Me: About what?

Adam: About the thing at the theater? About the passing out?

Me: Oh, it's nothing.

Adam: What do you mean, it's nothing? You blacked out. That doesn't just happen for no reason.

Me: He said it was a panic attack.

Adam: Bullshit.

Me: No, seriously. He said I had a panic attack and something about low blood pressure and blood pooling or something.

Adam: How can you not know exactly what he said?

Me: He didn't seem to think it was anything serious.

Adam: Oh, well . . . good. I'm all for "nothing serious."

Me: Yeah, me too . . . He said (*I need to have my fucking head examined*) to say hi . . . Hi.

A First Step

This is the message center for Dr. Thomas Lesaux. I'm either out of the office, on the other line, or with a client. Please leave your name and the most efficient way to get ahold of you. I'll get back to you as soon as possible. Have a wonderful day.

Beep.

Me: Um . . . hi, my name is Hillary Fogelson. That's Hillary, with two *l*'s, Fogelson: *F* as in "Frank," *o-g-e-l-s-o-n*. I got your name from Muriel Hager over at St. John's Hospital in Santa Monica. Um, I'm a melanoma patient over there . . . and Muriel said you work with a lot of . . . people like me. So, um, I thought I'd give you a call. Muriel doesn't have any young people in her melanoma support group right now, so I figured it might be good to, you know, find someone who—

Beep.

Me: Hi, it's Hillary Fogelson again. I think the machine cut me off. I'll make this short. The best way to reach me is on my cell. Or you can always leave me a message at home. I check my machine regularly. Okay. Talk to you soon. Bye.

Me: Hi, sorry, me again. I'm an idiot. I don't think I left my numbers with you. Cell: 310-xxx-xxxx. Home: 323-xxx-xxxx. That's it.

Okay. Call me when you can. And sorry about all the phone calls . . . and I really look forward to speaking with you. I've heard such great things about you from Muriel . . . and I'm actually *not* as insane as these messages have made me sound. Anyway, hope I haven't used up your whole tape. Okay. That's it. Hope to talk to you soon. Thanks, I'll look forward to—

Beep.

Ring. Ring.

Me: Hello, Dr. Lesaux? I'm—

Other: Who is this?

Me: Mom?

Mom: Hi, honey. I thought I had the wrong number for a second. Should I call you back? Are you expecting a call from a doctor?

Me: Oh, no . . . I just left a message for someone, and I thought—

Mom: Who is Dr. Lesaux? I haven't heard you mention him.

Me: He's just . . . someone I got referred to.

Mom: Another dermatologist? Because it probably wouldn't hurt you to have more than one.

Me: Mom, I already have a surgeon, an oncologist, a dermatologist, an internist, an ophthalmologist, and a gynecologist. I don't need another doctor checking for moles. My moles are getting plenty of attention, trust me.

Mom: Well, you can never be too careful.

Me: Yeah, well—

Mom: How did the appointment go with your internist? You were supposed to call me.

Me: Everything went fine. Nothing to worry about.

Mom: What did he say about the fainting? Did he say you needed a stress test? Did he have you walk on a treadmill? I hope he checked your blood sugar. Diabetes runs in the family, you know, and you might be anemic. You don't eat enough red meat.

Me: No, all that's fine. He thought it was a panic attack.

Mom: What do you mean? What are you anxious about?

Me: Mom.

Mom: Those brain scans can miss things. Maybe you should make the hospital do—

Me: Mom, it's anxiety.

Mom: But—

Me: Mom, seriously, you're giving me a lot of anxiety right now.

Mom: I'm just trying to make sure nothing was overlooked.

Me: Nothing was overlooked.

Mom: How do you know that?

Me: Because I've started to have these attacks all the time, but they only happen in real specific situations. Like, when I'm on the freeway, but only when I'm in the middle lane. I don't get them driving on side streets, or in the slow lane—only the middle lane. That's psychological. And I'm getting them more and more often, so that's why I decided I needed to see someone.

Mom: Like who? Like, a psychiatrist?

Me: He's a psychologist, actually. I need to try and get this under control. I don't think these panic attacks are going to go away on their own. The hospital recommended this guy. So, we'll see if he can help. At this point, I really don't have much to lose.

Mom: Well, what are you going to talk about?

Me: I don't really know, Mom. Whatever comes to mind, I guess. Don't worry. I'm not going to blame any of it on you.

Mom: You can, honey, if you want. If you think it will help.

Me: Is Dad around?

Mom: He's on a conference call.

Me: Oh, okay. Tell him I said hi. I've gotta go. I'll talk to you later.

Mom: I love you.

Me: You too.

The "In My Uterus" Device

I'm only slightly concerned. I'm only slightly concerned because the nurse I talked to on the phone said it wouldn't hurt. That I wouldn't need to take a painkiller. That I'd only feel pressure and then maybe a little pinch. Maybe a slight cramp or, maybe, nothing . . . She also said that everyone's cervix is different.

Dr. Goldberg: How are you? Are you ready for this?

Me: I think so. *The baby-faced Angel of Mercy. Dr. Goldberg, my gynecologist, looks like a fourteen-year-old playing dress-up in her father's work clothes. Rolled-up coat sleeves and oversize shoes to match. Even the pens and #2 pencils in her coat pocket look bulky compared with her diminutive frame. But she's young, smart, gentle, and understanding. She listens to my questions and concerns. Grabs my hand and tells me it's going to be okay. She makes me feel like it's only natural to be spread-eagle, crotch sky high, with my feet in bootie-covered stirrups.*

Dr. Goldberg: And you read all the pamphlets I gave you? Of course you did. The one with possible side effects? And what you can expect after the fact?

Me: Yep.

Dr. Goldberg: I just want to make sure. Don't want you to have any surprises. And you know there is always the possibility your body will reject it?

Me: What do you mean?

Dr. Goldberg: Some women expel the IUD within the first month or so. Their uterus never accepts it. If this is going to happen, it usually happens with your first or second period after the insertion. The muscle contractions push the device out. After each period, you should check for the strings.

Me: The strings don't hang out like . . . like tampon strings, do they?

Dr. Goldberg: No, no, no. If the IUD is in its proper place, you will feel them just below your cervix.

Me: My husband won't be able to feel the strings when we're having sex, right?

Dr. Goldberg: He shouldn't. Some men say they can, but I think it's psychological. The strings are made out of a superfine silica . . . see, here, feel. It's not like having two pieces of chicken wire hanging inside you.

Me: Good. *That's something to be thankful for.*

Dr. Goldberg: So, why don't we get started? I'll tell you everything I'm doing as I'm doing it. If it gets too uncomfortable, tell me.

Me: I have a high tolerance for pain, so I'm not worried. And the nurse said I probably wouldn't really feel anything.

Dr. Goldberg: Some women don't feel anything, that's true . . . okay, I'm just inserting the clamps . . . so far, just like a pap smear . . .

Me: Yeah, this isn't bad at all.

Dr. Goldberg: . . . and now I'm inserting the tool that will open your cervix, and now I'm opening your cervix . . .

Me: *Holy Mother Helen of God Jesusfuckingchrist Motherfucker . . .*

Dr. Goldberg: You holding up okay?

Me: Uh-huh. *Who is she fucking kidding? Mommy. Mommy. Shit fucker God bless it Motherhumper . . .*

Dr. Goldberg: You have a very stubborn cervix—it doesn't seem to want to open . . .

Me: *Be strong, be strong. I'm crying, suck it up. It's the only way. Remember the spermicide. Ouch, ouch, ouchum, ouchy . . . focus on a happy place . . . I'm in a field of poppies. There's a cool breeze blowing against my . . . my voluptuous c-cup breasts. Golden Retriever puppies are frolicking in the field. I skip over to pet them, but I can't move. Someone has shot an arrow into my vagina, pinning me to the ground. Dr. Goldberg is holding a bow, and she wants her arrow back. She starts yanking at the arrow, twisting it. The puppies are frantic, clawing at her as she slowly grinds the arrow out of me . . . fuck, fuck, fuck . . . she's Satan. The fallen angel. The Angel of Death. She's killing me . . . slowly. Fuck you, fucking asshole bitch. Fuck, fuck, fuck your mother . . .*

Dr. Goldberg: I'm not making much progress here . . .

Me: That's it. *Stop.* Stop doing whatever it is you're doing. I've never felt that . . . *level* . . . of pain, ever—

Dr. Goldberg: Why didn't you say something earlier? Since you're uncomfortable, would you like me to numb your cervix?

Me: That's an option?! Why didn't you tell me that was an option? Yes. Numb it. Please.

Dr. Goldberg: I don't typically start with the cervix numbed. I figure I'll wait and see if the patient is uncomfortable—

Me: I think you should stop using the word "uncomfortable" to describe my level of "discomfort."

Dr. Goldberg: Well, every woman's cervix is different.

Me: Apparently. *Pain level "eleven." It's "one" more.*

Dr. Goldberg: This is one procedure I do that I've never had done *to* me. So, unfortunately, I can't really tell my patients what to expect.

Me: Right. *You should have them call me.*

Dr. Goldberg: Let's try this again, shall we?

Me: Don't be afraid to use too much of that numbing stuff. Get it all over. Really rub it around. Be generous.

AFTER:

Me: Hello?

Adam: Hey, babe. How'd it go? How do you feel?

Me: Uncomfortable.

The Fine Print

So, maybe I didn't read *all* the pamphlets I was supposed to. Okay, I skimmed—fine, I glanced at—them before I folded them into small origami-like squares and stuffed them into my wallet next to sunscreen receipts. It's not like I had other great options, so what's the point? If I *had* read them cover to cover, I would have known I *might* experience:

- "Heavier and longer periods" (didn't think possible)
- "More painful periods" (didn't think possible)
- "Cramping and backache" (fun!)
- "Increased vaginal discharge" (no comment)

Golly, I can hardly wait!

The Shrink

Every doctor's office waiting room has its own distinctive smell.

Dr. Bach's:

> Rubbing alcohol
> Sweet-and-sour pork
> Old person's medicine cabinet

Dr. Gregory's:

> Lemon Pine-Sol
> Day-old Maxwell grinds

Dr. Braun's:

> Roses
> Chanel no. 5
> Chocolate croissants

The Shrink's:

> Parliament lights
> Stale urine . . . and . . . what else?

I can't quite place it. It's not sweet, exactly, or musky or old . . . or fruity or meaty, really . . . it's . . . I don't know if I've smelled it before, but it reminds me of . . . like a . . . maybe similar to . . . I don't know, it's like . . . a . . . like . . . "crazy." I've always heard crazy had a smell, but I've never really smelled it until now. It smells kinda nice. It smells *real* nice.

Jesuschrist, I'm sweatin' bullets. What's taking so long? I have a sneaking suspicion I don't want to divulge my deepest, darkest secrets and fears to a total, complete, and utter stranger. I need to be here. I need to be here. I've got to keep telling myself, I need to be here . . . I don't *really* need to be here. I could probably buy a book to help me with my panic attacks. *How to Conquer Your Fears; Attack of the Panic; You're Not Going to Die (at least not right now).*

I know shrinks aren't just for crazy people anymore. It's not only artists who seek psychological assistance these days. Not just the "creative" types, the "quiet" ones, the "I'm hearing a voice and no one's talking to me" types. Doctors, lawyers, investment bankers—they all go. Yeah, if they can, so can I. Right. I'm not crazy. I'm just . . . "sensitive." I need to be here. I need to be here. Everyone goes to shrinks. Everyone I know goes, has gone, will go again soon. Except my husband . . . and father . . . and brother. They'll never go. Ever. Still, everything is going to be okay. Remain calm, all's well . . . ooh, the door's opening . . .

Man: Take care. I'll see you next week.
Woman: Um-kay.

This woman standing before me appears to be in her early forties. Obese. Very obese. Morbidly so. Her hair, if in fact that *is* hair, is greasy and stringy and could very well be a host to several extinct organisms.

And she's wearing what are commonly referred to as "pj's." Flannel pj's. Flannel pj's with butterflies and ladybugs. And she's clinging to a mangled teddy bear, and she's wearing reindeer slippers. The reindeers' antlers have bells attached to them and make a Christmas jingle as she shuffles toward the exit. And she's crying, and giggling. A giggly cry, a whiny cryish giggle. Like that disturbing combination of sounds that leaks out from under the masks of madmen and killers in all those '80s horror movies I used to peek at through my index and middle finger at sleepovers. This woman scares me. She scares me bad. And she smells really fucking crazy.

Man: Hillary?

Me: Yes?

Man: Come on in. I'm Dr. Lesaux. Nice to meet you.

Me: Hi.

Dr. Lesaux: . . . and here we are.

Me: Great. *This office is so dark. Blinds closed, lights dimmed. Jesuschrist. Can we get some lights on in here before I go into a deep depression? Should I tell him I'm light-sensitive, that I need some overhead brightness, some footlights, or sidelights? A pin light could even do the trick if pointed directly at my face . . . something with a bulb, for fuck's sake.*

Dr. Lesaux: You can take this seat right here, if you like. Would you like me to open the blinds or keep them closed? My last client likes it dark.

Me: Whichever. I'm easy.

Dr. Lesaux: I'll open them. Just tell me if it's too much light in your eyes. And let me move this coffee table back a bit. You have slightly longer legs than my last patient.

Me: *Our only difference.*

Dr. Lesaux: So, let me get my notes. I know I wrote down how you got my name . . . ah, here it is . . . let me see . . . oh, you know Muriel.

Me: Yeah.

Dr. Lesaux: And you're a patient over at St. John's.

Me: Right.

Dr. Lesaux: Uh-huh . . . and . . . well, great. Great to meet you. Did Muriel tell you anything about my background or—

Me: Just that you have experience counseling younger cancer patients.

Dr. Lesaux: Yes, and Muriel and I go way back. She's been recommending patients to me for close to fifteen years now . . . So, I'd like to start by just getting some background information from you. How does that sound? Oh, and I have to set this alarm. It keeps me from running over with the time.

Me: Oh. Okay.

Dr. Lesaux: Great. Have you ever been in therapy before?

Me: Um, yes.

Dr. Lesaux: And when was that?

Me: Well, about four—no, um, like five or six—years ago.

Dr. Lesaux: Uh-huh.

Me: When I was in college.

Dr. Lesaux: Uh-huh.

Me: . . . in New York . . . at NYU.

Dr. Lesaux: And were you seeing someone to work through something specific, or—

Me: I was having some . . . weight issues.

Dr. Lesaux: I see. Like, anorexia? Bulimia?

Me: Um, yeah . . . bulimia. *He's a toughie.*

Dr. Lesaux: And did you feel like the therapy was successful?

Me: Definitely. My therapist, she was great.

Dr. Lesaux: Ok, good. I'm glad it was a positive experience for you. So, besides being treated for bulimia, you haven't been in therapy?

Me: Correct.

Dr. Lesaux: Uh-huh.

Me:

Dr. Lesaux: And family history. Has anyone else in your family ever been in therapy?

Me: Yes.

Dr. Lesaux: And what were they treated for?

Me: Depression.

Dr. Lesaux: Okay . . . let's talk about your family in more detail for a—

Me: Just so you know, I'm actually here because I've been having panic attacks and my internist thought you might be able to give me some breathing exercises or something. Aside from the panic attacks, I've been feeling pretty good. A little anxious, but good. And as far as my family's concerned, I actually worked out most of my issues with them when I was in therapy in New York. I've, um, you know, "changed my expectations" about certain relationships, and, well, I feel pretty comfortable with everything, my life and stuff. So we can just, like, focus on the panic attacks. I mean, I have trouble on the freeways. That's my biggest issue. It's starting to be a real bitch, having to drive in the slow lane all the time. I get the attacks when I'm in the middle lane. I mean, I'm normally a really fast driver. An aggressive driver. I've started to be able to live with the anxiety attacks. I know what they are when they're happening. And mostly, they don't interfere with my daily routine—just sometimes. So that's why I'm here. I wanted to make everything clear. I don't want to waste your time. Or my time. Anyone's time. So, yeah. Just the panic attacks, really. Don't need to get into much else. Just need a couple breathing techniques or whatever you normally recommend. Exercises or something. Because, on the whole, I've been feeling pretty good. Strong. Clear-minded. Together. You know, considering . . . everything.

Dr. Lesaux: I'm picking up a slight resistance.

Me: To?

Dr. Lesaux: To your being here.

Me: No, no, no. I want to be here . . . I just wanted it to be clear *why* I'm here.

Dr. Lesaux: Why did you want it to be clear?

Me: Because . . . I . . . don't want you to waste your time dealing with things that don't need to be dealt with. Things that have *already* been dealt with . . . before . . . by me.

Dr. Lesaux: I understand.

Me: Great.

Dr. Lesaux: You want me to understand you have everything under control.

Me: Right.

Dr. Lesaux: And that you are feeling "pretty good."

Me: Yeah.

Dr. Lesaux: That you just need some breathing exercises.

Me: Correct.

Dr. Lesaux: Well, I *will* be able to give you some breathing exercises. But first I think we need to take a look at a couple of things. In order for your anxiety to go away, we need to find the root of it. And I don't mean the cancer, necessarily. I wouldn't be a good doctor if I only treated the symptoms and not the problem. The panic attacks are the *result* of something deeper. That's what we must uncover. Together. I understand that this is scary, but you have already gotten over the biggest hurdle. You're here. You called me . . . several times . . . made an appointment, and came. So now we have to get to the "why" of why you came. And it's not because you're having panic attacks. That, I can guarantee. So, we must look closer. Chart the uncharted. So, I'd like you to start thinking about patterns. For the next week, keep a journal of your daily activities. Also, be aware of your thoughts and thought patterns: if you're particularly anxious, what you're anxious about, that kind of thing. I'd like to try to pinpoint the thoughts that precede your attacks. If we can get rid of the negative thinking, then—

Me: Ok. But—

Dr. Lesaux: I'd also like to give you this handout on patterns of negative thinking. I wrote this a couple of weeks ago. It was prompted by one of my callers—I host a radio call-in show once a week.

Me: "If You Build It, He Will Come: An in-depth look at the power of thought," by renowned radio personality Dr. Thomas Lesaux.

Dr. Lesaux: *Field of Dreams.*

Me: Yeah, I got the reference. It's one of my favorite—

Beep-beep-beep-beep-beep.

Dr. Lesaux: Time.

N.E.D.

Driving to Santa Monica from West Hollywood stands as a constant reminder of how very little I know about traffic in Los Angeles. Since I somehow arrived twenty-five minutes early for my appointment, I'm doomed to wander the hospital halls in search of something—*anything*—the least bit entertaining. I'd love to find a cart with a few dozen rubber gloves. I'd even be satisfied to round up some of those heavy-duty, hospital-quality round Band-Aids. I *love* those Band-Aids. So far, though, everything seems to be under pretty tight surveillance, lock and key and all that . . . Maybe I should check the fourth floor, the Joyce Eisenberg Keefer Breast Center (a.k.a. where the money goes). They have *all* the good stuff. Their snack area is always overflowing with lemon rose and peppermint tea, Keebler graham crackers, and Ghirardelli hot chocolate mix—*luxury* compared with the third floor's stash of generic saltines (I thought Saltines *were* generic) and Lipton iced-tea packets, which I can only assume are meant to be used with water from the drinking fountain. *They* have leather wingback chairs and decorative oriental rugs. *We* have worn sofa chairs and faded gray carpet. They even have a boutique up there on the fourth floor that sells . . . stuff. I'm not exactly sure what kind of stuff—I've never betrayed my peeps long enough to go in—but I know it's there. The Positive Appearance Center—you can't miss it. Its gold placard practically blinds you as you step off the elevator into the Joyce Eisenberg Keefer blah blah blah. Everyone and their grandmother bends over backward to raise money for breast cancer. Men, women, and children alike can't write checks fast enough in support of the good ol' breast. Long live the breast! Three cheers for the boob! Another round of applause for the tits! And the crowd goes wild! If they could pull themselves away from their pretty-in-pink ribbons for a goddamned second, they might be able to see that melanoma could use a little cash once in a blue moon.

Not that I'm bitter or anything. Not that I resent little miss popularity and all of her friends. Not that I *mind* being the misfit, the freak on the third floor, the one with the black ribbon, the one everybody laughs at and no one wants to eat lunch with just because I was a foot taller than the average middle-school gym teacher! I bet the breast cancer center has an abundance of those heavy-duty, hospital-quality round Band-Aids! I bet they're practically giving them away up there. I'm gonna go clean them out. I may even take a few extra packets of hot chocolate. So there!

Half an hour and four cups of hot chocolate later:

Not sure why I got dressed this morning. Not sure why I put on underwear, bra, T-shirt, sweater, jeans, socks, shoes, and watch, only to drive to Dr. Gregory's office, strip, and go back to sleep on the padded hospital table while desperately trying to cover my bare ass with this piece of tissue paper nurses refer to as a blanket. I'm still wearing my wool socks because I'd like to keep my toes . . . and I'm putting my sweater *back* on, over my hospital gown, because my nipples could cut glass right now.

Knock, knock.

Dr. Gregory: Are you decent?

Me: I'm naked. Does that qualify?

Dr. Gregory: Hello. Good to see you . . . that's quite a get-up.

Me: Trying to keep warm.

Dr. Gregory: So . . . let's take a look . . . uh-huh . . . great . . . scar looks good . . . let's see . . . don't see anything suspicious on your arms . . . I see a small place on your back that has a speck of dark pigment, but it's very small, so just keep an eye on it . . . Your dermatologist is doing regular body checks as well, correct?

Me: Oh, yeah. Also, I noticed a new mole the other day. It's right . . . at the very, very bottom of my lower back.

Dr. Gregory: Yes, I see it. It's very small. Let me get the light. It's kinda hard to get a good look at it. Lie on your stomach for a second.

Me: *Let's be honest here. Lower, lower back equals upper, upper butt crack. So, yes, let me let you focus a bright light on my ass so you can examine a mole in my crack. I have no dignity. None at all anymore.*

Dr. Gregory: I think it's fine. Just keep an eye on it.

Me: Okay. *That should be easy.*

Dr. Gregory: Lymph nodes feel normal . . . everything looks good. Go ahead and get dressed, and then head over to the lab and Howard will draw your blood.

Me: You got it. Actually, if you have time, I've been doing some research online and I have a few questions.

Dr. Gregory: Okay, shoot.

Me: I've got my paper here . . . somewhere . . . okay. One: Do you test my blood for ta90? Two: Would I benefit from interferon therapy? Three: Does this hospital conduct any melanoma vaccine clinical trials? Four: Will staying out of the sun reduce my risk for a recurrence? And Five: How do you know, or I know, or does anyone know, for sure that I'm cancer free? . . . I sound so . . . doctorly, huh?

Dr. Gregory: Someone's been doing her homework. You may have to repeat some of that . . .

Me: Would you like to take the last part first?

Dr. Gregory: No, that's okay, let's see . . . you mentioned ta90. Ta90 is a glycoprotein that researchers claimed could predict metastatic disease and survival for early-stage-melanoma patients. Years ago, we started testing our patients for the presence of ta90 and then followed them for three, five, seven years to see if the ta90 patients were, in fact, less likely to have a recurrence. Unfortunately, we didn't find any correlation. I can order the test for you, if you'd like, but the results won't mean all that much.

Me: Not necessary.

Dr. Gregory: And what else? You asked about chemotherapy, right? The interferon therapy would only be recommended to patients as a last resort. These drugs are hugely toxic to the system, and they offer minimal benefits, in my opinion. The treatment is a whole year. And the side effects are pretty awful. Really awful, to be honest.

Me: Really awful. Really.

Dr. Gregory: And as far as the vaccine is concerned, believe it or not, we were one of the first hospitals to do vaccine trials. We have patients who first received the drugs twelve years ago. And all of our trials, up until this year, were with Stage III and IV patients. This year, for the first time ever, we're doing a trial with stage II patients. Stage II means a melanoma depth of at least .75. Your .4 thickness puts you into the Stage I category, so—

Me: So I'm fucked, basically.

Dr. Gregory: No, it's good you don't qualify. And the better news is, the way things are going, the vaccine should be FDA approved within the next two years.

Me: That would be amazing.

Dr. Gregory: And something about staying out of the sun?

Me: . . . if that decreases my chances of a recurrence.

Dr. Gregory: No, not really. But let me say, your odds of a recurrence are very low—

Me: Great.

Dr. Gregory: —but you do have around a 30 percent chance of getting a *new* melanoma, considering your staging, age, the location of your tumor, etc.

Me: Thirty percent? If I stay out of the sun, does that go down?

Dr. Gregory: You could live underground and never see the light of day and still get another melanoma.

Me: Thirty percent—that sounds so . . . high. How can I have a three-in-ten chance of another melanoma if I'm never in the sun?

Dr. Gregory: Because you've already done most of your sun damage. And there is an "unknown" with melanoma. Sun damage plays a role, but it's not the only cause. There's more to it than that.

Me: Maybe I could be like one of those translucent creatures that live deep in the soil and slither around using their little hairy tentacles, or whatever it is they use.

Dr. Gregory: Bottom line: You need to stay out of the sun. But that doesn't guarantee you won't get another melanoma.

Me: Thirty percent.

Dr. Gregory: Let's get to your last question. The answer is, I don't know for certain.

Me: You don't know if you got all the cancer cells.

Dr. Gregory: Correct. Not for certain.

Me: Oh.

Dr. Gregory: You're n.e.d. No evidence of disease.

Me:

Dr. Gregory: Well, if that's it, I'm off. I will see you in a couple of weeks. Oh, don't forget to stop at the lab.

Me: I won't. *N.e.d., n.e.d.*

"Hi, nice to meet you. I'm N.e.d., and you are?"

"N.e.d., but I'm waiting for L.e.d."

"Never heard of him."

"You know, lots of evidence of disease.'"

"Oh . . . shit. Hope I never run into him."

Knock, knock.

Me: I'm getting dressed.

Other: It's your nurse. It's Dana. I wanted to say hi.

Me: Come on in . . . I like as many people as possible to see me naked.

Nurse Dana: How are you doing?

Me: Good. Oh my God, you're huge! When are you due? . . . Here, walk with me to the lab.

Nurse Dana: I'm at thirty-one weeks.

Me: That's incredible. My husband and I are actually getting really close to starting a family. I've been looking forward to big, voluptuous nursing breasts for a *very* long time.

Nurse Dana: You talked to Dr. Gregory about that?

Me: Ah, no.

Nurse Dana: About getting pregnant?

Me: Um, no. Why?

Nurse Dana: Maybe I should page him . . . I'll page him. He didn't say anything?

Me: About what? About me getting pregnant? No. Why?

Nurse Dana: He should talk to you about it. He's better at explaining it—

Ring.

Nurse Dana: That's him calling. You can pick up.

Ring.

Me:

Ring, ring.

Nurse Dana: Pick up.

Me:

Ring.

Nurse Dana: Hi. I've got Hillary, here. She has a question for you.

Me: Hey. I don't know what I'm supposed to be asking you. Dana and I were taking about having kids, and then she paged you . . . I don't know. Melanoma doesn't affect my ability to have kids, does it?

Dr. Gregory: No, no, no. You and your husband just have to wait a while, that's all.

Me: How long?

Dr. Gregory: Well, I usually say at least two years. Between two and five.

Me:

Dr. Gregory: . . . hello?

Me: . . . yeah . . . I'm here. I can't have kids for five years?

Dr. Gregory: You're at the highest risk for a recurrence within the first two years.

Me: You said I'm *not* at high risk, though.

Dr. Gregory: You're not, but about forty percent of melanomas have hormone receptors on them.

Me: So?

Dr. Gregory: Meaning, *if* you were to get pregnant, and *if* we didn't get all the cancer cells with the surgery, the hormonal changes during pregnancy *could* stimulate those cells, causing them to multiply and spread really quickly. Also, if you have a recurrence, your treatment options are greatly reduced if you're pregnant. I don't want you in a situation where you have to choose between your health—your *life*—and the life of your child. I've seen too many cases where the mother postponed necessary treatment in order to carry her child to term, and the mother—

Me: I don't understand. Why didn't someone mention all this before?

Dr. Gregory: I assumed you and your gynecologist had discussed it.

Me: I knew I couldn't be on birth control pills because of the hormones, but no one *ever* mentioned melanoma affecting pregnancy. *How is that possible?*

Dr. Gregory: Look, this is a very controversial topic. Some researchers say there is no connection between hormonal changes during pregnancy and an increased risk of recurrence. But you need to give your body some time.

Me: *Time?* Time for *what?* Time to see if cancer cells turn up in my lymph nodes? Time to develop a *new* melanoma and then wait another two years, only to have a third fucking cancerous mole and have to wait two more years, and on and on and—this doesn't make any sense.

Dr. Gregory: Try and—

Me: I've gotta go. I'll talk to you later.

Dr. Gregory: But—

Click.

Dana: Honey, it's—

Me: You know what? I don't want to talk about it. Howard, take my blood so I can get *out of this fucking hospital.*

My life is starting to feel more and more like a Lifetime (television for women) miniseries. *Confessions of a Survivor,* starring Tracey Gold, with Patty Duke and a Special Appearance by Meredith Baxter-Birney . . .

Tracey dashes out of the lab, trying desperately to hold back her tears. As she sprints down an endless hallway filled with children of all ages, the tears start to flow. Background music swells as we hear Tracey's thoughts aloud. "And so I ran," she says, her voice calm and reflective, "As hard and fast as my feet would allow." She is sobbing as she reaches the entrance to the hospital and frantically pushes through the revolving door, stopping on the other side just long enough to reach into her purse for her sunglasses. And her hat. And some sunscreen. With music pounding, we watch in slow motion as Tracey tilts her head toward the sky and with arms outstretched screams, *"Whyyyy meeee?"*

Fade to white, as "To be continued" makes a slow crawl up the screen.

THE DRIVE HOME:

Me: Is Adam around?

Marci: He just stepped into a meeting with Greg. Can I have him call you back? Are you on your cell?

Me: Could you pull him out of the meeting, please?

Marci: He's in with Greg, and the door's closed.

Me: Could you get him?

Marci: Uh . . . ah . . . okay. Just a second.

Adam: Hello? What's wrong? What happened? Are you okay?

Me: Yeah, I'm fine—

Adam: You scared me to death.

Me: I just wanted to say . . . hi.

Adam: Hi . . . What's going on?

Me: No, I just wanted to say hi and that I love you, that's all.

Adam: I love you too. Did you see Dr. Gregory this morning?

Me: Yeah.

Adam: I see. Are you going to tell me what happened?

Me: No.

Adam: What did he say?

Me: I don't want to tell you . . . before I tell you, I just want you to know that I'm *not* convinced he's right about any of this, and I'm going to do my own research on the subject, because I'm not going to trust every word he says just because he's a doctor, because they don't know everything and they can be wrong about a lot of things a lot of the time and this whole issue doesn't really make sense to—

Adam: What did he say?

Me: He said . . . and I can't believe it never came—

Adam: What did he say?

Me: That we have to wait to start a family.

Adam:

Adam: How long?

Me: At least two years.

Adam: What does "at least two" mean?

Me: Two to five.

Adam: And what's the reasoning behind this?

Me: It's the hormone issue again. Apparently, the hormonal changes during pregnancy can stimulate melanoma cells or something. If I still have some cancer cells in my body, they would multiply and spread really fast if I was pregnant—something like that. So I'm supposed to wait until I'm out of high-risk territory. The whole thing seems—

Adam: High risk for what?

Me: A recurrence, the cancer showing up in my lymphatic system . . . which doesn't really make sense, since he said I'm not really *at* risk for a recurrence. Either there's a risk or there isn't. It can't be both at the same time.

Adam: Then you're not getting pregnant.

Me: What do you mean? Of course I am. I just have to wait.

Adam: I'm not going to let you do anything that puts your health at risk. There are other ways to have children—

Me: I know. I just—

Adam: We'll figure it out.

Me: I know. I—

Adam: We'll figure it out. We always do.

Me: I love you.

Adam: I love you.

Me: Get back to Greg. He's probably busting a gut by now. We can talk about this later.

Adam: Don't worry.

Me: Yeah. I'll try.

Adam: And concentrate on the road.

Me: I'm not driving right now.

Adam: Where are you?

Me: I'm parked. I started to get a panic attack, so I pulled over.

Adam: Jesus.

Me:

Adam: Are you crying?

Me: I'm laughing.

Adam: What's so funny?

Me: This. This whole . . . thing.

I have moments. Moments within moments when I'm able to make things stop spinning just long enough to take a close look at things—my world, the events that are unfolding—and I'm able to get some perspective. These moments are few and far between, but when they happen they are brilliant, extraordinary, awe-inspiring, because for a split second I am able to see my life the way others see it, see it from the outside looking in. And so as I sit in my car—which is parked on the side of a busy Santa Monica street, after I just had a panic attack because my surgeon said I shouldn't get pregnant and that I have a 30 percent chance of going through all this over again—I get a peek, a glimpse, at what others see. At what my husband must see. And so I do the only thing I can think to do, the only thing that my body will allow: I laugh. I'm laughing so hard, tears are rolling down my cheeks and I'm getting a cramp in my side and my stomach is turning cartwheels and still I can't stop laughing. All of a sudden everything seems so fucking hilarious. Like the funniest moment in the funniest scene of a John Candy classic . . . it's hard to catch my breath . . . aw, shit, this shit is funny . . . aw, God . . . so funny . . . This is sick . . . I may . . . never . . . be able to . . . stop . . . laughing . . . except that . . . now . . . I'm pretty sure . . . I'm crying . . . there is no more laugh in these tears . . . yep . . . I am. I'm most definitely crying . . .

Knock, knock.

Cop: Miss, you can't park here. You need to move along.

Me: Okay. I'm trying to move along. Trust me. I'm trying.

One Big Cookie

After yesterday's festivities and an evening of nail biting and cuticle demo-lition, I find myself standing outside the door of my best friend's house. I don't know if she's home—I don't know if she's *due* home—I just know I need to talk. And I want her to be the one who listens.

Tess and I go way back. Our friendship started, slow, in seventh grade. I knew of her because she was "the gymnast," close to Olympic level, or so I heard. She knew of me, I'm assuming, because I was the tall new girl from Georgia. I was Big Bird, I was The Tree—names I was given lovingly by prepubescent boys who were nearly approach-ing half my size. I was a short five foot seven and a half. Or at least I liked to think so. I was the girl you didn't want to be friends with. The one you never wanted to be seen with, especially not in seventh grade. Not when one's very existence hinges on trying to be cool and popular and—if you are a girl—having boobs. I fell into none of the previously mentioned categories, and so I was on my own, destined to eat lunch by myself until something happened that made me cool or popular or develop . . . you know whats.

But while most seventh graders looked through me, over me, Tess didn't. She was different. She was nice. On the surface she seemed perfectly content hanging out with her popular buddies and watching quietly as they tormented the unsuspecting, the unassuming, but her smile spoke of other things, deeper things. But maybe that was because she was a freak, too. She had muscles. Gymnast pecs and all that. All the boys in my grade put together didn't equal the power in her two arms. She was small, solid as a rock, and, of course, flat as a pancake.

So, like I said, our friendship started slow. Friendly hellos developed into birthday party invitations, into sleepovers, into long yearbook entries—each year, our friendship growing and changing, changing with us, in spite of us, our lives becoming more intricately intertwined, until it felt as if we'd *always* known each other. Until we couldn't remember a time when we hadn't had each other to lean on, to laugh with, to confide in. A decade later, the core of our friendship remains unchanged, a time capsule. Because I am still, in many ways, the gawky new girl, and Tess, well, she's still solid as a rock . . . and a rock is just what I need right now.

Knock, knock.
Me: Tess? It's me. Tess?
Knock.
Me: Tess? Hel-lo?
Knock, knock.
Me: Shit—

Tess: I'm coming . . . hold on . . . I've got cookie dough on my hands . . . I'm—Sabrina, get off!—The cat is pouncing on my leg . . . Hi, sorry. Come in. Sorry about the mess. It's my turn to clean. I promised Jimmy I would have it done before he got home, but I'm not sure that's realistic. I've gotta finish these cookies for one of my patients. This is my second batch. I wanted to make one big cookie, but I couldn't get the inside cooked without burning the edges, so I had to go to the market and get more dough. In my head it seemed like a good idea. And the cat keeps trying to jump up on the counters. I'd be so embarrassed if my supervisor found a cat hair in one of the cookies. How was your doctor's appointment yesterday?

Me: Fine. It was fine.

Tess: What's wrong? Something's wrong.

Me: I'm trying not to freak out about it. It was really weird. I was talking to one of the nurses, and I told her I was thinking about getting pregnant—I already started taking prenatal vitamins and everything—and next thing I know, I'm on the phone with Gregory and he's saying I have to wait to get pregnant.

Tess: Wait, why? How long?

Me: First he said two years—

Tess: Well, two years isn't so bad, when you think about it. You and Adam can do all the traveling—

Me: No, I wouldn't mind the two, but then he said two to five. And that's assuming I don't get another melanoma between now and then. I mean, what if I wait, like, a year and a half and then get melanoma again? I'll have to wait another two years, and then . . . I don't know.

Tess: Did he say why you have to wait?

Me: It has to do with the hormonal changes during pregnancy. They can stimulate melanoma cells or something.

Tess: So, how does all this make you feel?

Me: You are such a therapist right now.

Tess: Sorry. How do you feel?

Me: I feel . . . sad. I feel really sad. And angry. I'm pissed because . . . I don't know.

Tess: Why do you feel—

Me: I'm pissed because—it's not about the two years, I can wait the two years—it's that I feel like this stupid melanoma is taking over everything. I can't get away from it. I can't stop thinking, worrying, checking every single little fucking mole on my body every single fucking day. I wake up, I check my moles. I shower, I look at my moles. I put on sunscreen, I look at them again. I step outside, and I am reminded. I get in my fucking car and I worry because my side windows aren't UV tinted because if I tint them I'll get ticketed . . . and now the whole pregnancy thing. It was something I had to look forward to. Something that seemed positive. Something that I've always wanted and . . . and something I had control over. I feel like I have no control over anything anymore.

Tess: I'm so sorry. I can't even imagine what it feels like.

Me: It feels bad. It feels really bad.

Tess: Well, I think we should do some research on this. I can talk to my aunt. Since she had breast cancer, she keeps pretty well informed on the cancer front. I'll also talk to some of the doctors where I'm doing the group-therapy sessions, see if anyone knows anything.

Me: I'm gonna go online and see what I can find . . . Adam was so great. He said, "We'll figure it out. We always do." I was really worried about what he was going to say. I guess at this point, nothing fazes him . . . So, I see Sabrina's still pouncing.

Tess: Yeah, but she's getting much, much better.

Me: What happened to your hand?

Tess: Oh, well, she still likes to attack me in the night. I try to stay covered up, but—

Me: You've gotta get rid of this cat.

Tess: I know. I know . . . you want a cookie? Or some dough? I've already eaten about a quarter pound of the dough. I'm starting to feel nauseous.

Me: No, that's okay. I think I'm gonna head home. Sorry I just dumped all that stuff on you.

Tess: You didn't. *I'm* sorry you have to deal with all this.

Me: I'll call you later. Thanks. Love you.

Tess: Love you too.

With Tess still a year and a half away from becoming a full-fledged psychologist at this point, I take an enormous amount of pleasure in pointing out all her "How does that make you feel?" and "What are you feeling right now?" inquiries. But to be fair, sometimes I like it. Sometimes it's nice just to be asked. Because no one ever asks that. Not in a real way. Not looking for an honest answer. Not really.

Worst-case Scenario

Dr. Lesaux: You came back. I wasn't sure I'd see you again.

Me: I've thought a lot about the appointment last week, and—

Dr. Lesaux: Let me just set this alarm.

Me: —to be honest, that really bothered me last week. Can't you just glance at the clock once in a while? The alarm—it's very abrupt.

Dr. Lesaux: I'm sorry. I just haven't found a better way of keeping track of the time.

Me: Yeah, well . . .

Dr. Lesaux: Let's see . . . where did we leave off last week? We talked about panic attacks. Did you have any this week?

Me: I have them every day.

Dr. Lesaux: How many times a day? Your best guess.

Me: Um, three or four times.

Dr. Lesaux: And do you feel they are starting to affect your daily routine?

Me: Yes.

Dr. Lesaux:

Me: Yes. I would say they do.

Dr. Lesaux:

Me: . . . affect my daily routine . . . are you waiting for me to say something in particular?

Dr. Lesaux: No, I was just listening. You know, I've got a handout that I think you might find helpful. It discusses common symptoms of panic attacks and different ways to address each symptom . . . let me find it . . . it's been a while since I've used it . . . Here it is.

Me: "Attack of the Panic," by Dr. Thomas Lesaux.

Dr. Lesaux: You're smiling.

Me: Catchy title.

Dr. Lesaux: I think it's good to try and address many of these types of issues with as much humor as possible.

Me: No, I totally agree . . . So, should I read this all now or—

Dr. Lesaux: No, take it home and really take some time with it. We can discuss any questions about it next week.

Me: *More homework. Great.*

Dr. Lesaux: I'd like us to start exploring *why* you're getting these attacks.

Me: Okay.

Dr. Lesaux: Last week I asked you to try to notice any patterns. Did you find "Build It and He Will Come" helpful at all?

Me: Well, I definitely understood what you were saying. I mean, I know I'm creating these attacks by what I'm thinking about, but *my* problem is, I don't know how to stop thinking the thoughts—without thinking about them. Ya know what I mean?

Dr. Lesaux: Yes, I do. Why don't we get back to what we talked about last week, and I think we might start to figure out ways to change your thinking. So . . . patterns. When or where do you typically get an attack?

Me: Well, I mentioned the freeway. I also get them in movie theaters, when the seats don't have headrests. I need those big stadium seats. I get them in the hair salon. I sometimes get them in restaurants, when the seats have low backs. I get them if I look down while walking up a staircase. And . . . um . . . I get them when I talk to my mom on the phone.

Dr. Lesaux: You mentioned seats with low backs. What do you think that's about?

Me: I don't know. If I don't have a headrest, I feel . . . out of control.

Dr. Lesaux:

Me: Like . . . I feel like my neck can't support my head . . . my head doesn't feel safe.

Dr. Lesaux: *You* don't feel safe.

Me: My head. My head doesn't.

Dr. Lesaux: And have you paid attention to what you're thinking about right before these attacks happen?

Me: Not really.

Dr. Lesaux: Do you find yourself worrying about having a panic attack?

Me: Of course. I sometimes think to myself, *this would be a* really *bad time to have one.*

Dr. Lesaux: You know, I think I've got an article you might find helpful. It's something I've used for quite a few years, not on my call-in radio show, but just as part of my private practice . . . here it is. Take it home; look it over. It lists the most common symptoms of panic attacks. I think you'll find it not only educational, but comforting as well. This sensation in your head, this light-headedness, is really very common. So, back to the hair salon: If you had an attack in the hair salon or movie theater, what's the worst that could happen? Let's really explore this . . .

Me: I don't know. The whole thing would be incredibly embarrassing, for one thing.

Dr. Lesaux: Okay, so, give me a worst-case scenario.

Me: Okay. Um, so, let's say I'm having my hair cut and I pass out from an anxiety attack. Except no one knows what happened; they think

I'm choking or something. So some slobbery patron suffering from advanced gingivitis starts CPR while the salon owner calls an ambulance. I am sprawled on a hairy floor with the entire salon hovering over me, staring down at my pathetic, anxiety-ridden carcass. And just as the firemen prepare to hoist me onto a stretcher, I come to. The man in charge shouts, "There's nothing to see here, folks. False alarm. She's a faker." It would be like the scene in *Terms of Endearment* where the grocery checker yells over the intercom, "She doesn't have enough money." That's the kinda thing I worry about, generally speaking. You know, total and utter humiliation. That sort of thing.

Dr. Lesaux: That's definitely a worst case. But, to be honest, it's very rare to pass out from an anxiety attack. One might feel dizzy, lightheaded, but people rarely lose consciousness.

Me: Really? That's a relief.

Dr. Lesaux: It *can* happen, but it's very, very rare. You know what, let's consider a more *realistic* scenario and see if we can reduce some of your negative—*beep-beep-beep*—I'm sorry. I thought I turned that off. That must be my backup alarm.

Me: What were you—

Dr. Lesaux: Time.

News

So, today's the day. Today's the day I tell my mother and father they aren't going to be grandparents. They're not gonna get to spoil the fruit of my loins, at least not right away.

I've been mulling over the exact verbiage. I'm not so worried about *telling* them I have to wait as I am about them asking *why* I have to wait. Actually, I'm worried about my answer to their question of why. Because no matter how I say it—casually mention it, give a shout-out to the waiting—my mother will inevitably throw herself back into the pit of despair she just recently clawed her way out of. She'll have an endless string of questions, most, or all, of which, I can't answer. Or won't answer. She'll call all my doctors. Demand a conference. Demand a recount. It's not going to be pretty. It's not going to be fun, but it's got to be done, and the time is now.

Okay. Deep breath. Maybe I won't tell her. Maybe I should wait. Yeah, wait for the right time. Okay, so, yeah, I'll wait for the right time, which clearly isn't now. I mean, I don't want to worry her. I don't want to cause me—I mean, *her*—any unnecessary anxiety. Yep, just gonna wait this bad boy out. Because I'm a good person.

Who the fuck am I kidding? I'm gonna blurt it out no matter what. I know me. Dial the number . . . okay . . . deep breath . . . and . . . I should ease her into it. I don't need to go into all the medical stuff—just stick to the facts. *I can't get pregnant now, Mom. Doctor's orders.*

Or I could just lie.

I'm sterile. I just found out.

Adam and I have decided we don't like kids.

A dog is a big enough responsibility.

Adam got fired. We can't afford to feed another mouth right now.

Adam can't get me pregnant. He's shooting blanks, but don't mention I said anything to you. He's very sensitive about it.

Me: Hello, Mom?

Mom: Hi, honey.

Me: Mom, I need to talk to you about something Dr. Gregory mentioned the other day. He . . . you aren't going to like this . . . said . . . but don't freak out, because I'm still investigating the issue . . . that . . . I know this comes out of left field . . . Adam and I have to wait to have children.

Mom: I have to start dinner. I'll put your father on. He has something to tell you.

Me: Wait, Mom—

Dad: Hi, hon.

Me: Dad, Mom was *really* weird just now. I was trying to tell her—

Dad: I got the pathology back today from that mole on my back.

Me: Finally. It took long enough. It really shouldn't take—

Dad: It's melanoma.

Me: *I'm spinning. Everything is spinning. Where am I? . . . okay, stay upright. I feel cold under my feet. Cold in my hand. I'm gripping something hard and cold. A countertop. Okay, hold on to the granite. Don't pass out. My legs are bending. Shit. Okay, I'll sit right here. I'll lie right here. My legs are curling up. Knees to chin. I'm safe. I'm safe. I'm safe. Focus. Be in the moment. Listen . . .*

Dad: Your mother's taking it really hard.

Me: . . . um . . .

Dad:

Me: Um . . . I don't understand. Your dermatologist said it looked fine. He . . . ah . . . he said it was nothing to worry about. Didn't he? Who the fuck is this guy? He said worst case it's basal, right? I don't understand. Who did you talk to? Did you talk to your doctor? Who called with the report?

Dad: The doctor did.

Me: The doctor who said it was nothing to worry about? *That* doctor?

Dad: He said he was surprised. But that's why he took it off, because he wasn't sure what it was.

Me: Did he tell you the thickness? What stage is it? Did he say?

Dad: I didn't ask.

Me: Didn't he tell you? What did he say, exactly?

Dad: Just that it was melanoma. I have an appointment set up for next week.

Me: Call him back. You need to get in there *this* week.

Dad: His schedule is all booked.

Me: If you can't get in before next week, you should at least call the office and have them read you the pathology report over the phone.

Dad: I'm sure he'll go over all that when I see him.

Me: But I . . . you don't want to wait that long, do you?

Dad: Now, I don't want you to worry about me. You need to focus on your own health—

Me: I'm fine.

Dad: You don't need the extra stress.

Me: Dad—

Dad: I'll be fine. I'm strong. We come from hearty stock. I don't want you to worry. Promise me.

Me: I—

Dad: It's your mother I'm worried about. She's been through so much already.

Me:

Dad: I have to be strong for her.

Me:

Dad: How do you feel?

Me: What?

Dad: How do you feel?

Me: Dad, *please* call the doctor.

Dad: I'll see him next week . . . I've gotta run, honey. I've got a conference call in a couple of minutes.

Me: Put Mom back on . . . Mom?

Mom: I'm here.

Me: Did you talk to the doctor?

Mom: No, just your father.

Me: Dad didn't seem to have any details. I'm sure the doctor must have told him something.

Mom: We'll find out everything next week.

Me: Mom, I want you to call the office back and ask a nurse to read you the path report over the phone. I want you to ask—get a pen; you need to write this down. I want you to ask the Clark level, the Breslow thickness, and if they got clean margins when they removed it.

Mom: Their office is closed now. I'll have to call back in the morning.

Me: *No.* I want you to call right now. I'm sure they have an emergency number on their answering machine. Page the doctor and have him explain everything in detail. I can't believe Dad didn't ask any questions.

Mom: There is no need to page the doctor when we'll find all this out next—

Me: —week. *I know. Jesus fucking Christ*—don't you want to *know?*

Mom:

Me: You know some of this information already, don't you? You're just not telling me.

Mom:

Me: Mom, tell me everything the doctor told you.

Mom:

Me: Mom, *for fuck's sake.* This isn't helping me. Not telling me is not going to keep me from worrying. This is bullshit. *Tell me what the fucking report said.* What was the thickness?

Mom: I promised your father I wouldn't—

Me: *Mom!*

Mom: Um . . . it was . . . two something.

Me: Point-two or two-point-something?

Mom: 2.43.

Me:

Mom: What was yours, again?

Me: I don't remember . . . . *4, .4, .4, .4* . . .

Mom: Your father didn't want to tell you any of this because he doesn't want you to worry about him.

Me: You don't understand. I want to know everything. I'll feel better knowing.

Mom: Okay.

Me: Is there anything else?

Mom: No. As far as I know, the doctor told your father the thickness and said we'd discuss everything else when he comes in for his appointment.

Me: I can't believe they can't squeeze him in this week. And this doctor. Do you think he's good? Maybe Dad should come here for his excision.

Mom: Let's just wait and see what this OSU doctor says; then we can decide . . . I've gotta go, honey. I'm making your father tuna fish casserole. His favorite. We'll call you tomorrow.

Click.

The fear. It's bubbling up. Creeping, sneaking, trying to make a break for it. Trying to take over completely. It's building an army. I feel the stomping of millions of little feet in the pit of my stomach. Their march is echoing to the tip-top of my ears, and I can't shake them. I can move them around, shift them from right leg to left, down to my toes and back up again, but I can't shake the army, not completely. I can't shake them out . . . off . . . I want to jump out of my skin. Out of the body that is curled up on the kitchen floor, shaking and twitching. My skin is crawling, and I want to follow suit. Crawl far and fast away, leave behind not just all that I've heard in the last five minutes, but all that has happened in the last fifty days.

Maybe I just need a good cleaning out. Maybe I could remove my head, clasp it firmly on either side, and shake the hell out of it. That might work. I'll empty it out. Because I know too much. I need shit out. And if in the shaking of my own head I lose other valuable information, so be it, because I don't want to know what I know. I don't want to feel how I feel. Everything I narrowly escaped and gladly pretended didn't happen is happening to my father. And I'm sick with fear. And I'm just going to lie here. And wait for something to happen. For something to happen that will help me figure out my next move. Because I have no more moves . . . I'm just gonna wait riiiiiight here. And pray.

Ring, ring, ring, ring.

You've reached Adam and Hillary. We're not in right now, but leave us a message and we'll get back to you as soon as possible. You can also try me on my cell. If you're someone I'd want to talk to, you already have the number.

Beep.

Adam: Hey, babe, it's me. I thought maybe I'd catch you at home. Just got a call from my bro. You won't believe it: Nancy's pregnant again. I wanted to give you a heads-up. I think Nancy's hesitant to call. She's afraid she might upset you. I understand. But you should call to say congratulations if you get a chance. I can't believe they're having another baby. I'm going into a meeting, but call me later. Love you.

Click.

Beep-beep-beep, beep-beep-beep-beep.

Ring, ring, ring, ring.

Hi. We're not in, so leave us a message and we'll call ya back . . . Jackie, honey, say bye.

"Byeeee."

Beep.

Me: It's Hillary. Adam told me your, um, good news. I'm, I'm really, really happy for you guys. I'm, um, sure . . . you guys are, uh . . . really, really happy . . . too. It's such good news . . . to hear. So, um, yeah. Just wanted to say congrats. Congrats to good, happy news.

Click.

The Sun'll Come Out . . . Tomorrow

I'm chopping onions and liking it. My eyes are burning and running, my nose is red and stinging, and I'm lovin' every second of it. Cryin' and choppin'. Cuttin' and sobbin'. *And in the red corner, standing in a pile of piss, with a snot bubble in her nose . . .* I can taste salt, and onion, and . . . pain. It's like a metallic taste in the back of my mouth. And my jaw is aching. It's aching because it's been clenched since one this afternoon. It's aching because I want it to. I want *everything* to ache. All at once. *Give it all to me!* I want to cut my fingers off with this knife and rub the bloody, stubby leftover digits in onion juice. I want to take a cheese grater to the tips of my toes and shave 'em down a bit. Not too much—just enough to know I shouldn't dip the leftovers into a bucket of Clorox . . . give it all to me. I want it all. I want it all now, today, this very second, because tomorrow I don't want any of it. Tomorrow's a new day. Tomorrow . . . will be perfect. Tomorrow will give me all the good that has piled up from my last couple months of bad. See, someone's fucked up. Someone, somewhere, has got the numbers wrong. Their fingers slipped off the keyboard and messed up my turn. 'Cause it's my turn for something good. My chance to hear something happy and nice and fun. I'm due. I'm due for a huge fucking good thing. Whatever it is, it's gonna be *good*. I just know tomorrow is gonna be great. Tomorrow's *good* will let me forget today's . . . *not* so good.

Tadpole Baby

Me: Will you spoon me? Ad? Ad? Adam? *Adam?*

Adam: Huh?

Me: Spoon me. I had a bad dream.

Adam: Your feet are freezing.

Me:

Me: I just had *such* a crazy dream.

Adam: Shocking.

Me: Can I tell you?

Adam: In the morning.

Me:

Me: I'll forget it. So, it starts out in this auditorium. It's like a high school theater or something, with lunch tables set up everywhere. And I'm walking around in this theater or wherever it is, and I've just had a baby. And there's this big stage, and all these people, all these friends from high school, like Stacey and Violet and I don't remember who else, are all up onstage giving a slide-show presentation about why I'm going to be a great parent. And they're using one of those things where you write on the thing and it—

Adam: Overhead projector.

Me: Right. They're using an overhead projector along with the slide show. And I'm walking around and I'm holding my baby. Except my baby is like a little worm or something, and it's in a test tube. I'm going up to people, and they're asking to look at my baby and saying congratulations, and they're holding the test tube and talking to the little tadpole baby inside. And then, all of a sudden, my parents are there. And my dad takes the test tube and he says he's going to fix it up for me. And when he hands it back, he has made a little outfit for the test tube. He put, like, pipe-cleaner arms on it, and a little pair of shorts and a little shirt. And a hat, too. Because the tadpole baby was a boy. Then, let's see . . . oh, then my mom and dad and me are all standing in this kitchen. Yeah, we're in this long, narrow kitchen, and my dad is holding my tadpole baby, and he drops the test tube, and the tadpole, like, slithers under the refrigerator, like a little worm or something. And I start sobbing and screaming, "My baby, my baby," and we try to move the refrigerator but it's too heavy. We can't move it. And I'm sobbing and sobbing. And my mom is saying something about "It's going to be okay," something like that, but all I keep thinking is that one day we'll move out of this house and someone will move in and find my poor little shriveled-up tadpole baby under the refrigerator, dead . . . Adam, are you awake?

Adam: That is the most fucked-up dream I have *ever* heard. Jesus Christ, honey.

Me: Good night.

Adam: How am I supposed to go back to sleep after that?

Me:

Adam: Hill? Hill?

Me: Yeah?

Adam: I love you.

Me: I love you too . . . I don't think I can go back to sleep.

Adam: I'm not sure I'll ever be able to go back to sleep.

Me: Ad?

Adam: Yeah?

Me: Do you think my dad's gonna be okay?

Adam: . . . I really don't know.

Me: Squeeze me tighter. You're more like a knife back there. Don't flatten out. Put your chest to my back and your knees in the back of my knees . . . yeah, like that. Just like that.

The Way Things Work

I'm sitting here waiting for my "head" doctor, frantically biting my cuticles, trying to distract myself from my life. I've been doing a lot of biting the last two days. I stare off into space while I gnaw on my digits, the sounds of Adam pleading, "Stop it! Quit picking!" echoing in my ears . . .

Oh, looks like I made it just in time. Reindeer slippers is *in* the building. She just jingled past me sporting a faded pink T-shirt with a picture of a kitty on it and the words GET WELL SOON stretched across the front. Her hair, somehow looking worse than last week, is gathered into two slept-in ponytails. She is clutching the same mangled teddy bear as before, except now it's dressed in an oversize shirt that reads DON'T PUT ME ON HOLD, PUT ME ON HUG.

I feel so sad looking at her. I wonder who gave her the kitty shirt. Whoever it was was disappointed long ago that the message never helped. And the bear. How long has she had him? It's like this woman is mentally frozen in time. Like she's completely unaware that any time has passed since she was six and getting tucked into bed by her father . . . my father . . .

Dr. Lesaux: Hi, Hillary. Come in.

Me: Would you mind opening the blinds? It's a little dark in here.

Dr. Lesaux: Of course.

Me: And could you turn on the lights?

Dr. Lesaux: Do you want the fluorescents on as well?

Me: Yes.

Dr. Lesaux: So, let me see where we left off last week . . . looks like we were talking about you getting pregnant and if—

Me: My dad has melanoma.

Dr. Lesaux:

Me: I just found out. He's having surgery in a couple of weeks, so I don't know if he has any lymph involvement yet. It was really deep. His melanoma was five times deeper than mine. I'm trying to prepare myself for the possibility it has gone into his nodes, but . . . I . . . I don't know.

Dr. Lesaux: I'm sorry to hear that.

Me: I'm scared he's going to die. And I can't stop thinking about it. I keep thinking about all this shit I've read online, all these numbers and statistics, charts and graphs I've seen. And the worst part is, I don't think my parents are telling me everything.

Dr. Lesaux: Why do you say that?

Me: Because my dad doesn't want me to worry. It's like pulling teeth getting any information out of him or my mom. I had to yell at my mom before she would even tell me his tumor thickness. I keep telling them I worry more *not* knowing everything. I figure if you know, you can make informed decisions. You can know all your options.

Dr. Lesaux: It sounds like your father is dealing with his diagnosis much differently than you did.

Me: Totally differently.

Dr. Lesaux: Well, he has the right to.

Me: But he's in denial.

Dr. Lesaux: Is he *not* doing something that he needs to do?

Me: Well, not yet, but . . .

Dr. Lesaux: Give him some time. Sounds like he's just trying to look out for your best interest.

Me: My best interest is to know what's going on. If I don't know, I assume the worst, not the best.

Dr. Lesaux: Have you explained to your parents how you feel?

Me: I tried to tell my mom, but she's a fucking wreck. And my dad won't even talk about it with me. He keeps telling me I need to think about *my* health. He keeps saying he feels fine. Well, *no shit, Sherlock!* I mean, if he already felt sick or was in pain, it would be over. It would mean the cancer had spread, and he would be dead. Melanoma's not like other cancers. There are no Stage IV melanoma survivors. Maybe a couple percent of Stage IV patients survive. And that's not even long term. That's, like, a year or something . . . I don't understand. I don't understand what's going on. I . . . I . . . don't understand why all this is happening.

Dr. Lesaux: Well, let's not get ahead of ourselves. Let's take this one step at a time. Is it possible your father's cancer hasn't spread to his lymph nodes?

Me: Of course it's possible. Unlikely, though.

Dr. Lesaux: And when will you know anything?

Me: Not till after his surgery.

Dr. Lesaux: Let's wait until then to worry about it. I know that's hard to do.

Me: Yeah, you could say that.

Dr. Lesaux: How did your father know he had melanoma?

Me: His dermatologist. This guy—who I don't trust in the least—removed the mole. He told my dad it was nothing to worry about. The doctor thought it could be basal cell or something. Nothing serious. And

then it took fucking *forever* for my dad to get the pathology. I want him
to come here for his surgery.

Dr. Lesaux: And why did your father go to the dermatologist?

Me: What do you mean?

Dr. Lesaux: Did he just decide, on his own, he should get checked out?

Me: He and my mom both went.

Dr. Lesaux:

Me: . . . I told them they had to go.

Dr. Lesaux:

Me: My doctors said I was probably genetically predisposed since I
got it so young. It tends to run in families.

Dr. Lesaux: How do you feel about the fact you saved your father's life?

Me: I don't know if I saved his life.

Dr. Lesaux: Your father doesn't sound like the type of man who would
go to a dermatologist of his own volition.

Me: Yeah . . . well. . . . A couple nights ago I remembered something
that happened the last time I visited my parents in Ohio. I guess it happened almost a year ago. I was sitting in the living room with my dad.
We were both reading. I can picture it so clearly. I was on the couch. I remember he was over by the fireplace. He was wearing a blue dress shirt. It
looked like it had been starched. I remember noticing that because Adam
never gets his shirts starched and his wrinkle so quickly. We were about
to go out to dinner at my parents' country club, I think. My mom was
upstairs, finishing getting ready, and my dad kept glancing at his watch.
He's like me—we hate to be late. We have to be on time. We need to be
early . . . anyway, my mom yelled downstairs that she wanted me to look
at a place on my dad's back. She wanted to know if I thought it looked
funny. I yelled back, "Okay." I distinctly remember looking over at my
dad, and before I could say anything, he said, "Later. We don't have time
now. We'll be late for dinner."

Dr. Lesaux: So, what happened?

Me: I never looked at it. I forgot. And of course he never brought it up to remind me or anything . . . a year, a whole year, went by, and that fucking thing was growing, and all I can think about is, why didn't I insist on seeing it right then? How could I have forgotten to look at it? How? Maybe I was embarrassed. Maybe I was afraid I would embarrass him. I don't know. I mean, looking at a mole on my dad's back wouldn't be at the top of my "Things I'd Like to Do" list. But if I had seen it, I'm sure I would have known it was something worth removing . . . a year, a whole year . . . you're the first person I've told that story to.

Dr. Lesaux: It's not your fault.

Me: I know, but . . .

Dr. Lesaux: Even if you had looked at it, who's to say you would have even thought there was anything wrong with it? Would you have even known what a melanoma looked like a year ago?

Me: I don't know. Probably not. But, I mean, if it looked really gross and black and abnormal, then maybe.

Dr. Lesaux: Is that what your father's looked like?

Me: No. His was pinkish, I think.

Dr. Lesaux: You saved your father's life by getting him to go to the doctor.

Me: I feel so guilty.

Dr. Lesaux:

Me: Maybe I had to get melanoma in order to save my dad from dying from it.

Dr. Lesaux: Maybe. Something to think about.

The Waiting Game

I'm starting to get the strange feeling I'm waiting my life away, bit by bit, moment by hellish moment, and I can't seem to do a good goddamn thing about it. Once again, I am waiting for a phone call that may or may not change the course of my entire life. My father's life. A call with which the news will most definitely be some version of bad, no matter how the information is delivered to me—packaged for my consumption by my well-meaning mother. I'm waiting to hear about my father's doctor's appointment, and I can hardly keep from pulling my eyebrows out, one by precious one (several of which are still stuck to my fingertip from my last vicious attack). My eyes are glazed, my arms are crossed, my feet have been asleep for nearly an hour, and still I wait by the phone, staring, believing that my looking at it will have some telekinetic impact on its ringing.

Rin—

Me: Hello, Mom?

Mom: Hi, sweetie.

Me: What'd the doctor say? Did you like him? Do you think he's good? What does he specialize in? When's Dad having surgery? Can he get him in this wee—

Mom: He can't operate till the third.

Me: The third! Of September! Are you fucking kidding me!

Mom: It's the soonest he had an opening.

Me: Dad's coming here, then. That's ridiculous. The third, my ass. I'll call Gregory, and I bet I can schedule something for next week, at the latest. Dad is not waiting two weeks to have surgery. The third. That's totally crazy.

Mom: You think Gregory could see him sooner?

Me: Definitely. I'm sure.

Mom: Well, I don't know if your father will like the idea—

Me: I don't give a shit . . . what else did the doctor say—the third . . . who is he kidding?

Mom: He didn't really have that much to say.

Me: *Mom!*

Mom: What?

Me: Jesus, what did he say?

Mom: . . . your father doesn't want you to worry. He doesn't want you to make a big deal out of this. You know how he hates people to fuss over him.

Me: Mom, Dad's sick, so he's gonna have to get over it. This is not something he can fuck around with, you know.

Mom: I know. I know.

Me: Well I don't feel like you're making this any easier. You've gotta stand up to him.

Mom: I don't want to scare him.

Me: He's already scared, trust me.

Mom: He seems to be doing fine. I'm the one who's a wreck.

Me: What else did the doctor say?

Mom: Well, he's going to do the dye thing.

Me: To his lymph nodes?

Mom: Yes. He said he can inject the tumor with a dye and then track where it drains. I think that's what he said. Some of it was hard to follow.

Me: If the cancer has spread to his lymph nodes, the dye allows them to remove the smallest number of lymph nodes. One of the doctors at St. John's developed the technique.

Mom: What happens if the cancer has spread to his lymph nodes?

Me: What do you mean?

Mom: What do they do then?

Me: They'd remove all the cancerous nodes and then . . . I don't know. It depends. It depends on how many are positive. It depends on a lot of things. Did they say what Stage they think Dad is?

Mom: I think they said Stage IV.

Me:

Mom: Is that bad?

Me:

Mom: Are you still there?

Me: *He's dying. My father is dying, and at this very moment, all I can picture is my dad next to me, holding my hand, as a surgeon tries injecting a vein between my little piggies in order to numb my broken leg. I'm fourteen, I'm still in my muddy soccer uniform, I'm shaking with fear, and I'm squeezing my father's hand for dear life. I've been squeezing it for two hours. I can't even tell where my hand ends and my dad's begins anymore . . . his hand is rough, callused from refinishing an old canoe that hangs, waiting oh so patiently to be finished, from the ceiling of our garage. I hear his voice, over and over: "You're going to be okay, you're going to be okay . . . "* Why do they think he's a four? Do they suspect he has metastases? *His breath smells like a mixture of Dunkin' Donuts coffee and halftime Gatorade.*

Mom: They didn't say anything about that. What stage were you?

Me: I was a stage I. *He chants, like a mantra, "The pain is going to be over soon . . . "*

Mom: I thought you were a II.

Me: I was a *Level* II, Stage I. *And I squeeze harder.*

Mom: Oh, I thought they were the same thing.

Me: Jesus, Mom, no—they're totally different! *The drugs are slowly creeping into my veins, after what seems like a lifetime of waiting.*

Mom: Oh, well, then, they said your father is a *Level* IV, not Stage IV.

Me: Oh my God, Mom, Jesus fucking Christ—you scared the shit fuck piss out of me. *My eyes are heavy with the weight of the drugs.*

Mom: I'm sorry, I thought they were the same.

Me: Stage IV would mean the melanoma spread to other parts of his body. Like, he had tumors in his brain or lungs or something. *The pain in my leg seems distant now, separate from my body.*

Mom: No, no, no, they don't think that.

Me: You know what, let's not waste any more time. I'll talk to Gregory and then I'll get back to you.

Mom: Okay, but I still don't know if your father would go for the idea of coming to L.A. for the surgery.

Me: I just want to see if it's an option. I'll call you later.

Mom: I can call. I don't want you to have to worry about this. I can—

Me: I should do it because I know all the questions to ask. I'll call you as soon as I've talked to Gregory.

Mom: I love you, sweetie.

Me: Love you too.

It's funny, the things that pop into one's mind at what seem like the most inopportune moments. How strange that hearing "Stage IV" triggered a memory from eleven years back, most of which I thought I had long forgotten, some of which I never knew I had noticed in the first place. I mean, coffee breath? But it all came back so clearly just now, like the whole mess happened only the day before yesterday. Maybe hearing that from my mother made me feel small again, or helpless, or . . . I don't know. But something happened, and I had a moment just now, brief as it was, where I knew my father was going to die. Someday he *is* going to die. There, I've said it. And by *some*day, I mean to say *any* day. We're all gonna die, as hard as it is to believe. But it seems to me most of us don't really *know* it, or think it, or ever really believe it—until it happens. I understand the natural progression of things—the cycle of life and all that. I know people die. I know parents die all the time. I just don't think I ever believed mine would. . . . Until just now.

NOT MUCH LATER:

Ring.

Me: Hello?

Other: It's Dr. Gregory. Is this Hillary?

Me: Yeah, hi. Thanks for getting back to me so fast.

Gregory: I'm really sorry to hear about your dad. So, on the machine, you said you wanted to talk about any openings in my calendar.

Me: Yeah. My dad's surgeon doesn't have an opening for, like, two weeks, and I don't think he should wait that long. If you could operate sooner, I was thinking I could try and convince my dad to come here. Also, I haven't been impressed with the care my dad's been getting in Ohio. I'm not all that confident in his doctors.

Gregory: Well, I talked to my nurse, and I could see your father in about a week and a half, but—

Me: Oh, that's great. That would be awesome—

Gregory: —*but* if he has surgery here, he's going to have to stay awhile for all the follow-up visits.

Me: He can't do those in Ohio?

Gregory: No, I'd want to see him myself.

Me: Oh. Well, it might still be worth doing. I think my dad should have surgery as soon as possible. I think I said on your machine, his tumor is over two millimeters deep.

Gregory: To be honest, Hillary, an extra few days, an extra few weeks—at this point—isn't going to make any difference. He's probably had that melanoma for years. Two weeks isn't going to change anything.

Me: Oh. For years? Really? So, you're saying a couple months wouldn't make much of a difference?

Gregory: No. Probably not. Why?

Me: . . . um . . . nothing . . . from what you know about my dad's tumor, what other treatment options does he have? I mean, besides surgery. Would that interferon treatment be good for him to do?

Gregory: I doubt it. Let's wait until after his surgery to talk about options. Are they doing a sentinel node biopsy?

Me: Yes.

Gregory: Okay, so we need to wait until he gets those results back, which will be after the surgery. If the cancer hasn't spread to his lymph nodes, he might qualify for one of our vaccine trials. We're doing one for Stage II patients. But that means his nodes *have* to be clear.

Me: God, that would be great if he could qualify. Does he need to get on a waiting list or anything?

Gregory: The trial is filling up fast. I'll see what I can do.

Me: Thank you so much. Do you have information on the vaccine that I could read? I could come by your office and pick it up.

Gregory: I'll tell Dana to pull some stuff for you.

Me: Oh, and 2.43 is deep. Right?

Gregory:

Me: I mean, the odds are good it has spread to his nodes, right? I'm just trying to be realistic. I need to prepare myself for the possibility. I want to be optimistic, but . . . I don't know. How did no one notice it before? That's what I want to know. How come, with all his regular checkups, no one thought it looked suspicious?

Gregory: I don't know. Fair question. And yes, 2.43 is fairly deep. Much deeper than yours, obviously. But it's not impossible that it's still contained. Try not to get ahead of yourself. We'll talk after his surgery, after they get the lymph node pathology. Okay?

Me: Yeah, okay. I . . . I'm just really, really worried. I know too much about this cancer now, is the problem. I know what he's up against . . . wish I hadn't done so much reading.

Gregory: I know. And don't believe everything you read on the Internet.

Me: I don't, I don't. Thanks for getting back to me so quickly. I'll call you when I know anything new.

Gregory: I'm sure you will.

Me: Talk to you later. Thanks again.

Why do I do that? Why do I have to know every little thing about every little thing? Why can't I leave well enough alone? I've royally fucked myself. All my research has jumped up and bit a big ol' hole in my informed ass. I know too goddamn much, and it's my own fault. I have no one to blame but myself. But I can't help myself. I must know. All of it. The bad *and* the ugly. Because without it, I'm . . . I'm . . . lost. Without it, I'm helpless. And I won't be helpless. Not if I can help it.

Left to Lose

I've been staring at a blank piece of linen stationery for the better part of an hour and a half. Actually, to be perfectly honest, I have sweat through two pages already; the linen buckled under the moisture coming off my hand. So, in an attempt to save my digits from an inevitable cramp and—truthfully—from completing this project without running out of this overpriced, thinly sliced tree, I have rightly chosen to keep my hand away from said paper until I have something worth penning. See, said paper is part of said project, which makes up half of unsaid care package I'm sending to my dad. I had this brilliant (if not unrealistic) idea of writing a simple letter of encouragement to my father, along with a few items that might come in handy after his surgery.

Care package consists of:

- New Stevie Nicks CD
- *For Whom the Bell Tolls*—first edition, thank you very much
- Pine-scented candle
- Three bottles of sunscreen

The only person my dad loves more than Hemingway is Stevie Nicks, so I've got the major bases covered. As for the candle, I was hoping for a "fresh-cut grass" scent. I remember my father saying one time that there's nothing better in this world than the smell of a freshly cut lawn. Maybe the smell has more to do with memories of his youth than anything else, but, as far as I can tell, no one, and I mean no one, makes a fresh-cut-grass scent. The floral scents are in abundance, all dessert foods are easily sniffed out, and even fruits are amply represented, but God forbid anyone should want "grass," just good ol' salt-of-the-earth, between-my-toes ground cover—you're shit out of luck.

So my dad will have to recover to the healing aroma of pine—ah, pine. I'm really hoping the candle doesn't remind him of some camping fiasco, or, worse, take him back to a time he'd just as soon forget . . . And then, of course, you haven't sent a care package—at least one of any substance—until you've sent one containing sunscreen. So I've given him three bottles, with explicit instructions on how, when, and where (everywhere) to apply. So all I have left to do is this goddamned letter. Maybe I should make it a note. I could get a teeny tiny note card and just scribble, "Thinking of you." Or what about, "My thoughts are with you," "Good luck," "Take care of yourself," "Love ya," "Get better soon"? Better yet, I could mail the fucking thing without a card at all. Just pop this sucker in the ol' box and move on with it. Oh God, I'm such a chickenshit, I can't even believe it.

Okay. Let's just take it slow. Slow and steady wins the race . . .

"Dear Father . . . " God, that sounds so stilted.

"Dearest Dad," Why am I so fucking lame?

"Dear Dad . . . " Yeah, that sounds right.

Dear Dad,

To be fair, I've been having the toughest time coming up with the right, or appropriate, or—I guess—adequate words to fill the better part of this letter. In my head, I know what I want to say (it all seems so perfectly clear), but I can't seem to get the ideas from my head to travel the distance down into my fingers and onto this piece of paper. If I *could* write all that I feel, I'd start by saying how sorry I am you have to go through all of this. I wish, like hell, I could have taken the burden for both of us. Having been in a somewhat similar position as yourself, somewhat more recently than I would have liked, I can say with some certainty that I know you are scared. I know with complete certainty I was. So I write this letter in hopes that you can share how you feel with me, as hard as that may be. I know you don't like to talk about any of this, and that's why I think it so desperately needs to be addressed. You can't go through this experience alone— so don't. I love you, respect you, and want you to always remember that being sick and being weak are not the same thing, not even close. Know you can tell me anything, anytime, and that I want to hear it, always. So as you recover from this surgery, gain strength and knowledge from listening to Stevie, hearing Hemingway's words—and bells—and smelling the always inspiring pine.

    Love forever,

    Me

I don't know. I just reread what I wrote, and I sound like a complete freak. My words of "wisdom" sound like I gathered them up from random Hallmark cards, like the ones with a father and daughter strolling hand in hand through a field of hay or something equally nauseating. I'd better load this shit into a box before I lose my nerve and throw the whole thing into my "waiting to (never) be sent" pile. Fuck it. What do I have to lose? I guess the answer could sometimes be—everything.

Good Game

As part of my continuing effort to distract myself from my father's impending surgery, I've decided to scour my melanoma networking list in search of at least one woman who had children soon after a melanoma diagnosis. I've highlighted possible candidates, establishing thirty-five as the diagnosis cutoff age. Taking age and year of diagnosis into consideration, I'm left with four possibilities. F-o-u-r. That's it. Three of whom I've already called. Two of whom had children before getting "the cancer," one of whom never had children—"I always kinda regretted it, though." So I'm down to the nitty-gritty. The short and curlies. In other words, I'm desperate.

> *Ring, ring, ring, ring.*
> **Young Child:**—let go—hew-wo, Peterson wesidence?
> **Me:** *Bingo.* Yes, hi. Can I please speak to Terry?
> **Young Child:** Okay. *Mom! Mommy!*
> **Me:** *Okay. Don't get overexcited. (Yippee, yippee,* yippee!*). Don't overwhelm the poor woman right off the bat. Take it slow.*

Terry: Hello, this is Terry.

Me: Hi! You don't know me. My name is Hillary and I'm a melanoma patient at St. John's, and I got your name off their melanoma networking list and the reason I'm calling is, I was recently diagnosed—Stage I, Level II—and my husband and I would like to start a family and I was told I needed to wait a couple of years. So I'm trying to find women who had successful pregnancies soon after being diagnosed, and I saw you were diagnosed at thirty-three, and I thought maybe you had kids after the fact.

Terry: Oh, hi—

Me: Yeah, I wanted to ask you a few questions, if you don't mind. Do you have a second to talk, or should I call back later? Is there a better time? Because I can definitely call back again or . . . not? I'm sorry. I'm talking a mile a minute.

Terry: No, no, this is fine. But, unfortunately, I don't think I can help you with anything. I had all my kids before I was diagnosed. I remember, though, my doctor asked me if I was planning on having any more kids. My husband and I were considering it before I got sick. We always wanted a big family. My husband and I both come from big families. But . . . well, we decided I needed to focus on my health. Focus on getting better before having more kids—God had already blessed us with two beautiful children. Two can be a handful as it is.

Me: I bet. Well, thank you for your time. Good luck with everything.

Terry: God bless you. Children are the most wonderful gift. If you want to have them, have them. That's what I say. I thank God every day for my family. They give me such strength.

Me: Yeah . . . well . . . thanks. You were first diagnosed what, five years ago? How have you been since then, if you don't mind me asking? *You know, since God blessed you with melanoma.*

Terry: A lot's changed. I was originally diagnosed as a stage II.

Me: Uh-huh. Did *you* discover the mole, or—

Terry: No, it was really strange how the whole thing happened. A parent from my son's soccer team needed a bone marrow transplant. So all of us—all the other parents—decided to get tested to see if any of us were a match. I went to my internist and when my blood workup came back, it showed I was anemic. My doctor didn't really think it was anything to worry about, since I don't eat a lot of red meat, so we decided I would try and change my diet a little bit and come back in a month or so to test again. Anyway, just as the doctor was leaving the room, this place on my back started itching—a mole I'd had for years. The doctor noticed me scratching it, and when he saw it, he must have known what is was. He had me meet with a dermatologist right away. They biopsied it, I had a wide excision, and they took several nodes from my groin, which all came back negative.

Me: That must have been a major relief.

Terry: Yes. Although, looking back, I didn't really know much about melanoma.

Me: So, you said a lot has changed since then? I'm sorry—do you mind me asking all these questions?

Terry: No, no, not at all. I'm just trying to remember the order of things. So, let's see. Yeah, so, the nodes came back negative. And because they were negative, I was able to participate in one of the vaccine trials at St. John's. Only it was a double-blind study, so I didn't know if I was getting the drug or a placebo. And then, maybe a few months later, I started having problems at the site of the groin incision. It almost looked like a keloid, like a lump. When I went in for my next appointment, Dana—I'm sure you know Dana—she took one look at it, and I knew from the look on her face something was seriously wrong.

Me: What was it?

Terry: It's kind of difficult to explain. See, we have several layers of lymph nodes, which I never knew. Apparently, the cancer had spread to the deeper nodes. These nodes were growing and moving up toward the surface of my skin.

Me: *Oh my God. Oh my God. Oh my fucking God.* I see.

Terry: Anyway, I was dropped from the trial. I would have dropped out anyway. It was clear I was getting the placebo. So, I had *another* surgery to remove the deeper nodes. It was much, much more involved than the first one. And because so many nodes were positive, my doctors recommended I do chemotherapy. Maureen Reagan and I started chemo at the same time, actually.

Me: Really. *And look how good well turned out.* So, did the chemo take care of it? I didn't think it was effective in treating melanoma.

Terry: Well, it wasn't. At least not for me. After my first two treatments, I started getting these tiny blue dots all along one side of my body. Turns out, all these melanoma cells were in my lymphatic tract. It looked like an army of ants running from my original site around my side and down into my groin. So they stopped my treatment. My doctor said it obviously wasn't working. I mean, if the cancer was showing up even with all the chemo . . . then, let me see, next I did radiation. It's been about a year and a half now since I stopped radiation. I had to quit the treatment earlier than planned, because my skin wasn't able to take anymore. It got really hard, the skin on my side. And it's incredibly sensitive. My kids can't really hug me anymore. Not on that one side.

Me: . . . and now? Where are you with everything?

Terry: Well, after the radiation my husband and I took a *long* vacation. I really needed some time away from everything. We went to Hawaii. My doctor said it was okay. I think he figured, what could it hurt?

Me: But now are you n.e.d.?

Terry: Well, no. My latest scans showed a mass in my stomach. And possibly something in one of my lungs.

Me: So, what are you going to do?

Terry: I've been praying a lot. I believe God has a plan for us all . . . there isn't really much medicine and doctors can do for me. Not at this point.

Me: But what about trials? There must be some clinical trials out there? Something?

Terry: Well, maybe. I heard of something at USC that I might qualify for. I just don't know if I want to go through anything else. The treatments I've had have been much harder to bear than the cancer itself. And plus, my family suffers so much when I'm in the hospital. I was in the ICU for weeks after the first two chemotherapy treatments . . . I'm just enjoying time with my family.

Me: But if there's a trial out there . . . something that could help you . . .

Terry: You're right. I know I should contact USC, but God has given me so much: two wonderful children, a loving husband . . .

Me: I don't think you should give up.

Terry: I'm not. I don't see it that way.

Me: But if there's—

Terry: I feel really good. With the exception of my side, I'm not in any pain—

Me: But what about your husband? What does he say about all this?

Terry: He supports me in whatever I choose to do.

Me: I see. *I don't see! I really don't!*

Terry: I'm sorry I couldn't be of more help to you. Good luck on your search. And check out the melanoma patient information page online. You could post something on one of their bulletin boards.

Me: Yeah, yeah, okay. That's a good idea, thanks. Please call USC.

Terry: I'll think about it. God bless you.

Me: . . . you too.

I wanted to shake her just now! If I had been sitting in front of her, I think I would have leaned in, grabbed her by the shoulders, and shaken the shit out of her. It took everything I had not to scream and yell and

say, "Wake the fuck up!" I wanted her to see that it's her life that's slip-
ping away! *She's* the one who will leave her husband and two "beautiful,
wonderful gifts" behind! And all the prayers and all the "God bless yous"
aren't going to change that. Only *she* can change that . . . she can't see
what's right in front of her. Death. At arm's length. Closer, maybe. One
misstep, a slight shift to one side, and she will be face-to-face with her
own mortality.

And yet she doesn't seem to be afraid. She's dying and she knows it,
and she doesn't seem to be afraid. Quite the opposite. She seemed peaceful. Strangely peaceful, like she'd seen something that wiped all the fear
and pain and horror from her memory. Like it was all someone else's story.
Like the events belonged to someone she just met or knew only briefly.

But why isn't she fighting? Fighting for her life? For a life with her
family? If I were her, I would fight like hell. If it were me, I would battle
till my last half-breath, till my heart arrested and my skin got cold and
pale—er. Because if I sense death is right around the corner, I will push it
away as far and as fast as I can. Because I don't want to die.

I don't want to die.

I don't think I've ever thought that before. Just now, just as I was vi-
sualizing myself stone cold, dead as a doornail, I started to feel like I may
have been laboring under a gross misperception for the last twenty-five-
odd years of my life. Something I thought I knew about myself, something I always took quite a bit of comfort in, may in fact be something of
a lie. Until several minutes ago, I think I may have been fooling myself
into believing that I wasn't afraid to die.

But I am! I am afraid. I really am. I don't want to die! I don't!

There, I've said it. It's out there, and I can't take it back. I really, really, really, *really* don't want to die. And the worse part—the real kicker,
the undies-in-a-bunch aspect of this whole fucking thing—is, I know I
will die. I am absolutely convinced of it. It *will* happen to me. As much
as I'd like to believe the contrary, I would be remiss to dismiss the actual,
inevitable end. My end. The end. Well, not the *end* end. I mean, things

will go on long after I have gone—which may be the hardest part to accept. I think I'd somehow feel better about all this death-and-dying stuff if I thought we were all going at once. It sure would be a hell of a lot easier to go if there wasn't anything left behind. If there weren't people to leave behind. If we could all just hold hands, count to three, and jump.

I think that's where I got screwed up before. I had somehow convinced myself that I was only afraid of other people dying. People close to me. People I love. I thought that that was the worse thing that could happen, much worse than my own death, because if someone I love died, I'd be left behind to miss them. But the piece I've been missing this whole time—my whole goddamned life—is that if *I* die, then I'm leaving *everyone* behind. So it's either get left or be the one doing the leaving. Both are horrible. Both put equal-size knots in my stomach and lumps in my throat. I don't want anyone I know and love to die—and that includes me!

I think I thought not fearing death would make life easier. But, in actuality, the not fearing has maybe kept me from fully appreciating. I couldn't fully commit to life because I always had one foot placed casually in the grave. I was saying, *see, see, I'm not afraid. Look at me. Look over here. I'm ready to go . . . whenever. See, look how brave I am. See?*

But what if Terry *isn't* blind? What if she knows the end is near and still she embraces it? What if she's made peace with her story? It's the fear of death that keeps us fighting. And maybe she isn't afraid. Not anymore. Not like the rest of us. Not like me. And so she can give up the battle. She can throw in the towel, wipe the sweat from her brow, nod slowly and purposefully, and with dignity and strength say . . . "Good game."

Good game, Terry.

Cake

I couldn't sleep last night. Not that that really distinguishes the night from any other. I sat in bed sipping a Corona and watching a program on a "revolutionary hair-removal system: It works with the heat from your own body," until I finally passed out around three thirty.

I'm expecting my mom's call any moment. Dad was scheduled for a 2:00 PM surgery, so that's 11:00 AM my time. I figure two hours in surgery, plus an hour in recovery, another half hour waiting to talk with the doctor, ten minutes to get to the car, and two minutes for my mom to locate her cell phone. That puts us at 2:42, Pacific Time. So any min—

Rin—
Me: Hello? Mom?
Mom: Hey, honey.
Me: How'd it go? How's Dad? Did they get clear margins?
Mom: Yes, they did. Your father did great!
Me: O-kay. Why do you sound so weird? Is he sitting next to you?
Mom: Yes!

Me: I see. I'll make this easy. Does he seem okay?

Mom: Yes!

Me: Did you see his scar? Is it big?

Mom: No, I didn't see it!

Me: Did his doctor say anything about his lymph nodes? When does he find out about them?

Mom: Friday. Do you want to talk to your father?

Me: Yeah, I didn't think he'd be able to talk.

Dad: Hel-lo?

Me: Hey, Dad. You did it!

Dad: Piece . . . of . . . cake.

Me: Yeah, see, it was over before you knew it. Get some rest. You need to get a lot of rest. Okay? I love you . . . Dad? Hello?

Mom: He fell asleep.

Me: How'd he *really* do?

Mom: I could tell he was scared. His doctor said everything went fine. They took five lymph nodes from under his right arm.

Me: How does the incision look?

Mom: I can't see much. He's all bandaged up. But they took a *lot* of skin. The incision goes from shoulder to shoulder, and he's got drains attached to it. They showed me how to empty the drains and how to change the dressing. I don't know how he's going to take a shower.

Me: Make sure he gets some rest.

Mom: He seems pretty knocked out at the moment.

Me: I know, but, knowing Dad, he'll be trying to mow the grass within the week.

Mom: Your father has a lot of pride.

Me: How are *you* holding up?

Mom: Good . . . I'm okay. Your father looked so weak when they wheeled him out.

Me: It's major surgery. You should try and get some rest, too. You sound exhausted.

Mom: Now, don't you worry about me. You have enough to think about. We're almost home. I'll call you tomorrow with an update.

Me: Okay. I love you.

Mom: Thank you for all your support. That package you sent meant so much to your father. You have no idea.

Me: I'm glad. I'll talk to you guys tomorrow. Bye.

Can't Hurt

I've been praying a lot lately. Not like on-my-knees-with-my-hands-clasped-under-my-chin praying—more like quiet whispers to myself as I make my bed, Swiffer the floor, wash dishes . . . like a continuous chant or something. Reminiscent of Franny's Jesus prayer in Salinger's *Franny and Zooey,* except slightly less incessant. I started about a week ago. I wouldn't say I've found God or anything, I just lump the praying into the "it can't hurt" category. See, the lymph nodes are a big deal. If they're clean, my dad has one whole set of options, including the vaccine trial. If they're not clean, well, there are options, but none of them is great. None is all that promising. So I pray. In hopes it will make a difference. In hopes I didn't start too late. In hopes.

Battle Cry

Whoever is listening, make it be okay. Make my dad be okay. Make his nodes be clear. No cancer in his nodes. No cancer no cancer no cancer. What can I do? Tell me what I can do to make everything okay. Good thoughts, Dad, I am sending you good thoughts. I am filling you up with health. You are healthy you are healthy you are—

Ring.
Good thoughts good thoughts—
Ring.
You are healthy, Jon is healthy.
Ring.
Me: Hello?
Other: Hi, sweetie.
Me: So?
Mom: They're clear.
Me: All of them?
Mom: All five of them were cancer free.

Me: Oh my God. I can't believe it. I thought for sure . . . I mean, the odds . . . what are the odds? Holy shit, I can't believe it. *I can breathe. My chest feels so much lighter, my shoulders looser. The nagging pressure between my eyes—constantly causing me to furrow and unfurrow my brow—gone. I'm even standing taller. The sandbags I've been lugging around, balancing on either shoulder, have been lifted. I'm a new woman. I'm a happy woman. I feel like running a marathon. I want to hug a stranger. I'm going to give my dog a big, fat kiss right on her wet, sloppy lips.* Thank God. I almost can't believe it. I—

Mom: I know. I've . . . I've, uh—

Me: It's okay, Mom . . . it's okay.

Mom: I was so worried. I've been so worried about your father. I haven't been able to sleep, I haven't been able to eat—

Me: I know, me neither. Can I talk to Dad?

Mom: Yeah, let me get him—Jon, Hillary wants to talk to you—you wouldn't believe your father. He got up this morning and started working at his computer. Can you believe that? And he won't take any of the pain medication. And I *know* he's in pain. The incision—I have to whisper; I don't want your father to hear—it looks pretty bad.

Me: How long is it?

Mom: About sixteen inches or so.

Me: Jesuschrist.

Mom: You wouldn't believe the pus that's draining out of it.

Me: *Yummy.* How long does he—

Dad: Hello?

Mom: I'll get off now. I'll talk to you later, Hill.

Me: Dad, congratulations!

Dad: Thank you. How are you? How are you feeling?

Me: How are *you* feeling?

Dad: Fine. I feel good. A little sore, but nothing too bad.

Me: Yeah, right. How do you feel about the news?

Dad: Good. I'm not surprised. We're tough, right?

Me: Yeah, well . . . God, this is such great news. I feel like a weight has been lifted. You must feel *so* relieved. You know, now that your nodes are clear, there's a vaccine trial out here that you can qualify for. I was talking to Dr. Gregory about it. It's a phase-three trial. St. John's has been testing a version of this vaccine for, like, twelve years, and they've had a lot of success with it.

Dad: I think I'm done with doctors and hospitals for a while.

Me: But this vaccine, it could really, really reduce your chance of a recurrence.

Dad: We can talk about it later. Why don't *you* do the trial?

Me: I would in a second, but I don't qualify. You have to be a Stage II.

Dad: We'll talk about it later. I don't want to think about it right now.

Me: Okay. *You're never gonna wanna talk about it, are you?* But Gregory said the trial is filling up fast, so—

Dad: I'm feeling tired . . . I'll talk to you later.

Me: Oh, um, okay. Remember, don't do too much. You need your rest. I love you.

Click.

The battle has just begun. The war paint is tacky; the battle cry still echoes for miles: "Never give up! Never surrender!" He *will* do that trial if I have anything to do with it. I will not turn away from the facts. I will not totally disregard the numbers and charts and statistics that say my father, with a level IV melanoma, will most likely have a recurrence within the next five years. I will not close my eyes to all arrows that point to the fact that it's only a matter of time before the cancer makes its way to his nodes. Because even though the numbers and charts and statistics don't mean *everything,* they mean *something.* He *will* put up the good fight, even if I have to stand behind him, holding his dukes high in the air. He will do anything and everything to remain cancer free. Because there is one thing I know about melanoma: It never gives up. And so neither will I. And therefore, neither will he.

I wonder which will be harder to overcome—the cancer or my father.

Stitches

Number of moles removed by Dr. Bach: 3

Number of stitches: 14

Number of days I'm likely to wait before calling to get the pathology, even though Dr. Bach promised to call me the moment she gets the results: 5

Odds of my calling Dr. Bach's office before number of days listed above: 8/5

September 11

I reached for my glasses, accidentally smudging the lenses with cuticle cream that I'd put on my fingers the night before. As I used my flannel pajama shirt to wipe the lenses clean, I turned the television to Channel 4. Just as my glasses came to rest on my nose, I watched a very large, very tall building disappear into a cloud of smoke. I pushed my glasses farther up my nose with the tip of my index finger, and I watched in horror as an open space was revealed that had, only moments before, been filled with two giant towers.

I've been glued to the television all day, flipping from news channel to news channel, listening with my mouth open and my eyes partially shut. No one seems to know exactly what happened or why, but everyone has a theory. I keep hearing newscasters question in disbelief, "How could this have happened? How does something like this happen? I can't believe this is happening . . . "

I'd like to join in on all the disbelieving. I'd like to say I'm shocked that something so horrible, something so tragic and unexpected, happened.

I'd like to say I'm surprised that this horrific event took place with so little warning, creating such devastation, but somehow I can't. I feel somewhat numb to it. I have sat in a waiting room with a sixteen-year-old girl dying from melanoma. I have talked to a forty-year-old mother of two who has an army of cancer cells eating away her torso. I have heard a woman I hardly know tell me I have cancer. I have heard a man—who just so happens to be my father—tell me *he* has cancer. So if someone asks me if I'm *surprised* by these events that happened today, if anyone wants to know what I think about 9/11, I think I'll keep my comments to myself. Because I'm *not* surprised or shocked. Because I *know* bad things happen. I know bad things happen *all* the time, for no apparent reason, to completely innocent people, and if you haven't already learned that for yourself, you're damn well lucky.

Why I Hate Fridays

4:30 PM:

Other: Dr. Bach's office, how can I help you?

Me: Yeah, hey, Julia, it's Hillary Fogelson. Wait, where's Terry?

Julia: Her son got sick, so I'm doing double duty.

Me: I was calling to see if you guys got the pathology back on the moles Dr. Bach removed.

Julia: No, sorry, not yet. I *promise* I'll call you the moment I hear something.

Me: Okay—I just don't want to have to wait over the weekend.

Julia: I understand, but there's nothing I can do.

Me: Does she always send the slides to the same place? Do you know?

Julia: No, there are several places she uses.

Me: Oh. Like . . . where? Like, St. John's, or . . . ?

Julia: Sometimes she sends them there. Sometimes she sends them to a private practice in Beverly Hills. She has several places she works with.

Me: Oh.

Julia: First Dr. Bach reads the slides; then she—

Me: She reads them *first? Before* she sends them out?

Julia: Yes, usually. She writes up her report, then sends the slides out for a second opinion.

Me: Is Dr. Bach available? I'd like to talk to her.

Julia: No, she's not in the office today. She's at a conference in San Diego. Dr. Ward is filling in.

Me: . . . okay, well . . . call me as soon as you hear anything.

Julia: I promise. And try not to worry. Remember how I had that lump in my breast and it turned out to be nothing? Try not to get too worked up.

Me: *Remember how I had that mole and it turned out to be something?* Yeah, okay.

One minute later, and a bad idea:

Other: St. John's hospital, pathology, this is Rachel.

Me: Hi, yes, I'm calling to get the pathology for a patient, last name Fogelson. *F* as in "Frank," *o-g-e-l-s-o-n.*

Rachel: Fogelson, you said? Let's see here . . . ah, here it is. Okay . . . it looks like . . . what doctor's office did you say you're calling from?

Me:

Rachel: Hello?

Me: Um . . . *white lie. Little white lie never hurt anyone, right? It's like telling the truth, only slightly different. A half-truth, really. Part reality, part . . . not . . .* um . . . Dr. Jovanka Bach's office.

Rachel: And you are? I'm sorry, I didn't catch your name.

Me: Um . . . Hillary. *Shit motherfucker. Not good. This is not good. I'm undeniably in over my head.*

Rachel: Let's see here . . . I don't see your name on the approved . . .

Me: *Abort. Enemy is in sight. I repeat, abort mission! Move to Plan B. Plan B is now under way. Stand by for further instructions.* Um . . . I'm not actually from the doctor's office. I'm the patient.

Rachel: Oh, I can't disclose—

Me: No, of course you can't, but this is a special circumstance. See, my doctor is out of town for a while, and her office told me I should call—they're really busy—so I was hoping you could just tell me the results over the phone. I already had melanoma, as you can see from your files—my files—and I need to get that report right away so my doctor can remove anything that um . . . might need to be . . . removed.

Rachel: I'm sorry, I can't help you.

Me: *Plan C! I repeat, Plan C! Do not repeat Plan A or B.* Look, I don't need specifics. Just, generally speaking . . . do I have melanoma?

Rachel: I can't disclose that information . . . I'm really sorry.

Me: *Oh God, why is she so sorry? Sorry? Sorry for what? Was that a sorry like, "Sorry you have cancer" or just a plain ol' "Sorry, I can't help you" kinda sorry? Her voice most definitely went down at the end of the sorry. Does down inflection mean bad? Maybe down's good. Or maybe she's trying to throw me off the trail. Maybe up inflection actually means bad, but she's trying not to give anything away, so she gives me the down instead. Although . . . she knows I tried to illegally obtain medical records—a risky move by anyone's standards—so maybe she inferred that I'd presume the worst, so she gave me the down inflection, which would counteract the worst, thus forcing me to expect the best, which I would never expect, so . . .* I don't understand. The slides are of my moles. This is my body we're talking about here. Look, if you tell me what the report says, I promise I won't tell anyone. You would be doing me a huge favor. *Pretty please.*

Rachel: I'm sorry, it's against hospital policy.

Me: Can you at least tell me if the slides have been read?

Rachel: I'm sorry.

Me: *Could you say sorry one more time for me?* Fine. Look, if the slides *have* been read, could you please fax the report over to Dr. Bach's office?

Rachel: I'm not in charge of that.

Me: Could I talk to the person who *is* in charge of that?

Rachel: I'm sure the report will get faxed before the end of the business day.

Me: Today? By the end of today? What time is generally considered the end of the business day?

Rachel: I really don't know. I'm—

Me: Sorry.

Click.

ENOUGH TIME LATER TO KNOW BETTER:

Other: Hello, Dr. Bach's—

Me: Hey, Julia, it's Hillary again. Sorry to bother you. I'll make this quick. I know you're really, really busy. This probably sounds crazy, but I was wondering if you could call over to St. John's—or wherever Dr. Bach sent the slides—and see if my report is finished. It's getting kinda late, and I'd hate to have to wait until Monday.

Julia: They haven't faxed me anything. Not since you called a couple of minutes ago. I'm sure they'll send the report over as soon as it's ready.

Me: It would be great if you could call and check.

Julia: They might already be gone for the day.

Me: I bet they're still around. Could you at least try for me? I'd do it myself, but—

Julia: Oh, no, they won't give *you* that information.

Me: Yeah, I know.

Julia: Okay. I'll call over there if it will make you feel better. I'm really busy, though.

Me: Oh, thank you so much. I really appreciate it.

Julia: I'll call you back if I hear anything.

Me: Call me back no matter what, even if you don't speak with them, just so I don't worry, because—

Julia: I will. I will. Give me a couple minutes, though. I have patients I need to take care of.

Me: You bet. Thank you so—

Click.

4:48

4:52

4:56

4:57

4:58 PM

Other: Hello, Dr. Bach's—

Me: Hey, Juli—wait, who is this?

Other: This is Dr. Bach's answering service.

Me: I need to speak to Julia. It's urgent.

Other: Everyone's gone home for the day. Can I take a message?

Me: It's not even five o'clock yet!

Other: There's no need to get excited, miss. Would you like me to take a message?

Me: Julia was supposed to call me with a pathology report. Maybe you could look around the office and see if you see anything. It should be a fax from St. John's. It might still be in the fax machine. It's for a patient, last name Fogelson: *F* as in "Frank," *o-g*—

Other: Miss, I'm just the answering service. I'm not actually *in* her office.

Me: Oh . . . well . . . do you have some emergency number where I can reach Dr. Bach?

Other: If this is a life-threatening emergency, hang up and dial 9-1-1.

Me:

Other: Either you can call back Monday morning at eight thirty or I can take a message.

Me: *Yeah, could you take this down: Go . . . fuck . . . yourself.* Um, no. No message.

Weekend Fun

It has taken all of my willpower, all of my good sense and head-on-straight-ness, not to track down Dr. Bach's home number and pry the information out of her. *My* information. I *hate* her. No, I take that back. I hate my life. No—shit fuck piss—I take that back as well. I hate . . . I don't know . . . something.

The Craziest . . .

Me: You awake?

Adam: Not really.

Me: I had the *craziest* dream last night.

Adam: You say that like you're surprised.

Me: Can I tell it to you?

Adam: If you feel like you need to.

Me: I don't want to forget it. It was *so* fucked up . . . it started out in a bathroom, and I was brushing my hair. Except it wasn't my hair, it was actually a long blond wig. So I'm brushing the wig, and then I take it off and start brushing my own hair, which, in the dream, was medium length—like, to my shoulders. So, I'm brushing and these huge chunks of hair start to come out in the brush, like, massive clumps of hair, but I'm thinking it's just because I'm wearing a wig and haven't brushed my hair for a while. So I start running my hands through my hair, and I'm, like, parting my hair in different places, and I see all these bald spots. And then, like, one whole side of my head is practically hairless. And then the dream gets *really* fucked up, because I notice all these big moles on my scalp. They're *really* big, and gross, and I just know in the dream that the rest of my scalp is covered with these moles, so I decide to shave my head, and sure enough, my scalp is *covered* with moles and I know one of them, at least, is going to be melanoma. So I call Dr. Bach and I tell her I have to come in immediately, but it's late Friday, in the dream, and she says she can't see me till Monday. So I'm on the phone, explaining to her what I found on my head, and I'm pleading with her to let me come in on Saturday. I tell her I could come over to her house or something, but she says no. So I hang up.

Adam: And then . . .

Me: Um . . . I don't know. It kinda got weird after that. I decided to go shopping with my mom, I think. And I was looking for hats and scarves and stuff because I thought my head would get cold.

Adam:

Me: Since I had no hair.

Adam: Uh-huh, right. Of course.

No News Is Bad News

I have been staring at the phone since eight twenty-nine this morning. I've checked its batteries twice. I even made sure the phone was hung up. Of course, to do that, I had to pick it up, thus blocking potential callers from getting through. I just hope Dr. Bach's office didn't try to call in those few precious moments when I had the phone pressed to my ear, listening for a dial tone. Two hours and fifteen minutes, and still nothing. And still I wait.

As crazy and as paranoid as I may be (as I *am*), there is some legitimacy to my craziness. See, melanoma isn't easy to diagnose. This I've learned. This I know. Tricky-looking cells prompt second and third opinions and all that. So, the longer it takes to get a pathology report, the more likely the outcome is to be melanoma. But, of course, no one tells you that. You won't read that in some melanoma brochure or even overhear nurses whispering about it in the sterile hospital halls. You can only find out about the correlation, about "the secret," the hard way. Sad, but true. So, with four and a half working days behind me, I'm feeling less than confident about the outcome of the impending result.

Not that four days is a long time, mind you. It's just that Dr. Bach would have already called me to say everything is fine—if everything *is* fine—'cause she knows who she's dealing with. She knows all too well I can be a little too . . . involved. A tad anxious. A touch obsessive. A bit of a fucking nut basket. So, as I sit here with the phone in my lap, I'm feeling slightly . . . fucked.

TWO HOURS LATER:
Ring, ring, ring, ring.
You've reached Adam and Hillary. We're not in right now, but leave us a—
Me: Hello hello hello?
—message and we'll get back—
Other: Hillary?
Me: Yeah. Hold on. Let me turn this machine—
—to you as soon as . . . beep.
Me: Hello? Are you still there?
Other: Hi, it's Dr. Bach.
Me: *Be cool. Remain calm. I'm healthy. Hillary Fogelson is healthy. I am full of health and free of cancer. Free of cancer free of cancer free of cancer.* Hi. Sorry, I was in the bathroom and I didn't hear the phone, for some reason. *I was shitting my brains out from the thought of having melanoma.*
Dr. Bach: I wanted to call you and talk about the places I biopsied last week.
Me: *I'm healthy I'm healthy . . .*
Dr. Bach: I know you've been worried. I would have called you sooner, but I wanted to get a second opinion before I spoke with you.
Me: I totally understand. Not a problem.
Dr. Bach: Before I go any further, I should tell you that none of the places were malignant. None were melanoma. But—

Me: *I knew it! No cancer no cancer no cancer!*

Dr. Bach: Two of the three *were* severely dysplastic. So I need to go back and do wider excisions because—

Me: Whatever you need to do. I trust you. *No cancer no cancer no cancer!*

Dr. Bach: I want to make sure we got all the cells.

Me: Of course. Yeah, definitely. Wouldn't want to miss any cells. Thank you for calling. I was starting to get a little worried. I mean, I figured everything was okay, but, you know . . .

Dr. Bach: Julia told me you called several times, so I wanted to get back to you.

Me: Oh.

Dr. Bach: Do you have any questions for me?

Me: I don't think so. As long as I don't have melanoma, I don't care what you have to do to me.

Dr. Bach: Well, you don't have melanoma. I'll let you go. Look at your calendar and figure out a good time to come in for the excisions. I'd like to do them sooner than later.

Me: Sounds good. I mean, not *good,* but . . .

Dr. Bach: How's your dad doing?

Me: Good, so far. Thanks for asking. I was so relieved when his nodes came back clear. I think it's a miracle, considering how deep his melanoma was. I'm trying to get him to come out here to do a vaccine trial over at St. John's.

Dr. Bach: I think that's a really good idea. I've got . . . let's see . . . four patients who've had wonderful results with the vaccine.

Me: Really?

Dr. Bach: They all got the vaccine in one of its earliest trials at St. John's, and they're all still alive. I guess it's been close to twelve years now.

Me: What level melanoma did they have?

Dr. Bach: They were all level IV.

Me: That's amazing. And none of them had a recurrence?

Dr. Bach: One patient had satellite tumors around the site of his original melanoma, but none had distant metastases.

Me: Wow. That's unbelievable.

Dr. Bach: Anyway, schedule something for next week, if you can.

Me: Will do. Thank you. Again.

Click.

St. John's Hospital (a.k.a. My Club)

I feel good today, dare I say happy. I don't know why, particularly. Maybe I'm still flying high from last week's clean bill of health, or maybe I'm just starting to assimilate to my new existence. I'm not sure what it is, exactly. I mean, I know I'm about to get poked and prodded, felt up with cold hands, inspected from my tippy-toes to the top of my head and back down again, in my crack and between my legs, and still I feel giddy.

As I showered this morning, I caught myself smiling at the thought of coming here, the corners of my mouth turning up—if only slightly—picturing Howard take my blood while I squeeze a foam object meant to resemble a cell phone. I was looking forward to scanning the photos that cover the walls of the lab, pictures of pale patients and their beloved pets, all done up in doggie do-rags and kitty raincoats. I even giggled with anticipation as I thought of sitting in a freezing hospital room in my gownette—back open for all those who care to see—staring at the tarnished cross above the goddamned double-thick door—and none of it seemed so bad. I was half looking forward to coming here this morning, as crazy as that may sound. The hills are alive with the sound of fucking music—it's the damnedest thing. I have a spring in my step and a twinkle in my eye. I'm not ashamed to say it, but I don't know why I do.

Me: Hey, Tom. How are you?

Tom: I'm doing good. And you?

Me: Really good, thanks.

Tom: Let's see. I've got you down for ten forty-five with Dr. Gregory, correct?

Me: Yep. Your family's good?

Tom: They're great. The girls are growing so fast, I can't believe it.

Me: Oh, I bet.

Tom: So, here's your chart. You can head on back to the lab when you're ready.

Me: Great, thanks—

Tom:—also, we've got a new chaplain introducing himself around this morning, just FYI. He might come say hello.

Me: Okay, not a problem. Thanks for the heads-up.

Everyone's so friendly here, in a "Great to know ya" sort of way. I don't know why I never noticed it before. Guess I had other, more pressing things on my mind. Tom's a really nice man, quite receptive for a receptionist. He makes me feel important. He makes me feel like I'm a part of something. A part of something big—really big, bigger than I've ever been a part of before. He looks at me and—for some reason—I feel like I'm a member of an elite club or something. It's strange, the way he stares at me, but strangely comforting, too. He looks at me as if to say, *yes, I understand.* I don't really know if he actually understands fuck-all, but he sure as shit gives the impression that he understands a lot.

Maybe that's it. Maybe that's why I feel so good—why I felt so excited to come here today. Maybe I smiled at the thought of all this freakishness because I knew I was going to the one place where I can let my guard down. The place where people are like me, where I fit in. The third floor. It's like a club. A cancer club . . . except I shouldn't call it that. I've got to work on a title. I've never really been in a club before, besides my high school ski club and drama club, but those more closely resembled mixers or even loose gatherings. I was briefly a member of the debate club, but that really had more to do with my preoccupation with a guy than it did with any actual skill or keen interest in debating. But now I've got me a club and a big-ass clubhouse. I even have a club secretary, who meticulously takes minutes and schedules meetings. Yep, life is good. Gotta love club livin'.

Me: Hey, Howard, how's it hangin'?

Howard: Can't complain. What about you?

Me: I'm doing really good, thanks.

Howard: Okay . . . you know the routine . . . your blood pressure looks good . . . your temp . . . normal . . . weight . . . one twenty—

Me: Don't tell me, don't tell me.

Howard: Right. I forgot. Sorry.

Me: It's stupid, I know, but I just can't help myself.

Howard: You're not the first woman to not want to know her weight, believe you me.

Me: I see you've got a new squeeze toy. What happened to the phone?

Howard: One of my vaccine patients took it. Can you believe that? I'm using this globe till I find another phone.

Me: I've got the whole world in my hand. I've got the whole wide world in my hand. I've got the . . . *hum hum hum hum hum hum* . . . I've got the whole world in my hand.

Howard: . . . I'm all done here. You can head on over to your room. Dr. Gregory should be with you in a minute.

Me: Thanks, man.

As I stroll down the hall to my room, I look around and am surrounded by all things familiar. I close my eyes, and I know there is a poster to my right—WHEN TO MAKE A MOUNTAIN OUT OF A MOLE—decked out with colored photos of benign and malignant tumors. To my left, a "What Cancer Can't Do" poem, its type faded and the page yellowing with age. I know this because I have read it, studied it with every visit. I have stood centimeters from it and stared till my eyes crossed and blurred. There is a bathroom straight ahead, a nurses' station up and to the left. Recognizable voices float up and down the hall, bouncing off the gray carpet below and fluorescent lights above, and I feel safe. I feel safe in my clubhouse. I feel for my membership badge, just under my left breast. It is there; I can feel its texture through my cotton shirt. I belong. I belong *here,* anyway.

Knock, knock.

Me: Come in.

Other: Hello, it's so nice to meet you. I wanted to introduce myself. I'm the new chaplain, and I wanted to meet all the wonderful patients on the third floor.

Me: *"Wonderful,"* no less. Oh, yeah, hi. *We're a club up here, did you know that? I'm in a clu-ub and you're-re no-ot.*

Chaplain: I'll be here on Mondays and Thursdays.

Me: Great.

Chaplain: It's such a pleasure to meet you.

Me: Hillary.

Chaplain: Peter.

Me: Nice to meet you.

Peter: So, how long have you been a patient here?

Me: Oh, about three months. I was diagnosed with melanoma in June.

Peter: You look like you're doing well.

Me: Yeah. Thanks. *Are you referring to the fact that I'm still alive?*

Peter: I haven't met many patients who have been here that long.

Me: Really? *Not many longtime members?*

Peter: You must be doing *very* well.

Me: I am. I am. *I'd like to take a vote: All those in favor of never having chaplain Peter back as a guest speaker, say aye . . . aye aye aye aye aye!*

Peter: I'm so thrilled to hear that.

Me: And I'm hoping my father will be a patient here as well. He was diagnosed with melanoma a few months after me. He had surgery in Ohio—my parents live in Ohio. I'd like to get him in one of the clinical trials that the hospital is running. *I think we can go ahead and schedule a next meeting. Thanks for coming, Peter . . .*

Peter: I see. Ohio, huh? The Western Frontier. Have you ever heard it called that before?

Me: No, I don't think I have.

Peter: It's strange, huh, to refer to Ohio as the Western Frontier, when in the olden days Ohio was as far west as one could go?

Me: Oh, wow, that *is* hard to believe.

Peter: Yes.

Me: How interesting.

Peter: Isn't it, though.

Me: I never knew that. *This is a test. God is testing me.*

Peter: Well, more accurately, I should say, it was as far west as most people *had* gone. In the late seventeen hundreds, when Thomas Jefferson wrote *Notes on the State of Virginia,* many blah blahs in America, as well as in Europe, knew little about blah to the west of the Appalachians . . .

Me: *I think it's time to adjourn this club meeting. Thanks, Peter, for finding the time to talk to us today. Clearly, many of us won't be here next meeting, according to you, so I guess this is goodbye . . .*

Peter: . . . won by the U.S., so, like I was saying, the first American west was the Great Lakes to blah blah Florida and from the crest of the blah blahs westward to the Mississippi river.

Me: That is really fascinating. Wow.

Knock.

Me: Come in. Please.

Gregory: What's going on in here?

Peter: Hi, I'm Peter, the new chaplain. I was just getting to know Heather here.

Me: We're just . . . having a little party.

Peter: All we need is one more person for a foursome.

Me: *Golf? You're talking about golf? Please say you are, because all I can picture is me, you, Gregory, and some snagglepuss from next door, all buck naked, having a pillow fight in the lab.*

Gregory: Well, it's nice to meet you, Peter. Thank you for stopping in.

Me: *Don't encourage him.*

Peter: Take care, Heather. It was a real pleasure speaking with you. May God bless you and your father. You'll be in my prayers.

Me: Nice meeting you . . . I don't even know what to say. He was making me so uncomfortable. He started saying something about how it was great I've been here so long—like, alluding to the fact that most patients don't make it to their three-month anniversary—and then he went into Ohio, and I can't tell you what he was saying about that except that it was in the west or something. And something about the Appalachians.

Gregory: He was nervous. It was his first day up here, and he saw some very sick patients today. I'm sure he had a rough morning. I don't think he'd spent much time up here before today.

Me:

Gregory: So . . . let's take a look at that scar, shall we?

Me: *Yeah, I'm proud of my membership badge. Get right in there if you need to. Toss it like a salad. I will show anyone and everyone my membership badge. Because I'm proud of it! I earned it! And I belong! I belong on the third floor!*

Gregory: Nodes feel fine . . .

Me: *But what if . . . let's say I decided, for the sake of argument, I wanted to take a break from my club—temporarily, of course. I'm not talking about a permanent move or anything—I wouldn't dream of it—but just on an intellectual/metaphysical level, how would one go about doing that, do you think? How would (how could) one leave the club if one were so inclined?*

Gregory: You might want to have your dermatologist remove this place here on your arm, just to be safe . . .

Me: *I guess, when I think about it, there's really only one way out of the club, as far as I can tell, one would have to . . . die.*

Gregory: Everything looks good.

Me: Good . . . okay.

Gregory: You okay?

Me: Huh? Yeah. Thanks. See ya soon.

Me: Tom, can I get my parking validated?

Tom: Oh, we don't do that anymore. Sorry. You can try the fourth floor. I think the Positive Appearance Center validates. It's directly to your left when you get off the elevator. You can't miss it.

Me: Yeah, I think I've seen it.

WELCOME TO THE POSITIVE APPEARANCE CENTER

Me: Excuse me, could I get a parking validation sticker from you?

Shopkeeper: Oh, I'm sorry, we don't validate anymore. Check with the third floor.

Me: I just came from there. Tom sent me up to you.

Shopkeeper: Gosh . . . you know . . . let me . . . look. Maybe I have an old sticker around here . . . somewhere . . . I saw one . . . the other . . . day . . . but . . .

Me: You know what, it's not that big a deal. I can just pay the four bucks—

Shopkeeper: It's gone up to eight.

Me: Wow. Okay . . . maybe I'll let you look . . . this store is pretty great.

Shopkeeper: We've got a little bit of everything.

Me: Yeah, no kidding . . . are these all wigs . . . patients can, like, buy?

Shopkeeper: Yeah. A lot of the breast cancer patients get their wigs here.

Me: I can't believe I haven't come in before. *This place is really fucking amazing. And even though I feel slightly ashamed about enjoying the guilty pleasures of the fourth floor, let me say again . . . this store is fucking amazing! It's got wigs and scarves, sunscreen and sun protective clothing, face-care products and . . . and . . . vaginal lubricants. I think I'm more surprised to find a store with informational brochures on the dangers of the sun than I am to discover the striking similarity between the sample packets of Vagisil and the Murad under-eye moisturizer . . . this store is a cancer patient's paradise. I feel right at home in this center for . . . positive appearance. I'm feeling more positive already! At least, I'm giving the appearance of positivity . . . they have all the good sunscreens with all the necessary ingredients; they even have the ever-elusive lip/eye sun protection stick by Murad . . . oh my God, I have the best idea: I'm going to work here. No, wait, I'm going to volunteer. Yeah, work for free! Give back to my fellow cancer compadres. "Giving back" is just what I need. This could be that "important something" I've been looking for! Maybe I could share my knowledge of sunscreen, sun protection products, and all things sun related with other melanoma patients. Or . . . or I could help chemo patients pick out a wig, one that looks natural—taking into consideration their eye color and skin tone, of course. Yeah, this could be good. This could be really good. Or I could even give weekly seminars on the dangers of tanning beds. "What the tanning salons don't want you to know!" or, or, or . . .*

Shopkeeper: You know, I can't seem to find that darn sticker . . . I just saw it the other—

Me: I was wondering, could you use a volunteer up here? I'm a . . . um . . . melanoma patient, and I know a lot about sunscreen. *And* melanoma, obviously.

Shopkeeper: You're so young. I was just going to tell you what beautiful skin you have.

Me: Ironic, huh, that it's trying to kill me? Thanks, though.

Shopkeeper: I could definitely use some extra help up here, but unfortunately, I'm not really in charge of hiring volunteers. Muriel Hager is the person you need to talk to. She's the head of the hospital's psychosocial care program. She runs all the cancer support groups. Actually, I think the hospital has a program you have to go through in order to become a volunteer.

Me: Oh.

Shopkeeper: I could connect you with the volunteer office if you'd like.

Me: Yeah, that would be great.

Shopkeeper: Let me find the number . . . here it is . . . okay, it's ringing . . .

Me: Hello?

Other: St. John's volunteer office . . .

Me: Yes, hi, I wanted to talk to someone about becoming a volunteer.

Other: That would be me.

Me: Oh. Great. So, what do I need to do?

Other: First, you have to go through our eight-hour orientation. I organize the volunteer orientations. Our next one is in three weeks. Give me your address, and I'll send you the information.

Me: I'd really like to get started right away. I could start now and then go through the orientation in three weeks.

Other: No, no. You *must* go through our orientation *first.* In *addition,* there are health requirements, blood tests, an *exam* on hospital *safety,* several psychologi—

Me: Oh. *Did you hear me say I'd like to work for* free?! Okay, then. My address is . . .

Other: Last name?

Me: Fogelson. *F* as in "Frank," *o-g-e-l-s-o-n.*

Other: I'll get this right out. Our orientations fill up fast. Do you want me to put your name on the list?

Me: Yes. Definitely.

Other: Now, don't have me put your name down unless you're really serious about this. I don't want you taking someone else's spot.

Me: I really want to do this.

Other: Fine.

Me: Thank—

Click.

Shopkeeper: So, what'd she say?

Me: *She can't wait for me to get started! She welcomed me with open arms! She appreciated my eagerness to help! She was a big fat fucking bitch, and I plan on telling her that as soon as I meet her.* "Hospital safety exam," *my ass.* I have to go through the orientation first. The next one is in three weeks. You know, I'd love to come and just hang out. You could teach me everything I need to know, so after my orientation I'd be all ready to start. I mean, how would they even know?

Shopkeeper: If you'd like to come in a couple times a week, that would be fine with me. I don't see the harm, and I'll talk to Muriel for you. I'm sure she'd be happy to have extra help up here.

Me: Great. Which days would be best?

Shopkeeper: Mondays are usually the busiest. Most of the breast cancer doctors see patients on Mondays, so I get a lot of women coming in after their appointments. Why don't you start next Monday?

Me: Great. What time?

Shopkeeper: We open at ten o'clock. We're open ten to twelve, then one to four. I'm Amy, by the way.

Me: Hillary. Nice to meet you . . . I'll see you at ten, then.

Amy: Perfect.

Me: Oh, could I get that sticker? I almost forgot . . . great, thanks.

Oh, one more thing: You might want to consider moving that, um . . . Vagisil a little farther away from the face-care products. Just a suggestion . . . see you Monday.

I'm going to become a volunteer! In other words, I'm going to give my time gladly and, more important, freely to one and all! Actually, I may be overstating the generosity of my intended effort. I *am* going to volunteer, but I'm *not* going to be "giving" willy-nilly to anyone and everyone who presumably needs help. I mean, really. Who do you think I am? I'm not *that* fucking positive.

My Really Big Pupils

No reindeer slippers today. I didn't realize just how attached I'd become to those monstrosities until I saw little miss "crazy smell" sliding toward the exit with nothing more than thin soccer socks covering her particularly large tootsies. I wish I could say the 'deer slippers are in the wash, but, judging from the sad state the soccer socks are in (worn toes to heels and a couple threads away from becoming full-fledged leg warmers), it's highly unlikely.

Dr. Lesaux: Hillary, you ready?

Me: Yep.

Dr. Lesaux: Blinds open, right?

Me: If that's okay with you.

Dr. Lesaux: And all the lights turned on. I have to try and remember how each of my patients likes it. Everyone's a little different.

Me: If it's not going to hurt your eyes, yeah, all on would be perfect. I like a lot of light because of my pupils. I have really big pupils. I don't know if you've ever noticed them before. They're really huge. Now you're probably going to be staring at them. Everyone always thinks I'm on speed or cocaine. Sorry, we're, like, totally off topic right now. I think my pupils might be messed up or something. I'm not really sure.

Dr. Lesaux: Some people actually consider it a plus to have large pupils. There was a study done years ago, and the participants were asked to make character judgments based solely on photos of people's eyes. Many of the pictures were of the same person's eyes, just with dilated pupils. What the study found was, people generally assign more positive personality traits to people with big pupils as opposed to people with small ones.

Me: Huh. So, I guess when people meet me they expect me to be really, really nice. I must be quite a disappointment. Most people don't know what color my eyes are because my pupils are always so big.

Dr. Lesaux: Brown?

Me: See? See what I mean? They're blue.

Dr. Lesaux: . . . let me look at my notes for a second here . . . last week, toward the end of the session, we started to get into how your dad's been dealing with his diagnosis. Actually, before we start talking about your dad, how were your panic attacks this week?

Me: Um . . . better . . . I think. I'm still taking the Paxil that my internist gave me. I can't tell if it's doing anything or not. When I get on the freeway, I do the breathing and relaxation stuff from your handout, but I still get really panicky in the middle lane.

Dr. Lesaux: And what is it specifically about the middle lane, do you think, that gives you such a problem?

Me: I think I get worried that if something bad *did* happen, like, if I started to pass out or something, I wouldn't have time to get over to the shoulder.

Dr. Lesaux: Uh-huh.

Me: Oh, but I did have one really big realization this week. Some freeways have a shoulder to the left of the fast lane, so now, on those freeways, I feel comfortable in the fourth or fifth lane, which is a huge relief because it was taking me so fucking long to get anywhere, since I was pretty much confined to the slow lane.

Dr. Lesaux: And what about transitioning freeways? Has that gotten any easier?

Me: No, that's still my biggest problem. The 101—oh my God, that freeway kills me. I usually just take Ventura Boulevard until I get past the transition, and then I get back on the freeway. When I go to my in-laws' in the valley, it takes me, like, an hour and a half. It's ridiculous. Oh, but I am working on a technique that may temporarily solve my problem. Yesterday I decided to *try* to transition; I figured I could always chicken out last minute and head toward Santa Monica if I had to. I pretended that the thick transition line was actually the shoulder. I know it doesn't make a lot of sense, and if I really started to pass out or something I'd be royally fucked if I used that lane as the shoulder, but somehow it helped me to think about it in that way.

Dr. Lesaux: Did it work?

Me: Yeah, I transitioned. I was panicky, but I didn't, like, totally lose my shit.

Dr. Lesaux: You know, I think it's really good what you're doing. You're finding ways to cope. They may be unconventional, but as I always say, "whatever works." You didn't happen to catch my radio call-in show on Wednesday, did you?

Me: No, why? *Did you provide handouts for all your listeners? Did you mail them postcards with sayings like "Get a Life" and "Only Freaks Call Radio Shows" scribbled on the back?*

Dr. Lesaux: Darn, I hate that you missed it. I broached this very topic on my live call-in show.

Me: Yeah . . . I hate that I missed it.

Dr. Lesaux: You know, I have an article on coping mechanisms you might find interesting. Remind me to print it out before you leave today. So, where were we? Last week we were talking about your dad and . . . let's see . . . you were saying how . . . how you feel like he's in denial and that you think he needs to talk about what he's feeling.

Me: Well, yeah. I think it's bad to hold stuff in. You can't just keep it all to yourself.

Dr. Lesaux: So, have you had any more thoughts about this topic since last week?

Me: No. Not really. Nothing new. I've just been feeling mostly frustrated.

Dr. Lesaux: Why?

Me: Because I feel like I have nothing to talk to my dad about. You know, we were getting along a lot better when I was first diagnosed—I felt like we were really talking and stuff—and now it feels like we've reverted back to our old relationship.

Dr. Lesaux: In what way?

Me: We're not talking about real stuff anymore. He doesn't want to talk about melanoma, except right now, it seems like it's the only thing *to* talk about. Other stuff seems trivial in comparison. Like, what can we talk about? I mean, I'm not doing any acting right now, and he's not working, so what are we supposed to talk about besides how we're doing and what we're feeling? We're going through this very uncommon experience together, ya know, and I don't feel like he wants to reach out to me. And I'm the one person who might actually understand how he's feeling. But he just doesn't want to talk about *anything* having to do with melanoma or sunscreen and . . . and . . . I don't know . . . we're just very different people, I guess. I want to know everything there is to know and read everything there is to read and talk about it with people who are going through it, but he seems content to ignore everything. It can't be healthy.

Dr. Lesaux: You said some interesting things. I can't imagine how difficult it must be for the two of you—let me start by saying that. And I'm like you: I like to talk about how I feel—it's one of the reasons I became a therapist. But you need to respect your father's feelings. He's trying to deal with all of this in his own way, and you shouldn't try to force him to deal with it in the same way as you.

Me: But that's the point. He's *not* dealing with it! He's not dealing with any of it!

Dr. Lesaux: How do you know that?

Me: What do you mean, how do I know? He doesn't talk about any of it!

Dr. Lesaux: Just because he doesn't talk about it doesn't mean he isn't dealing with it.

Me: You don't understand.

Dr. Lesaux: He's just dealing with it *differently* than *you*. And as long as he's not hurting himself, you need to allow him the space to do that.

Me: He *is* hurting himself! He's not doing all the things he should be doing. Like, like, he should be investigating and researching clinical trials. He needs to find a trial, another form of treatment; otherwise he's . . . he's got a really high chance of a recurrence. And the thing is, there's this really amazing trial at St. John's, but he doesn't even want to talk about it. He's completely close-minded. He's being stubborn and difficult, and I feel like the small amount of progress we made in our relationship is for shit.

Dr. Lesaux: In what way?

Me: We don't talk! We don't have anything to talk about. If we don't talk about melanoma, then we don't have anything to say to one another. How am I supposed to be close to him and talk to him *without* talking about the biggest thing going on in both of our lives?

Dr. Lesaux: It sounds like your dad is trying to be as normal as possible. He's looking for ways to feel normal.

Me: But his life *isn't* normal right now. What am I supposed to talk to him about? What I saw on television?

Dr. Lesaux: Maybe.

Me: That's so . . . lame.

Dr. Lesaux: If you want him to respect your ways of coping, you're going to have to respect his.

Me: It makes me so anxious. It's like the whole elephant thing.

Dr. Lesaux: What elephant thing?

Me: Like the elephant in the room and no one's talking about it, or even looking at it. You know, everyone's just pretending it isn't there. Were you staring at my pupils? I should never have said anything about them.

Dr. Lesaux: No. I wasn't aware that I was. No. Give your dad some time. You've had more time to adjust to all of this than he has. He's just getting started.

Me: I guess, but—

Dr. Lesaux: How's your mom doing?

Me: Hard to really tell. She's okay, I guess. Better than before. At least she's slowed down with the skin cancer articles. She was faxing me new articles, like, every other day. I'm worried she may be drinking too much.

Dr. Lesaux: Why do you say that?

Me: I don't know. It's not like I have proof or anything. She hasn't really done anything, but I know her. It's how she handles stress: She drinks. I mean, I do the same thing, so . . . I know how it works . . . I don't know. I can't do anything about it, not until she's out here and I can watch her. Maybe I'm just being paranoid, although I suspect she tries to be on her best behavior when she's around me.

Dr. Lesaux: Have you tried to talk to her about it?

Me: No, not yet. I don't even know what I would say . . . it's probably nothing. I mean, a couple of drinks at night never hurt anybody . . . maybe *I* have been drinking too much.

Dr. Lesaux: How much do you drink?

Me: I don't know . . . couple drinks a night.

Dr. Lesaux: And do you feel you really need those couple drinks a night?

Me: *Need?*

Beep-beep-beep.

Me: Time.

Dr. Lesaux: Let's not forget where we left off. I think we should look into this drinking a little further.

Me: Yeah, okay, well, see ya next week. Nice alarm, by the way.

Dr. Lesaux: I thought of you when I bought it. This one sounds a little less intrusive, don't you think?

Me: Um . . . not really.

Dr. Lesaux: Darn it. I'll see you next week. Oh, wait, let me get you that handout . . . here, look this over. It doesn't all relate to you, but I think you'll find at least a couple things helpful.

Me: Thanks.

Dr. Lesaux: And don't forget to work on your relaxation exercises.

Me: Why? Don't I seem relaxed?

OVER A DRINK WITH DINNER:

Adam: How was your day?

Me: Good. What do you want to drink?

Adam: I'm just going to have a Diet Coke.

Me: You don't want any wine? I opened a bottle of Pinot Grigio.

Adam: No, Diet Coke is fine.

Me: I had therapy today.

Adam: How was it?

Me: Well, interesting. Toward the end of the session—

Adam: Could you get me a napkin?

Me: You've got one. Under your plate. Anyway, toward the end of the session we started talking about alcohol—

Adam: This chicken is really moist. Did you do something different to it?

Me: It's organic.

Adam: This isn't tofu, is it?

Me: No, it's chicken, but it's raised hormone free or something. I don't know. I got it at Whole Foods. So—

Adam: It's super moist.

Me: Do you think I drink too much?

Adam: What do you mean?

Me: Do you think I drink too much?

Adam: How much do you drink?

Me: You know. You see me. Do you think I'm an alcoholic?

Adam: Yes.

Me: You do?

Adam: I'm kidding. I—remind me, why are we having this discussion?

Me: It was just something that came up today in therapy. Got me thinking.

Adam: Always dangerous . . . no, of course I don't think you're an alcoholic. I mean, you could quit if you had to.

Me: I could?

Adam: Sure you could.

Me: You think?

Adam: You're gonna have to quit when you're pregnant.

Me: Yeah . . . but who knows when that'll be.

Adam: If you're worried about it, quit.

Me: No, I just, I don't know.

Adam: Quit for a week. See how you feel.

Me: Yeah. Maybe I will.

Adam: Good.

Me: What will you give me if I quit?

Adam: Nothing.

Me: Oh.

Adam: You'll have the satisfaction of knowing you were able to quit.

Me: Great.

Adam: So, you gonna quit?

Me: What? You mean, like, now? I'm . . . I'm gonna do it . . . I've just . . . you know . . . gotta figure out when . . . and stuff.

Adam: Okay.

Me:

First Day of School

Ring, ring.

Me: Ad? Ad? Can you get that?

Ring, ring.

Me: Ad! Get the phone! I have sunscreen all over my—

Ring, ring.

Me: Hello?

Other: Good morning.

Me: Hey, Mom.

Mom: Adam left for work yet?

Me: Not yet.

Mom: Should I call back later? After he's gone?

Me: No, it's fine. We're not, like, having a family breakfast or anything. I'm just putting on sunscreen. I was thinking of wearing shorts today. Thought I might expose my legs to a little fresh air. Adam's right—they really are the color of skim milk. They're bluish . . . all this sunscreen—it takes, like, half a bottle to cover my legs. Maybe I should just wear pants to the hospital and be done with it.

Mom: The hospital? Did something happen? I thought you just had a checkup.

Me: Today's my first day of volunteering.

Mom: Oh, that's right. I can't wait to hear how it goes. I think it's great you're doing this. I just hope it isn't too depressing. Should I call back later? I don't want you to forget where you left off with the sunscreen.

Me: No, that's okay, I'm an expert. I can talk and rub at the same time—what are you up to?

Mom: Well, I worked in the garden some this morning.

Me: Still mulching?

Mom: Yes, if you can believe it. I don't feel like I've made a dent in that mulch pile. I bought too much, that's what it is. I guess I'd rather have too much than too little. I hate running out.

Me: Nothin' like runnin' out of dried shit. Remember when I used to play in the manure piles with Nina Pollock? Do you remember that?

Mom: Was that with Nina? I thought you did that when we lived in Kentucky.

Me: No, Georgia. Remember? Nina lived across the street from that farm. Remember? And it always had a humongous pile of manure next to the barn—God, that was fun. We used to climb to the top of that pile and just fly down the front of it. I remember going back to her house just absolutely covered in shit, and it didn't even smell. Not until we took a bath . . . the good ol' days.

Mom: Are you sure that was in Georgia?

Me: Positive. We moved to Atlanta when I was five. How could I have been sliding down a pile of manure before I was five?

Mom: Huh. I could have sworn you did that in Kentucky.

Me: Speaking of, why don't you hire someone to do the mulching? Your back's gonna go out.

Mom: I'm careful.

Me: It's not about being careful. You just shouldn't be doing it. And you can *afford* to hire someone.

Mom: I kind of like doing it. It's therapeutic. Very Zen.

Me: Yeah, I guess it's like how I feel about dusting.

Mom: And everything's bad for my back these days . . . did you get really sunburned in Cancun?

Me: What?

Mom: When you went to Cancun after your senior year, did you get a lot of sun?

Me: Um . . . yeah. I mean, I wore sunscreen—I had to, or else I would have been burned to a crisp—but, yeah, I still got a lot of sun. Why? What made you think of that? What the hell does mulching have to do with Cancun?

Mom: Nothing. I was just thinking that that could have been the reason you got melanoma. I was trying to figure out when you could have gotten a lot of sun on your stomach, and then I remembered Cancun and thought that might be the answer because you wore a two-piece bathing suit.

Me: Right . . . ?

Mom: So, you probably got a lot of sun on your stomach—when you were a kid you *never* wore a two-piece. Your stomach was never exposed.

Me: I wore a two-piece when I was younger. I had that one I always wore to Raging Waters. The one with the stomach cut out. It was blue, and it had Miss Piggy in the upper-right corner. I must have been around ten or so. It was one of my chubby stages, because I remember my stomach always hung out of the cutout.

Mom: I remember the Miss Piggy suit, but I thought it was a one-piece . . .

Me: How the hell did we get on this topic?

Mom: I was just trying to figure out when you got so much sun.

Me: I never got *that* much sun. In high school, whenever I went to the beach, I always wore sunscreen.

Mom: But you *did* get some bad burns.

Me: Yeeesss. So?

Mom: What?

Me: Huh? What?

Mom: I didn't say anything.

Me: Actually, I should probably go. I need to get all my sunscreen on, and I've gotta leave for the hospital in, like, twenty minutes.

Mom: Love you—oh, by the way, your father and I were thinking of coming out for a visit.

Me: Oh. Great.

Mom: We were thinking maybe the beginning of November. We were planning on coming out for your birthday, but I was afraid that would be a little too soon for your father to travel. Sitting, for any long period of time, is hard for him—are you guys going to be around in November?

Me: I'll check with Adam, but I'm pretty sure we're around. I don't think we have anything planned.

Mom: Well, talk to Adam. Your father and I don't want to be an inconvenience.

Me: Mom. Please.

Mom: I'll let you go. We'll talk about hotel options later.

Me: You guys are *not* staying in a hotel. We have plenty of room at the house.

Mom: Adam needs his privacy.

Me: What are you talking about? It's not like he walks around the house naked or anything. You're staying with us. That's what the guest room is for. No one else ever uses it.

Mom: We'll talk about it later.

Me: Fine, but you're staying with us.

Mom: Get back to your sunscreen.

Me: But you're staying with us.

Mom: If that will make you happy. I know you—if we stay at your place, you'll clean for a week before we get there.

Me: Well, I'd do that anyway. I've really gotta go.

Mom: Love you.

Me: You, too.

Click.

Me: Didn't you hear the phone ringing a second ago? My mom's crazy. Just thought you should know.

Adam: What happened? I mean, I agree with you—I'm just curious why you decided to say it.

Me: It was so weird . . . we were talking about mulching, and then all of a sudden she starts asking me questions about my trip to Cancun.

Adam: I have so many questions. How did you get on the topic of mulching, and what trip?

Me: My mom's mulching her garden, and I was telling her she should hire someone—she was referring to the trip I took right after high school.

Adam: What did she want to know about the trip?

Me: I'm not exactly sure. Something about sunburns, I guess.

Adam: Sunburns.

Me: Yeah—oh, and they're coming to visit.

Adam: Who?

Me: My parents. They're thinking about the beginning of next month. Do we have anything going on?

Adam: I'll be out of town.

Me: When?

Adam: When are they coming?

Me: Very funny. They're not that bad.

Adam: I was kidding. November sounds fine.

Me: So . . . how do I look?

Adam: I see you decided to let the out-of-bound stakes out for a little fresh air.

Me: Do my legs really look that white? Do they look ridiculous?

Adam: Not at all. And this is not a beauty contest.

Me: I just want to look good for my first day of volunteering—helping—whatever it is I'm doing.

Adam: You look great. Have a good time.

Me: Thanks—I'm off to make a difference.

Adam: I love you.

Me: Love you, too.

Adam: I'm proud of you.

Me: I haven't done anything yet.

Adam: You will.

No . . . What?

After a quick lesson on mastectomy bras and prostheses, a crash course on Murad face products, and an unfortunate study of vaginal lubricants and clitoral stimulants, I feel more than ready to start working for free. And even though I am a novice in the ways of wig maintenance and support stockings, I figure I can learn as I go . . .

Customer: Excuse me, can you help me? Do you work here?

Me: I'm a volunteer, actually, but if I can't answer your question, Amy can help you.

Customer: Well, I'll tell you, I have two young sons, both play Little League, and I need to get some sunscreen for them. Something that they won't sweat right through. Do you know which of these would be best?

Me: I highly recommend Blue Lizard. It uses zinc as its UVA blocker. You always want to get something with UVA and UVB protection. The main UVA blockers are Parsol 1789 (avobenzone), which is a chemical blocker, and zinc and titanium, which are physical blockers. Sunscreens with physical UVA blockers must contain a large concentration, more than five percent, of zinc or titanium dioxide in order for them to be really effective.

Customer: Okay—

Me: And remember, if you're perspiring, pretty much any sunscreen is going to need to be reapplied every forty minutes to an hour. Even the waterproof ones don't work much longer than that. And the skin *must* be dry when the sunscreen is applied. So make sure you towel off your boys *completely,* at halftime or whatever, before reapplying. Also, make sure you put enough of the lotion on them. You have to use more then you might think. I've seen so many people squirt a little dab on their hands, rub their hands together, then kinda pat themselves. That's not going to do anything. You've gotta really rub it in completely. Get it everywhere.

Customer: Yeah, I—

Me: You probably need about what, ten bottles to start with? You'll go through it pretty fast.

Customer: Actually, I'll just get the one bottle for now, see if my boys like it.

Me: But—

Customer: I appreciate your help.

Me: Sorry. I'm sorry, I totally overloaded you with information. This is my first day volunteering, and I'm a little overzealous. I'm just a big fan of sunscreen—it's really important to protect your kids when they're young. Especially if they're fair, like you—I'm going to stop talking now. Let me give you these brochures. They'll answer any other questions you might have. And Amy can ring this up for you.

Customer: Thank you.

Me: How did you hear about our store?

Customer: I saw one of your posters down on the third floor.

Me: Oh.

Customer: Thanks for all your help.

Me: My pleasure. Hope your boys like the sunscreen—and make sure you put it everywhere. Don't forget the back of their necks, their hands—

Customer: Their ears.

Me: Exactly.

Customer: Yeah, or this can happen . . .

Me: *Oh my God, she has no . . .*

With a flip of her wrist, she brushed her hair away from her face just long enough to reveal her ear.

Me: *. . . except . . . there is no ear, none to speak of, not really. Just the tiniest tip of a lobe, a bit of flesh more likely to be mistaken for a skin tag than recognized as the remnants of an ear. Where's her . . . where's your ear? What the—? Okay, stay calm. Don't look away, but do not stare. I repeat, do not stare. I need to get in for a better look, though . . . is there just a hole, or what, exactly, is going on? Could it sustain an earring, supposing she wanted to wear two? How does she keep her sunglasses from sitting cock-eyed? Can she use earphones? Surely not the wraparound ones. There's so many questions . . . I probably shouldn't ask to see it again. "Do it again—come on, pleeeeeeeease!"*

Customer: Melanoma.

Me: Me too.

Customer: Where?

Me: Stomach.

Customer: You're so young.

Me: Yeah, well.

Customer: Take care of yourself. Lots of sunscreen.

Me: Yeah, don't we know it. Good luck to you and your boys.

Customer: Thanks. You too. I'm Beth, by the way. I didn't catch your name.

Me: Hillary.

Beth: Hope to see you again, Hillary.

Me: Yeah, you too, Beth. You too.

Ah, Beth. Beth and I go *way* back. I love Beth. Beth and her two sons. Beth is . . . Beth loves to . . . well . . . *you* know Beth. Oh, she is crazy, that Beth is. You must know her. Red hair, about shoulder length; blue eyes. Beth. *Beth. B-e-t-h* . . . she has no left ear . . . yeah, *that* Beth.

OVER DINNER:

Adam: How was work today?

Me: Work?

Adam: You're not getting paid, but it's still work.

Me: Good point.

Adam: When are they going to start paying you, by the way?

Me: I just started. What, you think I should really work there?

Adam: I bet you could run that place.

Me: Yeah, but I don't *want* to. Work was good. Really good. I met some really amazing people . . . met a woman with one ear.

Adam: Excuse me?

Me: She had melanoma on her ear. So all she had left was a—

Adam: I'm eating.

Me: No, it's not gross. It was basically a hole with just a—

Adam: Okay, okay, okay.

Me: You don't want to know what it looked like?

Adam: No.

Me: You're not curious?

Adam: No. But thank you.

Giving the Finger

Adam: How'd you sleep?

Me: Okay.

Adam: Just okay?

Me: I'm still tired. I feel like I was working all night. I think working at the hospital affected my dreams.

Adam: Everything affects your dreams.

Me: True. I dreamt I was giving skin screenings . . . I don't remember where I was, but there was a huge group of people, all ages, and they were all milling around in this giant room, and somehow they all knew I'd had melanoma. I don't know if I announced it or how they knew, but they all seemed to think I was an expert on melanoma, so everyone started forming a line, and one by one they asked me to look at their moles. They wanted me to tell them whether I thought they needed to see a dermatologist or not. And it was amazing because everyone, every single person in the room, had at least one mole for me to look at.

So I started checking out each person. I told them what I saw and why I thought they should or shouldn't see a doctor. But I started getting worried

that I was giving them a false sense of security by saying I thought their
moles looked benign, so I made an announcement saying that anyone who
has been worrying about a mole should go see a doctor. I told them if they
had a mole that had changed in color or size, they definitely needed to get
it checked out by a professional. And in the dream, I started getting really
frustrated because I saw all of these people who had moles that had grown
or changed or whatever, and none of these people had taken the initiative to
call a doctor. They'd waited for some free screening by someone who isn't
even a doctor to tell them that everything was okay, or not. So anyway, I was
going from person to person, looking at mole after mole, making announce-
ments in an attempt to educate people about what they should look for, and
this woman came up to me and she was smiling and stuff, saying she didn't
really have anything for me to look at except this one little thing . . .

Adam: Oh no.

Me: No, it's not gross. She held out her index finger—she had acrylic
nails on, by the way—and she showed me her cuticle—

Adam: You said it wasn't gross.

Me: No, it just looked black. Her cuticle looked bluish black, almost
like she smashed her finger or something. But as soon as I saw it, I knew it
was melanoma. I must have gotten this horrible look on my face or something, because she tried to pull away from me. But I grabbed her by the
arms, I was squeezing her arms really tight so she couldn't get away, and I
looked right into her eyes and told her she *had* to see a dermatologist right
away. I kept staring at her until I was sure she understood the seriousness
of the issue. And then . . . I don't remember anything after that.

Adam: It was on her fingernail? You can get melanoma on your fingernail?

Me: Not on your *nail*. You can get in *under* your nail. I think it's
melanoma of the cuticle, but I'm not exactly sure. I don't really know
that much about it, but I've seen pictures. Most people have to have their
fingers cut—

Adam: Okay, okay, okay. I get it.

Me: —off.

Adam:

Me: I can't believe my birthday is coming up.

Adam: How did we get on that?

Me: Cuticle, melanoma, death, getting closer to death . . . twenty-six sounds old, doesn't it?

Adam: Don't talk to me about old.

Me: It's different for men.

Adam: It's not *that* different.

Me: This birthday feels . . . I don't know . . . I'm actually looking forward to it.

Adam: What are you talking about? You always look forward to your birthday.

Me: Because of the gifts. But I don't care about gifts this year.

Adam: Yeah, right.

Me: No, seriously.

Adam: Okay, then, I guess I don't need to get you anything.

Me: Well, I don't mean I don't want *any* gifts . . .

Adam: No, no, I think it's good. No gifts this year.

Me: But—

Adam: Good idea.

Me: You have to at least get me a card.

Adam: Oh, you'll get a card.

Me: I want a *real* card. One that you buy at the store. I don't want you scribbling something on a piece of computer paper. I want a card you have picked out from other cards at a store. A card you have *personally* picked—for me—for my birthday . . . I can't believe you're not getting me a gift.

The Day of the Birth

I feel old. Older. Older than my twenty-six years (as of today) would suggest. I feel wise. Much wiser than my twenty-six years would indicate . . . and I feel lucky. Luckier than my twenty-six years should know.

8:00 AM:

Adam: Bub?

Me: Yeah?

Adam: Happy birthday.

Me: Thanks.

Adam: You want your gift now?

Me: I *knew* you got me something.

Adam: Do you know what it is?

Me: Um . . . no.

Adam: Honestly?

Me: Um . . . no.

Adam: How could you know? You don't know.

Me: Okay, maybe I don't.

Adam: What do you think I got you?

Me: I don't want to say.

Adam: Come on. You can say it.

Me: You're gonna be upset if I guess right.

Adam: I won't. I promise.

Me: Fine. I think you got me a bracelet.

Adam:

Me: Am I right?

Adam: What would make you guess that?

Me: Because I lost the other one you gave me . . . and last weekend it took you longer than usual to get home from golf, which means you probably stopped at Altobelli jewelers. *And* you didn't ask me what I wanted, so you must have had something in mind that you knew I would like. Like jewelry.

Adam: Are you going to be disappointed if I didn't get you a bracelet?

Me: No.

Adam: Well, you can't have your gift right now.

Me: What? Why? Because I guessed right?

Adam: No, you just can't have it yet.

Me: Oh, this sucks! When can I have it?

Adam: Later tonight.

Me: You're probably going to go exchange it now or something.

Adam: I swear I didn't get you a bracelet.

Me: You swear on my life?

Adam: I won't swear on your life—because I don't like doing that— but I swear it's not jewelry.

Me: God, now you have me so curious . . . look at you. You're so proud of yourself, aren't you?

Adam: You're not an easy person to surprise.

Me: I know. But you're also not very good at surprises.

Adam: What does that mean?

Me: I can usually guess what you've—

Ring, ring.

Me: Hello?

Ma-in-law: Happy birthday to you . . .

Adam: Who is it?

Me: Your mother.

Ma-in-law: . . . Happy *birth*day, dear Hill-ary. Happy birthday to you . . . and many more.

Me: Thanks.

Ma-in-law: What do you have planned for today?

Me: Nothing crazy. Just hangin' out. I'm hoping Adam will make me a cake.

Adam: Oh, great. No pressure or anything.

Ma-in-law: Well, have a wonderful day celebrating.

Me: Thanks.

Ma-in-law: Did Adam give you his gift yet?

Me: No! He says I have to wait till tonight. Do you know what it is?

Ma-in-law: No, he wouldn't tell me.

Me: Really.

Ma-in-law: I think he was afraid I would ruin the surprise.

Me: So, it's some kind of surprise . . .

Ma-in-law: No, I don't know.

Me: I am so freakin' curious—Adam's over here grinning. He's so pleased with himself.

Ma-in-law: Have a great day. I love you.

Me: I love you too.

Click.

Adam: Did she sing?

Me: What do you think?

1:30 PM:

Ring, ring.

Me: Hello?

Other: Hi, it's Marci.

Me: Um . . .

Marci: From Adam's office.

Me: Oh, hey, sorry.

Marci: I hate to bother you on the weekend.

Me: That's okay—he's out right now. I think he's at the market, buying cake batter. I've pretty much bullied him into making me a cake.

Marci: Is today your actual birthday?

Me: Yep. Twenty-six. Hard to believe—you can try him on his cell if you want. I think he took it with him.

Marci: Actually, you can probably answer my questions. Couple of things. First, I *was* able to get the tickets for the show, and you guys are *not* going to have to stand in line. Second, Adam had me checking on flights, and I before I book the tickets, I wanted to make sure your schedule was open. How does leaving on October twenty-sixth sound?

Me: For what?

Marci: For New York.

Me: You mean, how does the date sound for *Adam's* schedule?

Marci: No, for you.

Me: I have absolutely no idea what you're talking about.

Marci:

Me: Does this have something to do with my birthday?

Marci: He's gonna kill me. He didn't tell me it was a surprise.

Me: Oh my God, he got tickets for *The Seagull?!*

Marci: I'm not saying one more word.

Me: Shit, I can't believe it. *The Seagull*—that's it, isn't it? I was just saying how much I wanted to see that play, and I remember—I totally remember now—Adam kinda, like, perked up when I said it. I *cannot* fucking believe it! I'm gonna see Meryl Streep! Oh my God, I'm dying! I'm gonna pretend like I don't know. Forget you told me.

Marci: I am so, so sorry.

Me: It's not your fault. He should have told you it was a surprise.

Marci: I feel *so* bad.

Me: Call him on his cell. Pretend like you never talked to me.

Marci: Okay—I'm so sorry.

Me: Don't worry about it.

Marci: I'm going to call him right now.

Me: I'll talk to you later.

Marci: Sorry. Bye.

I can't believe it! I can't fucking believe it! Meryl Streep! I'm gonna see Meryl Streep. The bestest actress in the whole wide world! I'm gonna see her. Onstage. Up close. In person. I think I'm gonna throw up . . .

Aside from my engagement, this is the biggest, best, and only true surprise of my whole entire life. My parents' one and only attempt at a surprise birthday party for me failed miserably: My mother spilled the beans about a dozen times in the week leading up to the blessed event. And even though a rhesus monkey probably could have guessed that something was in the works for my sweet sixteen, I can't deny the fact that I'm an impossible person to surprise, mostly because I'm always expecting one. Surprise parties, surprise trips, surprise gifts—I've played out all possibilities to the point that the only surprise I get every year is that another year has gone by and I haven't been surprised. I'm the type of person who walks into a room expecting people to jump out and yell, "Happy birthday!" "Congratulations!" "Just because!" At least ten times a year, I'm totally convinced my parents are waiting on the other side of my front door with balloons and a giant sign reading WORLD'S GREATEST DAUGHTER written in even giant-er pink bubble letters. I have (on more than several occasions) expected Adam to bring me flowers on his way home from work or pick me up a CD I've been not-so casually dropping hints about.

And even though my parents haven't once dropped in uninvited, and I have yet to have the privilege of receiving flowers unexpectedly from my husband (with the exception of when I'm in a play and I have to threaten him within an inch of his life), I still *believe* these things will happen. I still hold out hope.

Lately, though, I've started to think maybe life *isn't* one big, happy surprise party. Maybe it's because I'm older and I have more important things to think about than party favors and daffodils. Maybe it's because I finally accepted the fact that the only surprise party that will ever happen in my house is one that is thrown *by* me. But maybe, and more likely, the phone call a few months ago—the one that no one could have expected—maybe that call kind of turned me off to surprises for a while. Because when I really think about it, that was the biggest surprise of my life. That was the one surprise I never saw coming. The one I never dreamed about or smiled at the thought of or secretly wished would come true. I finally got my big surprise, and look how well that turned out.

So, these days, the tides have turned, and I'm not ashamed to admit that I often take pleasure in some good ol' predictable shit. I'm excited by the mundane and thrilled with the status quo. I guess, these days, I'm just happy with . . . "normal," whatever that is.

And then the inevitable:

Adam: Open it.
His eyes are wide and fixed as I unwrap a bracelet-shaped box.
Adam: I hope you like it.
Me: I'm sure I will . . . a note?

Adam: Read it.

Me: You're so tricky with the box and everything.

Where you love to go. What you've wanted to see.
We'll all take flight.
    Love always and forever,
    Big Bubba

Me: Oh my God! We're going to New York! To see *The Seagull!*

Adam: What?

Me: That's it, isn't it?!

Adam: How the hell did you guess it? I thought it would take you forever to figure it out—wait, you knew! How the hell did you know?

Me: What are you talking about?

Adam: You already knew. I don't know how, but . . . you swear you didn't know?

Me: Yeah.

Adam: "Yeah." You swear on my life you didn't already know the surprise?

Me: Yeah.

Adam: "Yeah" what?

Me: Yeah . . . I knew.

Adam: Goddamn it! How?

Me: Marci called me. She didn't know it was supposed to be a surprise.

Adam: What! Why would she call you?

Me: She was about to book the tickets and wanted to confirm dates. Don't be mad at her—and I was surprised. I was *soooo* surprised when she told me.

Adam: *I* wanted to be the one to surprise you.

Me: But you did, you did. It's the most unbelievable gift *anyone* has *ever* given me.

Adam: Well . . .

Me: Thank you. I love you.

Adam: I love you too.

Me: Your voice went up at the end . . . don't be mad.

Adam: I worked so hard to surprise you.

Me: I know. I'm sorry.

Adam: Anyway . . . Happy birthday. You want some cake?

Me: You made me a cake? You didn't need to do that . . . kidding.

Adam: Happy birthday to you. Happy birthday to you. Happy birthday, dear Hill-ary. Happy birthday to you. And many more . . . make a wish.

Me:

I'm becoming more and more superstitious, I realize, as I stand over my birthday cake and prepare to blow out all twenty-six candles in a single breath. I'm taking my time. I'm not risking a half-breath fuckup or an accidental partial blowout from an overly airy laugh. Not today. Not on my watch. All candles must be extinguished simultaneously in order for my birthday wish to come true, and I'm not taking any chances. This is not the time to take a walk on the wild side. Not the time to ignore old wives' tales or folklore—any lore, for that matter. This is the time to be practical. I need my wish to come true, so why mess with said tradition?

As I lean in, eyes wide and cheeks full, I pull all thoughts toward my intended target. I visualize my wish, imagine it coming true, repeat it to myself one last time, slowly and clearly, close my eyes, and . . . blow.

The One-Day Itch

Woke up this morning with an itch. A tingly, burning kind of itch. A belated birthday itch. An itch that just so happens to be emanating from a dysplastic mole scar. A scar that shouldn't be itching. Not now. Not like this. So as I lie in bed and stare at the blades of my ceiling fan going 'round and 'round and 'round, I know I've got to call Dr. Bach. I know she will tell me I have to come in. And I *think* I know what she's going to say . . .

Competitive Waiting

Dr. Bach's waiting room is a fully realized zoo for the aging. For the last half hour I have sat quietly, staring at a pamphlet on rosacea, while all the old people battle it out over who has the worst cancer story. I have purposely kept my trap shut in order to avoid adding logs to the raging skin-cancer wildfire. I've been privileged to hear how one woman had a squamous cell carcinoma on her shin the size of a baseball. She wanted to show all of us her scar, but she had support stockings on to help with her circulation, which, by the way, has gotten much better since her daughter-in-law gave her a foot stimulator for her eighty-fifth birthday.

Another patient felt the urge to tell us how he had this enormous black thing growing on the inside of his lip. For years he just watched it grow, until one day he couldn't close his mouth anymore, so he decided it was time to see a doctor.

Black tumors, red oozing sores, lumps and bumps and dry flaky skin—it's all been covered. One particularly vivid description disgusted me to the point of triggering my gag reflex. I had to bolt into the hallway for some fresh air to avoid dry-heaving on the woman and her handy-dandy support stockings.

Other: . . . and you should have *seen* the size of it. And it was black as night. And it bled like a son of a gun. Dr. Bach *really* is a savior. Quite the lady. One *smart* cookie.

Terry: Hillary, we're ready for you.

Me: Thank you.

Julia: We've got you in room 1. Where is the place that Dr. Bach is looking at?

Me: My upper stomach.

Julia: Take off everything above the waist. I've got a blanket in there for you.

Me: Okay. *Above the waist. Below the waist. What if every time I went in for a skin check, I stripped either above or below my waist, and what if I had a row of melanomas along my waist that went untreated for years, until one finally grew large enough to peek its little cancerous head above or below my waist? "Young actress dies of melanoma—and you won't believe where doctors found it." "Rare waist melanoma: What your doctors aren't telling you!"*

Knock, knock.

Dr. Bach: Hi, Hillary.

Me: Hey. I feel like I was just here.

Dr. Bach: You were.

Me: How have you been the last couple of . . . weeks?

Dr. Bach: Good. Busy, but good. What about you?

Me: I've been good. Counting the days until I leave for New York. Adam got me tickets to *The Seagull*.

Dr. Bach: That'll be nice.

Me: The cast is amazing. Meryl, Kevin Kline, Philip Seymour Hoffman, Marcia Gay Harden, Natalie Portman . . .

Dr. Bach: Sounds wonderful.

Me: Yeah, I can't wait. I told Adam I hoped this trip wasn't part of the Make-A-Wish Foundation or anything.

Dr. Bach: So . . . show me what itches.

Me: Right here. This scar. The place you took off about a month ago.

Dr. Bach: It's probably itching because it's healing. When did it start itching?

Me: A little last week, and then yesterday morning it started feeling kinda tingly. At first I thought maybe the scar was healing, like you said, but I know what that feels like, and it feels different than that.

Dr. Bach: Let me look at it under my magnifier . . .

Me: What do you see?

Dr. Bach: . . . well, it's pigment.

Me: What do you mean?

Dr. Bach: The redness is pigmentation, not scar tissue.

Me: So . . . what? What does that mean? The mole came back?

Dr. Bach: It appears it has.

Me: But you removed a lot of tissue with this one. I thought you got clear margins.

Dr. Bach: Let me look in your chart for a second.

Me: How could it have come back so quickly? It started getting red, like, a few weeks after you removed it.

Dr. Bach: Well, according to the pathology report, I got clean margins. I read the slides and I sent them out for a second opinion, and we both agreed I got all the mole.

Me: I don't understand. How could it have come back?

Dr. Bach: To be honest, I'm not sure. I've never had a mole come back like this. Not one that I did an excision on.

Me: *You know me. I like to be different.* So . . . what do you think this is? Because it came back so quickly, does that automatically mean it's a melanoma?

Dr. Bach: No, but it does mean that there is some kind of activity going on on the cellular level. I'd like to remove it as soon as possible.

What does your schedule look like? Could you come at the beginning of next week?

Me: Yeah, that's fine. I want this thing out before my trip.

Dr. Bach: Okay. Tell terry to schedule extra time for the appointment. Do you want to use the numbing cream before you come in?

Me: Am I gonna need it?

Dr. Bach: The excision won't hurt any more than all the others I've done, but the injection of anesthesia will be more painful, since I'll be injecting scar tissue.

Me: I think I'll be okay.

Dr. Bach: You're tough.

Me: Yeah, maybe you shouldn't numb it at all.

Dr. Bach: I don't think that would be a good idea.

Me: I was kidding—I'll see you next week.

Dr. Bach: And try not to worry.

Me: I'll try.

Me: So, Terry, next week what does Dr. Bach have available? And she said to schedule extra time for the appointment.

Terry: I've got Tuesday at one thirty or Friday at—

Me: Tuesday.

Terry: How did I know.

Me: Okay. See ya Tuesday at one thirty.

Terry: Have a good weekend.

Me: *Fat fucking chance.* Thanks. You too.

A Positive Appearance . . . Center

Me: Hi. Welcome.

Customer: Thank you.

Amy: Hello, Ms. Peterson. Aren't you looking beautiful today.

Ms. Peterson: You're such a doll to say that. How are your boys?

Amy: They're fine. They hate to be back in school, but they're doing good.

Ms. Peterson: Boys will be boys.

Me: If there's anything we can help you with, just let us know.

Ms. Peterson: Oh, thank you, dear. I'm just looking.

Me: Take your time.

Ms. Peterson: Do you carry this hat in another color?

Me: Let me ask . . .

Ms. Peterson: I thought you worked here. I'm sorry.

Me: Oh, don't be sorry. I'm a volunteer. A helper. Amy, do we carry this in another color?

Amy: Look in the cabinet in front of you. Bottom drawer in the center.

Me: Okay . . . let's see here . . . we've got it in navy and white. That seems to be about it.

Ms. Peterson: No black, huh?

Me: Appears not.

Ms. Peterson: I'm looking for something in black that will match my bathing suit. I'm about to go to Hawaii with my daughter and grandkids, and I need a hat I can wear to the pool.

Me: What about this one?

Ms. Peterson: Oh, no, dear. The inside of that one is too itchy. I won't be wearing my wig, so I need something that will be soft on my scalp. My head is still really sensitive.

Amy: This Kangol hat is really soft. It's cotton, so it's breathable, but it will still give you good coverage.

Ms. Peterson: You don't think it looks too young for me?

Me: No, I like it. Makes you look stylish.

Ms. Peterson: Would you mind if I tried it on without my wig?

Amy: Of course not. Hillary, you want to help Ms. Peterson?

Me: Um, sure . . . okay, why don't you sit down right here and I can . . . let's see . . . I don't want to hurt you . . .

Ms. Peterson: Don't worry, dear. My wig's not clipped to anything—I don't have anything to clip it *to*.

Me: O-kay . . . there you go. I'll hold it while you try the hat on.

Ms. Peterson: I'm embarrassed. My daughter hasn't had time to shave my head lately. I don't usually let it get like this.

Me: Don't be silly. You look fine. *My heart is breaking. This little woman, barely five feet tall, no more than eighty-five pounds, is brushing a few wisps of gray hair (and I mean, like, three strands) to one side as she slowly slides the hat down onto her head. Her head is so small, the hat could easily slip from its intended position, completely covering her bulging eyes and elfish ears. She raises her head, turning it from side to side, trying desperately to see beneath the brim.* How 'bout I get you the smaller size?

Ms. Peterson: Thank you, dear. I don't think I would have seen a durn thing the whole trip with that one. I would have been running into walls.

Me: This one should be better.

Ms. Peterson: . . . ah, there we go. What do you think?

Me: I think you look wonderful.

Ms. Peterson: I'll take it.

Me: Do you want me to wrap it up for you?

Ms. Peterson: You don't need to. Would you mind helping me put my wig back on? I'd hate to walk out of here with it on sideways and have everyone in the elevator think I've got a few screws loose.

Me: I bet no one even knows you wear a wig.

Ms. Peterson: You're sweet to say that, dear.

Me: Okay, this is my first time putting a wig back on, so you'll have to bear with me.

Amy: The easiest way to do it is to use one hand to grab it in the front, by the part, and then the other hand should hold it steady in the back. Put the front of the wig on first, and then, holding the part in place, slide the rest of it on.

Me: Oooo-kay . . . part . . . don't want to put this on over your ears . . . almost . . . got it. There.

Ms. Peterson: Perfect.

Me: Not too bad for my first time.

Ms. Peterson: You're a dear. Thank you both so much. I'll look so hip in my new hat, I bet my grandkids won't even recognize me.

Me: Have a wonderful time. Do you have sunscreen for your trip?

Ms. Peterson: I'm sure my daughter has plenty.

Me: Just make sure the bottles are no more than a year old. Sunscreen doesn't stay good much longer than that.

Ms. Peterson: Oh, really? I had no idea. Maybe I should get a little just in case. Amy, what would you recommend?

Amy: Actually, Hillary would be the best person to ask. She's the sunscreen expert.

Ms. Peterson: Well, Hillary, what do you think?

Me: How old are your grandkids?

Ms. Peterson: Two, five, and seven.

Me: I would go with the Blue Lizard. It's a great UVA blocker; plus, the bottle turns blue when it's exposed to UV rays, so kids always like it. See . . . look . . . if I hold it up to the window . . .

Ms. Peterson: Well, what do you know. Blue Lizard it is.

Me: Will five bottles be enough?

Ms. Peterson: Oh, dear. I don't think I'll need that much. We're only going away for ten days.

Me: Honestly, you might need more than five bottles. Remember, you should be applying about one to two ounces of sunscreen every time you apply it. And the sunscreen only lasts about 80 minutes if the kids are swimming. Three kids, two ounces each, then multiply that by—

Ms. Peterson: I hate to cut you off, dear, but I'm going to be late for my appointment if I don't get out of here soon.

Me: Of course. Here, let me give you these brochures on sun safety. They've got everything you need to know about how to apply sunscreen, when, how much—all that. Make sure you have your daughter read these.

Ms. Peterson: Thank you, dear. And I'll take three bottles. That should be enough to get us started.

Me: Well, if you have any more questions, you know where to find me.

Ms. Peterson: I sure do. Thank you both—see you when I get back.

Amy: Have a great time.

Me: Enjoy your trip.

Me: She was so cute.

Amy: She's not doing well.

Me: Oh.

Amy: She's very sick. I think this trip . . .

Me: Is like a . . . ?

Amy: I think so.

Me: She seemed to be in good spirits.

Amy:

Me:

Amy: So, why don't I show you how I organize the support stockings . . .

Dr. Bach's Blue Thread

Julia: You ready?

Me: Let's do this.

Julia: Take everything off above your—

Me: Waist. Got it.

Julia: I've got a blanket in there for you. You want juice or anything? I know sometimes you get a little light-headed.

Me: No, I think I'll be okay.

Knock, knock.

Dr. Bach: Hi, Hillary. Julia, I'm going to want to use the dye.

Julia: What kind of stitches do you want?

Dr. Bach: Get me the blue ones.

Me: How many stitches am I gonna need?

Dr. Bach: Only about five or six.

Me: You might want to do more, because the places on my stomach always tend to stretch. The scars always spread.

Dr. Bach: We'll give you some Steri-Strips to take home so you can keep it taped up until it heals. Are you ready?

Me: Yep.

Dr. Bach: Okay . . . little prick . . .

Me: *Ow ow ow ow . . .*

Dr. Bach: One more . . .

Me: *Ya ya ya la la la. Eyes watering. Heart pounding . . .*

Dr. Bach: Okay, the worst part's over. Now you'll just feel a little pressure.

Me: *Uh-guh-guh-guh . . . breathe . . . relax . . . don't think about what she's doing and don't look down.* How's it going down there?

Dr. Bach: Good. I'm just about to start the stitches.

Me: *Don't look. Stay focused on the ceiling. Don't look at the . . . oh God, I can feel my stomach skin getting pulled. I can feel her pulling then tying, pulling then tying . . . don't look . . . don't look . . . stay away from the light . . . how many stitches is she . . . d'oh! I looked. I just saw my stomach skin being pulled up off my stomach by a long piece of blue thread . . .*

Dr. Bach: Hillary, you doing okay?

Me: *I'm gonna throw up.* Fine. You almost done?

Dr. Bach: Just one more knot.

Me: *Breathe . . . I'm dizzy . . . I need to get out of here . . . my palms are sweating . . . I'm gonna jump off the table . . . I've gotta get out of—*

Dr. Bach: All done.

Me: Piece of . . . cake . . . could I . . . um . . . have some juice?

Julia: Here's your juice.

Me: I didn't know they still made Capri Sun.

Julia: You okay? You look a little pale.

Me: Fine . . . this is my normal color.

Julia: I'll call you as *soon* as I get the pathology report. I promise.

Me: *Where have I heard that before?* I swear I won't call you. Dr. Bach, did you hear that? I'm swearing I will *not* call and bother you guys.

Julia: We should have the report by Friday. Maybe even Thursday.

Me: Okay. You all heard me. I will *not* call. Thanks, Dr. Bach.

Dr. Bach: I'll call you as soon as I know anything.

Me: Have a good week.

Julia: You too. And try not to worry.

Me: Me? I have the sense I may be developing somewhat of a reputation.

Making Myself Sick

Ring, ring.

Me: Hello?

Other: Hey, girl, it's Gladys.

Me: Hey, what's up? It's been forever.

Gladys: I know. I know. I can't believe it. Work has been *so* crazy. Plus—you're going to think I'm insane—I started skydiving on the weekends, so that's been taking up a lot of my time. It's *so* amazing. You're gonna *have* to come with me sometime. It's the most orgasmic thing ever. So, I wanted to see how you were doing and plan a dinner. We need to have a tile rummy night.

Me: Totally . . . you're still down a game.

Gladys: No kidding. So, what's your schedule like?

Me: Well, maybe next week. Like, Wednesday or Thursday?

Gladys: I'm taking a class on Wednesday nights, but Thursday would work. I'll bring my chess timer. I've started playing speed rummy. It's totally wild. I play five-minute games. With speed rummy you can win either by running out of tiles *or* by running down your opponent's clock.

Me: Sounds right up my alley. Let's plan on Thursday, then. What class are you taking?

Gladys: It's like . . . it's part psychology, part spirituality. It's kinda hard to explain. I'll tell you about it when I see you.

Me: Sounds interesting.

Gladys: It's really cool. Actually, I was thinking of you the other day in class when we started to talk about the body's ability to heal itself. We were talking specifically about cancer.

Me: Really.

Gladys: My professor was talking about the mind-body connection and how we can heal ourselves without traditional medicine. The class deals a lot with how our mental outlook affects our physical body. Plus, there's a lot of talk about energy and healing hands and all that.

Me:

Gladys: I'm sure you have an interesting perspective on all this.

Me: I probably do.

Gladys: I really believe we have the power to heal ourselves.

Me: Yeah.

Gladys: And that we just have to learn how to tap into that power.

Me:

Gladys: If you think about it, there's so much we don't know. I mean, there is so much about our bodies that is a complete mystery. There are so many things doctors don't know. So many illnesses that traditional medicine can't fix.

Me: But that doesn't necessarily mean we should avoid medical doctors just because they don't know *every*thing.

Gladys: But think about it: If we are the *cause* of our disease—meaning, our outlook and how we choose to live our life can make us *sick*—then it stands to reason that with the *right* mental outlook we can make ourselves *well*.

Me:

Gladys: What do you think?

Me: I'm not sure I'm the right person to talk to about this kind of thing. Particularly right now.

Gladys: I'd love to hear what you think.

Me: I think—well, you have to understand that it's hard for someone like me to agree with what you're saying, because then it's kinda like I'm saying that it's my fault I got sick.

Gladys: But don't you think your mental health played a large part?

Me: Well, I guess it's possible it played a part, but I don't *blame* myself for getting melanoma. I don't believe I did it to myself, if that's what you're saying.

Gladys: No, I think you're misunderstanding me.

Me: I'm not sure I am. Look, has this professor of yours ever had cancer?

Gladys: No. Well, I don't know. I don't think so.

Me: Exactly. It's really easy to point fingers when you've been healthy your whole life. Of course *he* wants to believe that the "sick" make themselves sick. I'm sure it gives him a sense of security to believe that. And I bet it made you feel better when you heard it. I bet it made a lot of people in your class feel better. It made them feel like they have control. Like they have control over their health, their well-being, their—I don't know—life. But that's the thing. We *don't* have control. Not all the time. Sometimes shit just happens and it's nobody's fault. And that's the thing *I'm* still trying to come to terms with. This professor of yours, what he's saying, it's all very empowering and all that, but I just don't totally buy it.

Gladys: But the good thing about all this is, if you believe we have the power to cause sickness, then we also have the power to cause wellness.

Me: I'd like to think I could heal myself, but I can tell you with complete certainty that there was nothing I could have done to make my melanoma go away. It wasn't going to just miraculously disappear without the help of a doctor and a very sharp carving utensil. *That,* I'm fairly sure of. But, you know, some people need to believe. I mean, terminal patients—people who are dying and have already exhausted all their options—these people *need* to believe that there is something left for them to try. So for those people, this whole theory is probably great. It gives them hope. I've heard of a lot of patients doing yoga and meditation and all that Pac-Man-eating-the-cancer-cells stuff. It gives people hope, but, in my opinion, a lot of times it gives false hope.

Gladys: I didn't mean to suggest that you caused your disease.

Me: Well . . .

Gladys: I don't think I explained myself very well . . . I'll give you this book to look at; then we'll—

Me: Actually, I hate to cut you off, but I've gotta run. I have a million errands to do. Call me next week and we'll set up a dinner or something.

Gladys: Yeah, sounds great. I really want to catch up with—

Click.

God damn these ignorant fucking "healthy" ignoramuses.

I mean, what about all the wonderful, horribly sick children? How does Gladys's theory stand up against all the sick kids, all the wide-eyed, innocent, upbeat Hello Kitty–loving, Lego-playing kids skipping around in their sparkly pink princess gowns and Superman capes? According to her new life guru, everyone (kids included) plays some role in their illness. I just don't buy it. I'd love to buy it. I'd love to buy it hook, line, and sinker, but I know better. I've met too many sick people with the most positive outlook. Sick people, dying people, people like the kind of people I can't stand. People who smile at kitten bumper stickers and long for nothing more than a double rainbow. These people have done *nothing* to create, or deserve or manifest or inspire—whatever you want to call it—illness. It's just not how it works.

These healthy people and their healthy-person theories make me wanna puke. They think they're *so* great because they haven't had cancer or some other life-threatening disease. They think they're doing everything right and that we "sicklings" are doing everything wrong. They can take their shit-eating grins and chipper well-adjusted healthy bodies and shove it.

I don't think I have an unhealthy mental attitude. I mean, not generally. Just because I'm passionate, interested, and sometimes a tad reactive doesn't mean . . . I . . . I . . . I . . . make . . . myself . . . sick!

Note to self: *Kick Gladys's ass at speed rummy.*

Trying and Not Trying

In light of recent events (refer back to previous healing-hands discussions, blue-thread nightmares, and impending tile rummy playoff), I'm turning over a new leaf. I'm done worrying. I've had it up to here (I'm referencing the top of my head, by the way) with all the goddamned worrying because it doesn't make *any*thing *any* better. What a fucking gargantuan realization! Worrying doesn't help. I can't believe it has taken me twenty-six years to identify something so basic. My worrying won't keep my father healthy, or keep Adam from looking at his Blackberry while driving, or help me book a job, or even keep my dog from eating her own crap. It doesn't matter. Either these things will happen or they won't, and my worrying is not gonna make a damn bit of difference one way or the other. I'm not a better person for worrying—just a crazier, more neurotic one.

This realization came to me as I was thinking about a Spanish teacher in high school who used to say that trying and not trying are the same thing. It used to make me crazy when she would trick some kid into *trying* to pick up a pencil without *actually* picking it up. She just reveled in a student's saying he or she really *tried* to do well on a particular test. Oh, she just ate it up.

"You tried?! There's no such thing! . . . I'll give you something to try . . . you see this pencil?! Huh? You see it?"

"Um . . . uh . . . yeah. I guess."

"Try to pick it up."

"Uh . . . Ms. Martine, do I have to?"

"Go on, try to pick it up . . . no, no, no . . . I didn't say *pick* it up. I said *try* to pick it up."

"Um . . . how?"

"Go on, *try.*"

"I *am* trying"

"*No,* don't pick it up. Just *try* to."

" . . . can I have the bathroom pass now?"

Now, I always thought this particular teacher was slightly nutty. Maybe it was her affinity for hard candies, which she insisted on shimmying out of their wrapper with her teeth. Or maybe it was the hearing aid she wore perched on top of her head, disguised as a decorative flower. Whatever it was, I never really took her seriously. Not until now. If I've got this right, she seemed to believe that an action (like trying) has no purpose if it doesn't make a positive impact on an outcome (like a test). So, if you follow this same line of reasoning, worrying is pointless if it has no positive impact on the "thing" you're worrying about. And not only does worrying not have a *positive* impact on that special something, it has no impact at all! Worrying and not worrying are the same goddamned thing!

So I'm making a pact with myself. No more worrying. No more obsessing about pathology reports or swollen lymph nodes or funny red itching scars, because if worrying and not worrying are the same thing, I've already wasted a lot of years of my life worrying about a lot of things that I didn't have a lot of say in. Years I could have spent doing something much more constructive. So, no more worrying. At least, not excessively. No—no worrying. Not all the time. It's not worth it.

But . . . what if worrying and not worrying *aren't* the same thing?

What if (by some chance) worrying about something actually *keeps* that something from happening? Like, what if worrying contains some hidden power, something that can't be seen but exists nonetheless and helps us out when we need it most? What if, by *not* worrying, I am denying myself the power? I mean, I have a responsibility to my family, my friends, myself. I wouldn't want to leave everyone high and dry just because of some bad information I got back in tenth grade.

Yeah, I've gotta think about this one some more before I carelessly throw out worrying with the bathwater . . . but what if it's already too late? What if by *questioning* the power, I have inadvertently *lost* the worry power? Oh, shit. Fuck piss motherfucker . . . who ever is listening . . . I'm worrying, okay? I haven't given up on the worrying. I'm sorry I ever doubted it . . . or you. Please don't give up on me. I need you. Don't leave me when I need you the most. See? I'm worrying. I'm worrying, see?

See?

. . . *hello?*

THREE MINUTES LATER:

Me: Hello? Terry, it's Hillary.

Terry: I thought you weren't going to call. You promised. You swore, didn't you? I can't believe you.

Me: No . . . I'm . . . um . . . not calling about that. I . . . I . . . I realized I didn't set up my next appointment. Dr. Bach wants to see me every couple of months, so I need to book an appointment for the end of November.

Terry: Okay. Well, right now, her schedule's pretty open in November.

Me: Put me down for, like, November thirtieth. Is that a weekday?

Terry: Yeah, that's a Friday. Okay, what time?

Me: One thirty. That's the first appointment after lunch, right?

Terry: I've got you down for one thirty on Friday, November thirtieth.

Me: Great. Thanks. Okay, well, have a good weekend. Tell everyone to have a good weekend.

Terry: I will.

Me: All right. I guess I'll . . . talk to you later.

Terry: Bye.

Click.

Me: Bye.

Ring.

Me: Hello? Terry?

Other: No, it's your father-in-law. I can pretend to be Terry, if you'd like.

Me: No, that's okay. Thanks, though.

Pa-in-law: Who's Terry?

Me: She's the receptionist at Dr. Bach's office. I'm waiting on a pathology report, and I was hoping to get it before the weekend. I hate worrying over the weekend.

Pa-in-law: So, the report's not in yet?

Me: No. Well, I don't know. I just called the office, but I didn't ask. See, last time I was there I swore I wouldn't call. I swore I'd wait for them to call me. And they promised to call me the moment the report came in. It's just that I know they don't call right away. They say they do, but they don't. This weekend's gonna suck ass.

Pa-in-law: Call them back. See if it came in.

Me: No, I'm determined to wait it out.

Pa-in-law: Why would you make yourself crazy like that?

Me: I know, but they already think I'm insane. I'm always calling all frantic and everything.

Pa-in-law: Who gives a shit what they think?

Me: Yeah, but—

Pa-in-law: Call them, then call me back.

Me: I'll call them later.

Pa-in-law: Call them *now*. Call me back after you talk to them.

Terry: Dr. Bach's office, how can I—

Me: Hey, Terry, it's Hillary again. Okay, so I swore, but I still need to know . . . did you get it yet?

Terry: No, I *told* you we will call you the moment—

Me: I know I know I know, but I just thought . . . maybe . . . I don't know . . .

Terry: We're really busy right now.

Me: Yeah. Sorry. Bye.

Pa-in-law: So?

Me: No news. They don't have the report yet.

Pa-in-law: Well, make sure you try again before the end of the day.

Me: No, I'm not gonna bother them again.

Pa-in-law: You know how I feel about it. You know what I would do.

Me: Yeah.

Pa-in-law: Call me as soon as you hear.

Me: I will.

Pa-in-law: Try to do something to distract yourself.

Me: You mean, staring at the wall with the phone in my hand isn't good?

Pa-in-law: I know the feeling.

Me: Yeah. Thanks.

Pa-in-law: I love you.

Me: Love you.

And he *does* know the feeling. More than most. A raised PSA, a bi-opsy, then scans and ultimately surgery to remove a cancerous prostate. Last year he had a catheter for three weeks and didn't complain (at least not to me). Last year he shuffled around his house with a bag of urine strapped to his hip and felt lucky. Last year he wore adult diapers for the better part of a month and felt fortunate they weren't a temporary solution to a permanent problem. I imagine nothing can wake you up to the fact that you must be proactive in your own health care (in your own life) more than diapers can. So my father-in-law now lives by the mantra "fuck it—life's too short." And he's right. About a lot of things. Especially the "too short" part.

I have no self-control. I admit it. I'm impatient and nervous. I admit all of these things. I'm admitting them because I'm about to call Dr. Bach's office for the third time today, and I'm sure to the outside observer I seem slightly . . . unstable. But I'm not. I'm very stable. I'm incredibly focused and steadfast in what I do and why I do it. And the *reason* I'm calling Dr. Bach's office for the third time today is that I'm desperately trying to keep from spending my weekend in a cold sweat, pulling out my hair and biting my cuticles until they bleed. Plain and simple.

Terry: Dr. Bach's office, how—

Me: Hey, it's me again. I know you think I'm crazy, but I just need—

Terry: I'll let you talk to Julia.

Me: Oh . . . hello?

Julia: Hi, Hillary. I was just about to call you. I got the report right as I was leaving for lunch, and I just got back into the office.

Me:

Julia: Let me just . . . find . . . your report . . . I thought I put it . . . ah, here it is. Right where I left it. So, everything is . . . fine. It's not melanoma. It *was* the same mole that she removed a month ago, and it *did* come back more dysplastic than before, but Dr. Bach and the other doctor agree that she removed it all this time. She took pretty good-size margins, so you shouldn't have a problem.

Me: *You got the report* before *lunch.*

Julia: Anyway, I wanted to get back to you. I know how you worry.

Me: *No, you don't.* Yeah. Thank you. Have a good weekend.

Julia: I will . . . I will.

Click.

Very Official

Well, it's official. I have officially finished orientation and am well on my way to becoming an official volunteer for the hospital. In other words, I officially wasted an entire day wedged in between a group of inmates on work release and a gaggle of senior citizens, all in order to get a laminated plastic volunteer badge and the hospital's seal of approval that I am "officially" fit to work for free.

Judging from my fellow orientation-ers, I can see why such a day of instruction is necessary. The work-releasers were mostly illiterate, from what I could tell, and the seniors . . . well, they were just old. And not like grandparent old, like great-grandparent and, in one case, great-great-grandparent old. The seniors seemed to relish the orientation hoopla. It took many of them the entire four hours prior to lunch to fully complete their registration forms. They were like a team of science geeks at an academic decathlon. They rallied around one another and carefully debated the implications of questions like "Age Range" and "Sex" before they committed to checking the appropriate box. They read and reread *all* the fine print and asked endless strings of questions about what they should and shouldn't include under the "Medical Conditions" section.

I mean, disclosing hip replacements was a given, whereas the impact of gallstones on one's ability to effectively volunteer plagued even the most senior orientation leaders.

So, with orientation behind me (I passed my open-book final exam with flying colors), I am left only to complete a tuberculosis skin test. Compared with eight hellish hours of lectures, slide shows, and teamwork-building "games," a skin prick seems like *luxury*.

Nurse: So, you're going to be a volunteer, I see.

Me: Yep.

Nurse: Hoping to become an Angel? Work with the preemies?

Me: No, I'm going to be working in the Positive Appearance Center.

Nurse: That's great. Most volunteers wanna work with the babies. I've never been in that store. I keep meaning to stop in.

Me: Yeah, you should come by. I'm a melanoma patient here, so I wanted to work where I could potentially meet some young cancer patients. The melanoma support group is lumped in with the lung and prostate groups, so, you know, not a lot of young people for me to talk with.

Nurse: It's funny you say that—I know another young melanoma patient, whose parents were looking for a group for her. She's eleven.

Me: Wow, that's really, really young to have melanoma.

Nurse: I know. It's so sad. I've been working with her the last couple days. She just had surgery.

Me: Where was her melanoma?

Nurse: Thigh. Well, it's other places, too, but the thigh is where it started. What about you?

Me: Stomach.

Nurse: She's such a sweet girl.

Me: What do her doctors say?

Nurse: Doesn't look good. This is the second surgery she's had on her leg. She doesn't have much thigh left.

Me: Eleven years old . . .

Nurse: Melanoma's a *real* bitch.

Me: That it is. That it is.

Nurse:

Me:

Nurse: Well, I'm all done here. You may notice that the spot itches a little bit. Nothing to worry about. Here's an information packet for you. It tells you when you need to come back and have your arm checked. Make sure you come within the time frame, or else we'll have to do the test again.

Me: Got it.

Nurse: I'll have to stop by the store and see you. See how you're doing.

Me: Yeah, that would be great. You can stock up on sunscreen and stuff.

Nurse: Remember, make sure you come see me so I can sign off on your volunteer papers.

Me: Okay.

Nurse: And good luck with everything.

Me: Thanks. Oh, and tell that girl if she wants to come down and talk . . . or anything . . . my name's Hillary. I'll be working Mondays and probably Wednesdays. If I'm not around, tell her to leave a number or something.

Nurse: Okay. Yeah, that would be great if you two could talk.

Me: Yeah. Okay, well, hopefully I'll see ya around.

Nurse: You'll see me. I'm always around.

The Instigator

Mom: Hello?

Me: Hey, it's me.

Mom: Hey there, chickadee.

Me: You sound relaxed.

Mom: I am. I'm sitting here in my corner of the couch with a gin and tonic, watching *Frasier.* What about you?

Me: I was just about to make myself a good stiff drink.

Mom: Long day?

Me: Just stressful. They all seem to be stressful these days. I'll let you get back to your show. I was just calling to see how Dad's feeling.

Mom: He seems to be feeling good. He's still sore, but he's getting around good. You should see his back, though. There's all this fluid around the incision. When you push on it, it looks like a water bed. He may have to go in and have them drain it. I don't know if that amount of water will absorb naturally or not. I can't believe how quickly he's bounced back. I'd put him on the phone, but he's downstairs on a conference call.

Me: Okay. When you get a chance, I want to talk to you about the vaccine trial. Has Dad mentioned it at all?

Mom: No, not really.

Me: Maybe when you guys come out here he could meet with Dr. Gregory. He should at least hear about the trial, find out what it's all about.

Mom: I'll mention it to him again. Can I call you tomorrow? My favorite episode is on. It's the one where Niles faints every time he looks at the cut on his finger.

Me: I'll call you from the city. We're leaving early tomorrow morning, so I probably won't talk to—

Mom: I didn't know you guys were going somewhere.

Me: New York, remember? We're going to see *The Seagull.*

Mom: Oh, that's right. Have a fabulous time. That's Tennessee Williams, right?

Me: Chekhov.

Mom: *The Seagull* . . . didn't Tennessee Williams write something about a bird?

Me: Um . . .

Mom: A pet bird or an evil bird? Something with a bird . . .

Me: No, I don't think so. Are you thinking of *Suddenly Last Summer?*

Mom: Does it have a bird?

Me: Well, sort of. It has this really disturbing scene where this guy is running away from these vagrant kids and the kids attack him and eat his genitals and then the guy's cousin—I think she was his cousin—finds him and he's all bloody and there are all these birds picking at him and stuff . . . is that what you're thinking of?

Mom: Kids ate his genitals? They *ate* them?

Me: It was this whole thing like he was gay, and nobody knew it, of course, and he would take these vacations and find young boys to have sex with . . . I don't remember exactly how the whole thing happened, but I think he was eating dinner with his cousin and these boys, who he'd sodomized, were begging for food and he wouldn't give them any food or anything so they followed him out of the restaurant and they killed him.

Mom: No, that's definitely not the play I was thinking of. I never knew of any play where kids ate genitals. This is really going to bother me now . . . maybe it wasn't a bird . . . maybe it was a—

Me: I really should go. I need to finish packing. Talk to Dad about the vaccine. Gregory said the list is filling up fast. Dad really needs to get going on this if he's going to do it.

Mom: Well, I can't force him. He's going to have to make this decision on his own. How long is the trial?

Me: From beginning to end it's about two years, but it's not like he'd be getting injections that whole time. I think for the first couple months he'd get shots every week, but then, after that, every couple weeks. He'd probably have six months of shots and then about a year and a half of follow-up, something like that.

Mom: That's a big time commitment.

Me: *So is death.* Not when you consider that it could save his life. We're talking about his life here! Jesus. This is a once-in-a-lifetime opportunity, and you guys are fucking it up!

Mom: You get so upset with me . . .

Me: Yeah, because neither you nor Dad seems to understand the severity of the situation! I feel like Dad thinks now that the operation is over, he's all better. He has *got* to be proactive. I don't think you guys have done all the research that I've done. I *know* what he's up against. Doesn't he want to do everything within his power to beat this?

Mom: Why don't *you* do the trial?

Me: Oh my God! I don't fucking qualify! Jesuschrist! How many times do I have to tell you? I *don't* qualify! There are very specific qualifications for these trials. I'd do it in a second if I could—trust me. Dad qualifies; he may not get another chance to do something like this. With the depth of his melanoma, the odds of him having a recurrence are—

Mom: Very high. I know.

Me: I don't think you do. Or else you don't care.

Mom: I can't make him do it, Hillary! We've talked about it; I've told him I think it's something he should try. He's got to make the decision. I can't force him.

Me:

Mom: Your father's got a lot of pride.

Me: What the fuck does that have to do with anything? He's being stubborn. You have to stand up to him . . . you're always so *worried* about upsetting him—

Mom: I don't care about that.

Me: Yes, you do. You *really* do. How can you say that? You never stand up to him. You're so worried you're going to make him upset, but honestly, who gives a fuck? Of course he doesn't *wanna* do the trial. It's a pain in the ass, it would be a lot of travel, he would have side effects, but it could save his *life*. If it were me, I'd do it in a second.

Mom: You and your father are very different people.

Me: *I'm just one of those "crazy" people who would like to live as long as possible.* No shit.

Mom: He's a very private man.

Me:

Mom:

Me: Get back to your show. I'll . . . I'll call you when we land.

Mom: You get so worked up.

Me: Yeah . . . well . . . I'll talk to you later.

Mom: I love you . . . I'll talk to your father.

Me:

Mom: I love you.

Click.

TWENTY MINUTES LATER:

Ring, ring.

Me: Hello?

Mom: You wanna call Gregory and set up an appointment for when we're in town, or should I?

Me: Wha—

Mom: He'll meet with him. I can't guarantee anything beyond that.

Me: What . . . what did you say?

Mom: I told him he had to do it.

Me: O . . . kay. Yeah, I'll call Gregory's office on Monday and get something set up.

Mom: You didn't think I could do it.

Me:

Mom: So, now it's up to your father, I guess.

Me: I guess.

Mom: You're awfully hard on me sometimes.

Me: I'm sorry. I can't help it.

Mom: You always were the instigator.

Me: I thought I was the peacemaker. Kidding.

Mom: Your sister was the peacemaker. You were the instigator. I'm gonna head on up to bed.

Me: I love you.

Mom: I love you too.

Me: I'm really proud of you. I think it's really important that he do this trial.

Mom: I know. I know. 'Night.

Me: 'Night.

Click.

I *am* the instigator—a title coined by my sister some fifteen years ago and one that I have since earned with blood, sweat, and tears . . . tenfold. I openly admit that I have a tendency to incite, agitate, provoke. Yes, I often officiate, dictate, even dominate. But it's who I am. It's what I *do,* what I've always done. And now, with my most important mission at hand, I must continue full speed ahead. I won't wait for the miracle to happen. I won't waste time hoping and dreaming and telling myself everything is going to be okay. I will do what I do best. What I was born to do. I will fight. I will fight my battle *and* his battle—*simultaneously*—if I have to. Because someone has to. Someone. Some one. Me.

A Taste of the Big Apple

I saw Meryl Streep do a cartwheel! My life is now complete.

I'm still reeling from the blessed event. Poor Adam may never fully recover, but for different reasons. Once he noticed that the rustic theater seats lacked anything even resembling a headrest, he was so petrified I was going to suffer a massive panic attack in the middle of "I'm the seagull. No . . . I'm an actress" that he spent the whole play focused *not* on the brilliant stage happenings but on *my* beaming mug. He kept squeezing my hand, whispering, "Are you *sure* you're okay?" Every time I made the slightest adjustment in my seat, he nearly shit himself. When I had to crack my neck in the middle of the third act, I kept one hand wrapped tightly around the armrest just in case he got overzealous and decided to throw me over his shoulder like a sack of potatoes and lug me from the premises.

Regardless, it was truly a remarkable night. For two and a half hours, I sat mesmerized. And aside from the four panic attacks I had preceding the show, attacks brought on by an unrelenting fear of losing the irreplaceable tickets, I was cool as a cucumber.

There was something about the show, a feeling I was left with, that I can't seem to shake. All of Chekhov's protagonists, all his pasty "artists" struggling to find meaning in their lives—whether personally or professionally—they all seem to be questioning the point of things. I mean, we're all headed to death, the unavoidable end. And so we're just supposed to keep pushing and struggling and sweating it out until . . . what? Until we're happy? Fulfilled? Until we're . . . dead?

I've read *The Seagull* more times than I'd like to admit, butchered it, watched it open-mouthed as I sounded out the words, and yet this was the first time I really felt connected to "the struggle." I think *that's* the point Chekhov's trying to make: Life is about the struggle. It's that struggle, and our need to persevere, that make life worth living.

I've always focused on the end result, the final act, questioned what all those crazy Russians were ultimately fighting for, but I've been at it all wrong. It's not about the end, maybe not about the result or the finish line. It's about the middle. Because the end is the end, and it's all the same, for all of us. It's only the middle stuff, all the crap between point A and point B, that we have some say in. The middle—that's where all the action is. That's where we really find out what we're made of. It's about the race. It's all about how we choose to get there—the process, not the result. It's about going through the process . . . the middle. Huh.

I guess I'm in it, then. The middle. And that's exactly where I should be.

The Parents Are Coming! The Parents Are Coming!

Adam's been rolling his eyes all morning as I race to complete the parental-visit cleanup regimen. His contribution to the effort at hand: heavy sighs, head shaking, and the occasional grunt. But with or without him, I've practically got it down to a science. With limbs working independently on their preassigned tasks, I'm able to dust, Windex, and polish the hardwood floors all at the same time. I work with a duster in my left hand, paper towels in my right (Windex bottle conveniently hanging from my right hip), and rag booties on both feet that I've rigged out of an old pair of cotton leg warmers. When time permits, I plan on creating a battery charged "emergency cleanup" belt I can wear, which will include a holster for a toilet bowl brush along with an outlet for a vacuum. This way I'll be able to avoid all the plugging, unplugging, and cord-swinging nonsense that wastes so much fucking time. Plus, I've always wanted to be my very own power source.

I've gotta hurry up and finish the cleaning because I've yet to put together a list of planned activities. I must be ready and waiting with an abundance of scheduled "doings," or else my father will inevitably start tinkering with anything around the house that happens to be too tight, too loose, or the least bit askew. And if he has time to adjust the sliding mechanism on the bottom drawer of my bedroom dresser, my mother surely has time to load the dishwasher and vacuum the entire downstairs. See, they don't come to visit; they come to work. I usually find myself running around yelling, "Stop that" and, "Would you please sit down for two seconds!" It's like having kids in the house. I need eyes in the back of my head. They sneak around whispering, plotting, scribbling to-do lists on the back of napkins.

My mother is the worst offender. From the moment she arrives, I'm entangled in some sort of strange cleaning competition. She'll tiptoe around with a dust rag tucked under her arm, and when she "accidentally" spills something on my kitchen floor, she'll subsequently have to disinfect the *entire* kitchen. She'll sneak into my bedroom at 7:45 AM and make my bed. I honestly don't know how she does it. She's like the Tasmanian Devil. In the amount of time it takes me to walk the two steps to the bathroom, pee, wipe, and walk back, she has the ability to make my bed, perfectly arrange the throw pillows, and be downstairs, innocently sipping her reheated, lukewarm coffee.

So, I must have every minute filled. Because even with my dad's back in its early stages of recovery, I'm sure he's found alternate ways of doing all the handyman work he so passionately adores. And in light of recent events and the amount of stress my mother's been under, I'm sure she's more possessed than ever.

TWO HOURS LATER:

Me: Babe, you should go ahead and hop in the shower. My parents are gonna be here any minute.

Adam: I will. I just want to see this shot.

Me: Babe. Shower. Please.

Adam: Why don't you take the first one.

Me: Because I still have a few things to do around here.

Adam: What's left to do? You've done everything. Twice.

Me: I've gotta put the gate up so the dog stays in the kitchen so I can do one final Swiffer.

Adam: You're crazy. You know that, right?

Me: Yeah, I know.

Adam: Okay. Just so you know.

Ring, ring.

Me: Hello? Mom?

Mom: We made it. We just pulled out of the airport.

Me: Great. We'll see ya soon.

Mom: Do you need us to pick anything up?

Me: No, I think we're fine. We've got everything we need.

Mom: Nothing from the market?

Me: No. I went this morning.

Mom: What about your dry cleaning? You want us to grab it on our way?

Me: Nope.

Mom: Okay, then. If you're sure you don't need us to stop—

Me: Nope.

Mom: So, we'll see you soon. We're going to stop at In-N-Out-Burger on the way. Do you want us to order you guys anything?

Me: No, that's okay. We'll eat the lunch meat and stuff I already picked up.

Mom: Oh, well . . . we can have that. We don't have to stop.

Me: No, it's fine. Take your time.

Mom: Are you sure? You went to all the trouble of—

Me: It's fine. We'll see you soon.

Click.

Knock, knock.

Me: Coming . . . hold on. The dog is freaking out. Barrow, sit! No jumping! No jumping!

Me: You made it.

Mom: Hi . . . you look so skinny. Have you lost weight?

Me: Hey, Dad. It's so good to see you guys.

Dad: Hey, babe. The house looks beautiful.

Mom: I bet you were down on your hands and knees all morning. You work too hard.

Adam: Welcome.

Me: Here, let me take your bags into the guest room.

Dad: I've got them.

Mom: Jon, you know you're not supposed to be lifting those. Let Adam help you. Is this a new rug? Every time I come here you have something new. Oh, what a life.

Dad: Your mother doesn't let me do anything anymore.

Me: Um, yeah, new rug. Here, Dad, I'll get this bag. You take the carry-on.

Mom: It's so unique. I'm sure it cost a fortune.

Me: So . . . after lunch, if you're up to it, I thought we'd go for a walk around the neighborhood. Thought you guys might want to get a little exercise after the plane ride.

Mom: Don't you want to rest? You do too much. You run yourself ragged.

Me: What are you talking about? I'm fine. I want to do whatever you guys want to do.

Dad: *I'm* up for a walk.

Me: How's your back?

Dad: Fine.

Me: How does it feel?

Mom: The plane was tough. All the sitting.

Me: I bet. Those airplane seats are the worst.

Adam: I don't know about anyone else, but I'm starving.

AFTER LUNCH, CLEANUP, AND A BRIEF DISCUSSION ABOUT THE BEST STAINLESS-STEEL CLEANER:

Me: You guys ready?

Mom: Yeah, let me just find my sunglasses. Jon, have you seen . . . never mind . . . I found them. Hillary, you should try this sunscreen. It's from Australia. Actually, I'd love for you to see if it has all the right ingredients. You should try it, though—it's not greasy at all. It soaks right in.

Me: I'll try it later. I've already got stuff on. Dad, you ready to go?

Dad: You bet.

Me: Ad, you ready?

Adam: I've been ready for the last fifteen minutes.

Me: Mom . . . *Mom!* Let's go.

Mom: I was just getting a hat. You need a hat?

Me: No. I've got one. Let's go.

Mom: Anyone want sunscreen?

Me: We've all got it. Let's go. Dad, you have sunscreen on, right?

Dad: Yep.

Mom: What did you put on? I didn't see you put any on.

Dad: I used that stuff in the blue bottle.

Mom: I didn't bring that bottle with us.

Dad: I've still got some on from yesterday. I put it on yesterday.

Me: Jesuschrist, Dad! It only lasts a few hours! How long do you think it stays on?

Dad:

Me: You have to put it on *every* day. And why aren't you using the stuff I got you? That stuff you have in the blue bottle isn't even any good. It doesn't have a UVA blocker.

Dad: All right. All right! Jesuschrist! I'll go put it on. We're never going to get out of here.

Me:

Mom:

Adam:

Mom: It's a struggle. Every day I have to remind him. I have to treat him like a child to get him to do anything.

Me: How can he *not* wear sunscreen? And it's not like it's such a hard thing to do. I mean, how much time does it really take to put on?

Dad: Okay, let's go.

Me: Did you put it everywhere?

Dad: Yes. Let's go.

Me: Did you put some on your ears?

Dad: Yes.

Me: And on the back of your neck?

Dad: Yes yes yes. Let's go.

Me: We have to wait thirty minutes for the sunscreen to soak in.

The Trial

My mother says she and my father make me nervous. She's right. I have chewed my nails to the quick, and my cuticles, well, I'm just hoping they'll grow back someday. Everything turns into a struggle with them. Why is everything always a fight? We argued for twenty minutes this morning over who was going to the hospital with my dad, which car and/or cars were to be taken, who'd ride with whom, and what time we needed to leave in order for my dad to get there early enough to feel on time.

To make matters worse (and in a desperate attempt to keep us from fussing over him), my mom and I were assigned the "late" shift. We weren't allowed to leave with him because he didn't want to "inconvenience" us. We were instructed to wait at least half an hour after his departure before heading to the hospital. We were told to proceed to the third floor. If upon our arrival Father Figure was not done with his appointment, we were to immediately proceed to preassigned meeting place for lunch. If upon arrival at lunch place we had not heard from Father Figure via cell phone, we were instructed to order, eat, and then go about our day as if none of the above had ever happened. Father Figure would "catch up" with us at "some point," and then we would all live happily ever after . . .

My mom and I are currently sitting in the waiting room on the third floor. We've been twiddling our thumbs for half an hour—so much for the preassigned, predestined, prepubescent plan. We're both starving to death, and the thought of sneaking up to the Joyce Eisenberg Keefer breast center for cookies and milk is sounding better and better. My mom's already made three cups of lukewarm Lipton tea using water from the bathroom sink, and I'm fairly sure she has single-handedly finished off St. John's supply of saltines.

Mom: You sure you don't want any of these?

Me: I'm gonna wait for lunch.

Mom: It might be a while before we eat.

Me: I'll wait for Dad to come out if you wanna go get something.

Mom: No, no, I'm fine.

Me:

Mom:

Me:

Mom: I could eat my arm.

Me: Go get something. It'll take you, like, seven minutes to walk to Koo Koo Roo from here. Go pick up sandwiches or something. I'm sure Dad's gonna be at least another half an hour.

Mom: Your father might want something when he gets done . . .

Me: Yeah, so go get the sandwiches, and he can eat his as soon as his appointment is over.

Mom: It's right around the corner?

Me: Yeah, walk north on Twentieth, and it's on the corner of Twentieth and Wilshire. Get me a rotisserie chicken breast sandwich with steamed vegetables and macaroni and cheese on the side.

Mom: You sure you don't mind waiting here?

Me: Mom, go.

Mom: I've got my cell with me, so call if there's a problem.

Me: What, are you anticipating some kind of problem?

Mom: In case the doctor needs to talk to me.

Me: I'll call you if there's a problem.

Mom: North on Twentieth, then . . .

Me: It's on the corner of Wilshire and Twentieth. You'll see it. You can't miss it.

FIVE MINUTES LATER:

Lahhhhh dah. Lah dee dah dee dah dee dahhh. Misty watercolored memmmmm-ries . . . of the . . . way . . . we were . . .

FIVE MINUTES LATER THAN THAT:

Scattered pic-*tures* . . .

Papa, can you hear me? Papa, can you see me? Papa, can you something *in the nighhhht?*

I need to rent that. Papa . . . Papa . . . Papa!

Nurse: Helen . . . I'm looking for Helen . . .

Me: Helen?

Nurse: Her husband said she's short, with short grayish-blond hair . . .

Me: *Oh, and wouldn't she just love* that *description.* I think you're looking for my mom. I'm the daughter. She went to grab some food.

Nurse: If you could come with me for a moment.

Me: Yeah, sure.

Nurse: . . . right in here.

Me: Hey, how's it going?

Nurse #2: This must be your daughter. You two look just alike. Is this your natural color hair? It's beautiful.

Me: Actually, my natural is a little lighter.

Nurse #2: I haven't met many women who dye their hair darker.

Me: Yeah . . .

Dad: Okay, I'm done filling out this one.

Nurse #2: If you could help us out, it—I'm sorry, what's your name?

Me: Hillary.

Nurse #2:—Hillary. You look like a Hillary. We just need another witness to sign this.

Me: Okay. What is it?

Nurse #2: It just states that your father is agreeing to participate in the vaccine trial and that he will blah blah blah blah blah. All expenses will be blah blah, and so we want to make sure he blah blah blah blah blahs.

Me: Uh-huh.

Nurse #2: So if you could just sign here . . .

Me: Uh-huh. Should I put "daughter" where it says relation, or—

Nurse #2: You don't need to worry about that part. You know, you look familiar to me.

Dad: She's an actress.

Nurse #2: Oh? What have you done?

Me: Um . . . mostly TV.

Nurse #2: Anything I would have seen?

Me: I don't know. Maybe. The last thing I did was *ER*.

Nurse #2: You know, I've *never* seen that show.

Me: Before that, I did a couple episodes of *Once and Again*.

Nurse #2: Who's on that?

Me: Sela Ward . . . Billy Campbell . . . Jeffrey Nordling . . .

Nurse #2: I don't think I've seen that. To be honest, I don't really watch that much TV.

Me: You've probably seen me in the halls. I'm a patient here. Melanoma.

Nurse #2: Oh, well, there you go.

Me: Gregory's my surgeon. That's how I heard about the vaccine.

Nurse #2: Jon, you are all set. I'll see you in two weeks.

Me: Dad, did you have a chance to ask questions?

Dad: Yeah. Yeah. Let's go. Where's your mom?

Me: She went to pick up sandwiches at Koo Koo Roo. I'm so excited you decided—

Dad: How long have you been waiting?

Me: Not long. Maybe half an hour.

Dad: Jesuschrist!

Me: Less, less. Fifteen minutes.

Dad: I told you girls I didn't want you waiting for me!

Me: I know, but we wanted to. We wanted to be here to support you.

Dad: You wasted your whole day sitting around—

Me: It's only eleven forty-five.

Dad: I just wish you girls hadn't come all the way down here.

Me: Well—

Mom: There you two are. I've been looking all over. You all done?

Dad: Yep. Let's get out of here.

Mom: What did Gregory say? Does he think the trial is worth your time? Did you ask him all the questions we—

Me: He's doing the trial.

Dad: What kind of sandwich did you get me?

Mom: What? You're doing it?! Chicken. So, you're doing it?

Dad: Why don't we find a place to sit down and eat. Someplace outside.

Me: I'd prefer inside. It's really sunny right now.

Dad: I've been inside all day.

Mom: It's awfully hot out there . . . and you didn't bring your hat.

Me: I'll do outside if that's what Dad wants. I might have an extra hat in my car.

Mom: I know—how 'bout we head *back* into West Hollywood. Then we can—

Dad: I haven't eaten since six this morning! You want me to wait until we get back into the city!

Mom: I just don't know a good place to sit around here, and I thought . . .

TEN MINUTES LATER:

After a final round of our version of *Family Feud* (Category: Places You Eat Chicken Sandwiches), we have all caved to our hunger and decided to devour our bounty on the benches outside the hospital valet stand. Parking attendant Paco had a few napkins to spare, so we're eating in silence with Benitos Taco Shop napkins tucked in our shirts, protecting us from Koo Koo Roo's special sauce. My father refuses to divulge *any* information pertaining to the vaccine trial. All my mom and I know is that he's doing it. And as much as I'd like to hear every detail of everything Gregory said to my dad, I'm keeping my lips focused on the sandwich in hand. He's doing it, and that's all that matters . . .

I'd kill to know what they talked about, but it's my fear of my father's marching back upstairs and scratching out his name on all those forms I just witnessed him sign that's overriding my desire for a stimulating round of twenty questions. But I sure am curious. I figure Gregory must have said something pretty damn convincing in order to persuade Pa Peterman to go through with the vaccine "inconveniences." Whatever happened up there behind those double-thick doors must have put the fear of God in my father. I can't imagine much else that could or would convince such a man to do such a thing. He has made a decision *so* against everything he stands for. The man I know, the man who circled a roundabout in England nine times before admitting he *might* need navigational assistance, the man who never took a sick day in his twenty-odd years as a stock broker, the man who has little patience for weakness and no patience for defeat—this man is not a man to volunteer for a medical trial. He's not the man to sign up for *any* trial, as far as I can see, unless it's being underwritten by Orvis. So whatever was said up there—whatever secrets passed between my father and Dr. Gregory—must have been awfully significant.

The Positive Appearance Center
and Rose's Hair

I did it! I passed my boards! No tuberculosis! I am a certified (certifiable) volunteer for St. John's Hospital. My very official-looking laminated name tag is strategically clipped to the breast pocket of my light blue polyester volunteer coat so one and all can read my name and raise their voices in praise of me. It's all very glorious—glamorous, really, you know—being surrounded by Vagisil and thrush mouth rinses and . . . death.

Me: If there's anything we can help you with, just let us know.

Customer: Oh. All right.

Me:

Amy:

Customer: It's such a beautiful day today.

Me: Has it burned off? It was really foggy when I drove in this morning.

Customer: Oh, it's gorgeous out. Just ga-orgous. Not too hot. There's a little breeze.

Me: It's always so hard to tell once I'm in the hospital. They keep it so cold.

Amy: Oh, I know. I'm always freezing.

Customer: This is a great store you've got here.

Amy: Thank you. Yeah . . . we've got a little bit of everything.

Me: Is this your first time coming in?

Customer: It is.

Me: How did you hear about us?

Customer: Well, it's really funny . . . I was sitting with my doctor and—today I found out that I'm going to have to have chemotherapy—

Me: Oh, I'm sorry.

Customer: —and I was asking him about losing my hair, and I said that the hospital should have a place that sells products for chemo patients, and he said, "We do." He must have thought I was loopy. I've come up that elevator about a hundred times—well, it seems like a hundred times, anyway—and I've never noticed this place. I can't believe it.

Amy: We're kinda hidden.

Me: I'm glad you decided to check us out . . . and did your doctor say you would definitely lose your hair?

Customer: He said I would, but I'm not so sure. I've got *so* much hair. It's like a helmet. It's really, really thick. See? Feel . . . feel all this . . .

Me: It looks very thick.

Customer: No, feel . . .

Me: Yeah, wow. That's a lot of hair. But . . . you know . . . that . . . um . . . doesn't really make a difference once the chemo starts.

Customer: We will see, I guess. I'd hate to lose it. I don't think I'm going to. I really, really don't. I've always had such healthy, thick hair. He also said I'd probably start feeling fatigued, but, again, we'll see. I'm tough. And I like to stay busy. It takes a lot to get me to stay off my feet. I plan on working throughout my entire treatment.

Me: Don't you think it might be a good idea to take it easy for a few weeks, give yourself some time to rest?

Customer: What? You mean sit around and feel sorry for myself? *Noooo,* thank you.

Me:

Amy: If you have any wig questions, we're here to help.

Customer: Thank you. I think I'll wait. See what happens.

Me:

Amy:

Customer: To be honest, I'm still trying to get adjusted to the whole thing.

Me: Losing your hair is a big deal.

Customer: I mean the cancer. I was diagnosed a week ago, and I still don't think it's sunk in.

Amy: That's totally normal.

Customer: Oh, I've gotta run. I can't believe I've let the time get away from me. My husband is in the lobby—he insisted on coming with me, even though I begged him not to—he's probably wondering what happened to me. It was nice meeting you ladies.

Me: You too.

Customer: My name's Rose, by the way.

Me: Hillary. Nice to meet you.

Amy: Amy.

Rose: Have a great day. I'll come say hi when I start my treatment.

Me: Sounds good.

Me:

Amy:

Me: Wonder how she's gonna feel when her hair starts falling out.

Amy: I was just thinking the same exact thing.

Dinner at Eight

Me: What do you want to drink?

Adam: I'll have some red wine, if we've got it.

Me: Sterling okay? Grab a glass for me.

Adam: So, I thought you were going to stop drinking for a week. What happened to that idea?

Me: I'm still gonna.

Adam: When?

Me: Soon . . . what? You want me to stop right now?

Adam: I didn't say anything.

Me: I need to . . . you know . . . prepare myself . . . and stuff . . . I can't just . . . *start* . . . without warning . . . or anything.

Adam: Uh-huh.

Me: What? I'm *gonna* do it.

Adam:

Me:

Adam:

Me: I can't start tonight, anyway. I had a drink before you got home.

Adam: Okay. What*eeeeever* you say.

Me: Fine, I'll start tomorrow.

Adam: You do what*eeeeever* you want.

Me: Tomorrow. I'll start tomorrow . . . happy?

. . . Tomorrow

I'm quitting. For a week. Baby steps. "Baby steps to the elevator" . . . I will go without because I need to know I *can* go without. I need to make sure I'm still the one in control, because sometimes, if I'm perfectly honest with myself, I'm not entirely sure.

I feel it right now: "The Pull." I've felt it my whole life, and sometimes I think it's stronger than everything. First in high school, before I really knew what it meant and why I should be afraid of it, I felt it. It started slow, with drinks at parties spilling over into drinks after parties and culminating in drinks without parties. At freshman parties, I'd chase Bacardi with Kool-Aid. I became known as the queen of the beer bong and the princess of tequila shots. My tolerance was legendary. I'd follow Jell-O shots with more Jell-O shots. I'd drink till I passed out or threw up, whichever came first, and then I'd either wake up or wipe myself off and drink some more.

Many weekend mornings, I could be found drooling on someone's bathroom linoleum with most, but usually not all, of my clothes on. I'd wake up to stories of all I'd done the night before, none of it sounding all that familiar, but then again, I couldn't account for the better part of the evening, so anything was possible. I drank enough Peppermint Schnapps back in the day that the smell of mint Scope still triggers my gag reflex, and I can't look at Zima or peach wine coolers without my stomach turning cartwheels.

So as I stand in the kitchen, eyes glued to our liquor cabinet, salivary glands firing while I study the beautiful bottles on the second shelf, I know I need to quit drinking. At least for a while. Just to be safe. Just to be sure I still can.

Me: So? You notice anything different?

Adam: No, what?

Me: Guess.

Adam: Um . . . you . . . cut your hair.

Me:

Adam: I give up.

Me: No, you have to guess.

Adam: You . . . um . . . dyed your eyelashes.

Me: It's not something on my body.

Adam: You . . . I have no idea.

Me: Notice anything I'm not *doing?*

Adam: Something you're not doing . . .

Me: Drinking! I'm not drinking!

Adam: Well, what's that, then?

Me: Oh, that's just tonic and lime.

Adam: Now, how the hell was I supposed to guess that?

Me: I don't know . . . I figured . . . I don't know. Don't bother me. I'm sober.

Adam: This is going to be a long week—I can already tell.

The Shakes

Me: Ad? You awake?

Adam: Huh?

Me: I think I ate something weird last night. Is your stomach fucked up? I totally had diarrhea last night.

Adam: No. My stomach's fine.

Me: Maybe I'm coming down with something. Great. My parents are coming into town and I'm gonna be sick.

Adam: When are they coming, again? I forgot.

Me: Not tomorrow but the next day.

Adam: I feel like they were just here.

Me: They were. They're going to be here a lot for the next two years.

Adam:

Me: I think I'm gonna throw up.

Adam: Well, don't do it in the bed.

Me:

Adam: You need me to bring you a bucket or anything?

Me:

Adam: Hill?

Me: Don't talk to me. I'm trying to keep from yakking.

LATER:

Ring, ring.

Me: Hel-lo?

Adam: Feeling any better?

Me: No.

Adam: You throw up?

Me: No, but I still have diarrhea. And I've just been feeling kinda shaky.

Adam: Drink lots of fluids.

Me: I am.

Adam: I've got a screening tonight. You gonna be okay by yourself?

Me: Yeah, I'm just gonna rest.

Adam: Okay, well, get some sleep, and I'll be home around ten or so.

Me: Love you.

Adam: Love you. Feel better.

Click.

TEN OR SO:

Me: Hey.

Adam: How you feeling?

Me: 'Bout the same.

Adam: You need anything?

Me: Could you just get me some water . . . and Ad? I think I figured out what's wrong with me.

Adam: What?

Me: No alcohol.

Adam: Noooo.

Me: Yeah, I think so.

Adam: No, it couldn't be. You don't drink *that* much.

Me: I'm just telling you what I think it is. I was trying to figure out the last time I've gone twenty-four hours without a drink . . . it's been a long time.

Adam: Good thing you quit.

Me: I didn't quit. I'm just taking a break. Seven days. I'm stopping for seven days. I'm not stopping for good. Let's not get crazy.

Adam: Maybe you *should* stop.

Me: I'm fine. I'm sure by tomorrow I'll be fine. And when I start drinking again, I'm gonna really make an effort to cut back. I am. I promise.

On the Rocks

It's like I'm on a hamster wheel, running 'round and 'round till my little rodent paws are bruised and raw, and even though I'm working up quite a sweat, I seem to be passing the very same plastic water bottle over and over again. My parents are in town *again*. They stopped for In-N-Out Burger *again*. Their whirlwind entrance consisted of me looking too skinny, the house looking too clean, and my life looking just too damn perfect . . . *again*.

I'm going to start tape-recording their entrances so I can save them the breath. It'll be armed and ready to push play the moment they touch down. We can all mouth along with the recording like we're listening to an episode of *Barney*. We'll dance around my living room, clapping and chanting, "I love you, you love me, we're a fucked up fam-i-ly." I hate that goddamned purple dinosaur and the horse it rode in on. And that show . . . all those kids laughing and dancing around that fuchsia monstrosity. Word to the wise: *He's not fucking purple! He's fucking fuchsia!*

I'm a little tense. My parents are making me a little tense, and they have been here for less than four hours. I may not make it to the end of my week of sobriety . . . sober. Seven days might have been a tad ambitious, considering the amount of alcohol that flows through this house when my parents are in town.

I'm currently standing on the threshold of my kitchen, watching my mother try to reach the Tanqueray 10, which I have purposely stashed on the top shelf of the liquor cabinet. Standing a mere five foot two, she looks as if she's about to dislocate her arm in the attempt. Even when she's on her tippy-toes, her middle fingertip merely brushes the edge of the bottle.

Me: You look like you might need some help with that.

Mom: Oh! You scared me to death! I was just about to make your father a drink and . . .

Me: Here.

Mom: You like that top shelf so high? You know, your father could adjust it for you.

Me: No, I like it where it is. I thought Dad said he didn't want a drink yet.

Mom: Oh . . . well, I guess *I'll* just have to drink this one, then. You have any lime, sweet pea?

Me: *I can taste the sweet sting of the lime.* Bottom shelf. I'm gonna go to the market and get something to make for dinner.

Mom: You don't need to do that. Why don't we just order in?

Me: No, it's fine. I was going to make that chicken dish with the olives.

Mom: Let's just order in. I don't want you to have to make anything.

Me: It's fine. I need to go out anyway. I need to pick up laundry.

Mom: You want me to make you a drink before you go?

Me: I'm okay for now. You put a lot of gin in that.

Mom: Saves me from having to make another one right away.

Me: *I can feel the sizzle of the tonic bubbling up and tickling my nose.* I'm gonna go ahead and run out. You and Dad need anything?

Mom: Nope. Why don't you let me do your running around? You never sit down for a second.

Me: Oh, yeah, you're one to talk. I'll be back soon.

Mom: Drive safe.

Me: I will.

I'm starting to feel like the roles are reversing: With an ever-quickening pace, my parents are becoming my responsibility. And I don't want to be the parent. Not to my parents. Not yet. I'm too young. I'm not ready for the responsibility, and I wouldn't want it even if I were. I don't want to have to remind my father to wear sunscreen and then have to worry that he won't. I don't want to have to tell my mom to slow down on her gin and tonics as I hover in the doorway, keeping track of how much tonic is actually involved in the making of her favorite drink.

I'm not ready to be the parent, but I feel like I'm being forced into office prematurely. This is all supposed to happen much, much later. After they've become grandparents several times over, after hip surgeries and dentures, arthritis and osteoporosis—that's when I'm supposed to step in. That's the time for me to take over and help these ancient people find a peaceful way to spend their few remaining years. But not now. Not when I'm twenty-six years old and haven't even really begun my own life yet. I don't want to have two kids—whom I also happen to call Mom and Dad—before I have two kids. It's not right. It's not natural. It's all out of order. It's not the way things are supposed to happen. But it's happening. *I* know it. *They* know it. We *all* know it. And . . . I'm scared.

The Big Day and Car Trouble

I'm exhausted. I spent the first half of the night wondering if I could sneak a quick drink after midnight without *technically* falling off the wagon. I concocted some bizarrely complicated rationale involving the Chinese New Year, but, alas, I decided if a tree makes a drink in the forest and there's no one around to hear it, the tree's still an alcoholic. The second half of the night was spent figuring out how to broach this whole gin-and-tonic conversation without my mom freezing up, shutting up, or breaking down. I want to let her know I'm fighting the good fight. She won't want to hear it. She won't really listen. She will deny, question, and then fix. She's got a weak constitution when it comes to these kinds of problems. She's not up for discussing any "-ism," particularly this one. In her my mind, they all come down to one common denominator—her. She blames herself for all of the pain her children suffer/have suffered/may suffer some time in a land far, far away. She can't help herself. She sucks up pain. She feeds off it. She's like a pool sweep, always sifting through the dirt and grime, fighting an endless battle to try and keep things neat and clean.

So, what to do, what to say? Unfortunately, I failed to wake up with any usable material for the "g and t" chat. Instead, my head is inexplicably filled with blueprints for a sweatshirt-lined jean jacket. So, as I sit buckled securely into the passenger seat of my PT Cruiser, armed only with a design for a jean jacket for the new millennium, I feel anything but prepared for the looming discussion. Palms moist and mouth bone dry, I notice that I'm silently moving my lips—rehearsing—hoping something worthwhile will accidentally spill out.

Mom: I don't know how you put up with all this traffic. I can't believe how much worse it's gotten in the past five years. I think I'd go batshit if I had to drive in this every day.

Me: . . . huh?

Mom: I said the traffic would drive me batshit.

Me: Oh. Yeah. It's bad. I told you I'd drive.

Mom: I wanted to give you a break. You never get a chance to relax. Is my driving making you nervous?

Me: No, I'm okay . . . Tanqueray 10 is really good, huh?

Honk-honk-honnnnnk.

Mom: Jesus! Do you see this?! *Move! Move out of my way, asshole!*

Honk-honk.

Me: He's about to parallel park.

Mom: Well, he should have his blinker on, then. And—*oh, loooook at this! Can you believe this guy? Use your blinker, asshole! What do ya think it's there for?!*

Honk-honk.

Me: Mom, roll up your window. Roll up your window! You're gonna get us shot. Jesus!

Mom: You have to be an aggressive driver. I hate people who can't make up their mind. I think they're the most dangerous . . . and some people drive like they've got all the time in the world. Your father—I don't know the last time you've ridden with him—he's become an awfully slow driver in his old age.

Me: I hadn't noticed.

Mom: Oh, it's terrible. He makes me so nervous. You know, the Land Rover people got on him about it. They said he wasn't driving his car hard enough.

Me: What do you mean?

Mom: They said he needed to drive it faster, or else he was going to blow out the engine.

Me: Are you serious?

Mom: Oh, yeah. I have to constantly get on him to pick up the pace.

Me: I didn't know you could blow out an engine from driving too slow.

Mom: I told him he should let *me* borrow his car for a while.

Me: Yeah, that would probably do the trick.

Mom:

Me:

Mom:

Me: . . . so, do you and Dad usually drink the Tanqueray 10 or the regular Tanqueray?

Mom: Mostly the 10. Why?

Me: Yeah, Adam and I like the 10, too.

Mom: We first got hooked on the 10 because your father liked how the bottle looked. But I really do like the taste of it. I think it's mellower than the regular Tanqueray.

Me: Yeah, the 10's good. *I love gin. Do you love gin? Yummy . . . gin.* I think gin and tonic is the perfect drink.

Mom: Your father and I can't live with*out* it.

Me: . . . yeah. *Tanqueray good. Me Tarzan. You Jane.*

Mom: So, where should we eat lunch? I bet your father's starving. He didn't have any breakfast this morning.

Me: I bought that granola he likes. The one with, like, a million grams of fat.

Mom: I showed him where it was. He said he wasn't hungry. He just had coffee. He must be absolutely famished by now.

Me: Didn't they tell him to stay away from coffee before his appointment?

Mom: I don't think so.

Me: A lot of caffeine can make your veins collapse.

Mom: Is there an In-N-Out Burger around here?

Me: You've *got* to be kidding.

Mom: And you don't have Wendy's out here, do you?

Me: Not close by, no. Let's just wait and ask Dad what he wants. I'm open. I don't really care where we eat.

Mom:

Me:

Mom: I don't know how you stand this traffic . . .

Me: Do you ever feel like you drink too much?

Mom: What?

Me: Lately . . . lately, I've been feeling like maybe I drink too much, and I was just wondering—

Mom: What? Why? How much do you drink?

Me: I usually have a couple drinks a night.

Mom: Not every night.

Me: Not every night, but almost. You and Dad drink every night.

Mom: Not every single night—no, we certainly do not.

Me: When you're *here* you drink every night.

Mom: Oh, well, that's different. We're on vacation. We don't drink every night when we're at home.

Me: When I come to visit you drink every night.

Mom: Well, you're talking about Christmas or Thanksgiving . . .

Me: Okay, whatever . . . my point is, I was just wondering how one knows one is an alcoholic.

Mom: Why? Do you think you're an alcoholic? How long have you felt this way? I didn't know you've been feeling like this.

Me: No, I don't know, I just—

Mom: Do you think you need to talk to someone? Maybe you should talk to someone about this. I don't think you drink too much, but you would know. I bet there are a lot of doctors you could talk to about this. What about your therapist? You're still seeing him. If he can't help you, I bet he can recommend someone—

Me: No, Mom. I was just . . . I was just wondering how one would know, because usually alcoholics don't ever think they have a problem . . . have you ever thought *you* were?

Mom: What?

Me: You know . . . that maybe . . . you might have a drinking problem?

Mom: Well, there have been times when I thought I needed to cut back, but—

Me: How do you know you're not an alcoholic? How does one know?

Mom: I don't *need* it.

Me: But how do you *know* you don't need it if you drink every night?

Mom: Do you think *you're* an alcoholic?

Me: No . . . I don't know. That's my point. How does one know? I decided to quit drinking for a week—

Mom: That's why you didn't have any last night.

Me: I decided to quit and see how I feel. I'm on day four.

Mom: How do you feel?

Me: Okay. The first few days I felt like total shit. I was nauseous and shaky. I felt like crap.

Mom: Shaky?

Me: Yeah, you know, my hands and stuff.

Mom: I don't think that's a good sign.

Me: Yeah, well . . .

Mom: And what about now?

Me: I feel better . . . I'd like a drink, but I feel better.

Mom: It sounds like a good thing you stopped.

Me: I haven't *stopped*. I'm not, like, stopping drinking forever or anything. I just wanted to prove to myself that I could stop for a week . . . you think you could stop for a week?

Mom: If I wanted to. I'm very careful about how much I drink. Trust me. There have been times in my life when I've thought maybe I was drinking a little too much, and I . . . if I start to feel that way again, I promise I'll cut back.

Me:

Mom: You think you should join AA?

Me: *No.* Jesus. No, I'm fine. I was just, you know . . . I don't know . . . talking out my ass. I'm fine. I've been able to not drink for four days, so . . . so . . . so that proves something. I'm fine. Last thing you need is something else to worry about . . . if anyone should be cutting back, it's Dad. Alcohol is really hard on the immune system. It's an immune suppressant. Dad should, at the very least, watch the hard liquor and drink more red wine.

Mom: I think your father's doing just fine. He really doesn't drink that much, and you can't expect him to give up all his vices.

Me: He smokes cigars.

Mom: Once a month.

Me: I *know* he smokes more than once a month.

Mom: The man has to have one guilty pleasure.

Me: He eats red meat, always has dessert, drinks alcohol, smokes cigars, and doesn't exercise. I don't think he's exactly lacking vices.

Mom:

Me: I just want him to be healthy.

Mom: I know. You just have to understand that this is all very hard for your father.

Me: I understand, but if he wants to live a long life, he's gonna have to change his lifestyle.

Mom: He's doing the vaccine.

Me: Yes.

Mom: That's a big step.

Me: I agree, but in my opinion he didn't really have a choice.

Mom: Of course he did. He didn't have to do it.

Me: I know. I know. But he would have been an idiot not to. I still can't believe he's doing it. Did he ever say anything to you about what Gregory said to him?

Mom: . . . no.

Me: You're the worst liar. Your nostrils are flaring. What did Dad say? What did Gregory say to him?

Mom: He didn't tell me anything Gregory said. All he said was, he did it for you.

Me: What do ya mean, he did it for me?

Mom: He did it so that maybe the vaccine would get approved earlier and you could get it.

Me: What are you talking about?

Mom: I'm just telling you what he said.

Me:

Mom: Your father never would have done the vaccine if it wasn't for you.

Me: What about all the stuff Gregory said to him? Gregory must have told him it was something he needed to do.

Mom: Your father decided he would do it for you. He thought if he could contribute—even in some small way—to the vaccine getting approved, well, then it would all be worth it.

Me: You're telling me he did this trial, he signed on to do this whole thing—the traveling and all this shit—because of me.

Mom: That's what he said.

Me: That's bullshit. He did it for himself. He's using me as the excuse.

Mom: Maybe.

Me:

Mom:

Me: Maybe he needs an excuse.

As my mom and I pull into the hospital motor court, I am reminded of rotisserie chicken and sticky fingers covered in mayo and ketchup . . . eating sandwiches. I remember we were all eating in silence, and I was looking at my dad, and he was looking at his sandwich, and my mother was looking for her napkin (which was tucked in her shirt collar), and I was curious as hell about what had inspired him to do the trial. I wanted to ask him a million questions. I wanted to know everything he was thinking about. I wanted to know what Gregory had said to him. I wanted to understand. I wanted to be on the inside. In "The Know."

Turns out, I *was* "The Know." I *was* on the inside. I was the answer to all million questions, the inspiration, and the explanation. It was all me. The excuse. The instigator.

Me: Hey, Tom. Is my dad still back with Dr. Gregory?

Tom: I think he's in the lab. You, um, may want to go back there.

Me: Oh. Is he okay?

Mom: What happened?

Tom: He just started to get a little light-headed when they started the injections. I think the nurse is trying to get him to eat some crackers. He's in the lab. You two can go on back.

Me: Hey, Dad. How's it going in here?

Mom: Honey, you look so pale.

Howard: We're doing okay. His veins aren't cooperating this morning, and with all the poking around I had to do, he got a little light-headed.

Mom: What can I get you?

Dad: Nothing.

Me: Can I get you some more crackers or something?

Dad: No.

Nurse: I haven't been able to get him to eat much. I get the feeling he didn't have any breakfast this morning.

Mom: How 'bout I run over to Koo Koo Roo and pick you up a sandwich?

Dad: I'm not hungry.

Me: Dad, you've gotta eat something.

Howard: His veins collapsed. I told him he needs to stay away from caffeine before his appointments.

Me: I'll run down to the café outside the front entrance and bring up some—

Dad: No. Jesuschrist! I told you. I don't feel like eating anything!

Me:

Mom:

Howard:

Nurse:

Dad: Howard, let's do this. Let's get it over with.

Howard: I'm gonna need you to drink a little more fluid before we start again. We need to try and get your veins pumped up.

Dad: Girls, go home.

Me: We're not going home. Mom and I will wait in the lobby.

Dad: I don't want you spending your whole day—

Me: Tough shit. We'll be in the lobby. The sooner you drink some juice or something, the sooner we can all get out of here. Mom, come on, let's go.

Mom: I'm gonna stay here with—

Me: Mom! We're not helping this situation. We'll be in the lobby.

Me: I told him. I told him this morning to watch the caffeine.

Mom: I think it was his nerves. He didn't say anything, but I could tell he was nervous this morning.

Me: He needs to start taking responsibility for his health. On the mornings he's getting the vaccine, he needs to have a good breakfast and drink lots of fluid. He needs to stay away from the coffee and all that shit until after his shots.

Mom: He's gotta have *some* coffee in the morning; otherwise he'll get a headache.

Me: So he gets a fucking headache. You treat him like he's five . . . okay, yeah, you're right. He should be able to have his morning coffee. That's only fair. We wouldn't want to deprive him of anything. We wouldn't want him to alter his life in the *least* to accommodate this little "problem" he has. You know what, I don't think I want to wear sunscreen anymore! I like the beach. I like getting burned. I should be able to get burned. I shouldn't have to wear sunscreen or hideous sun-protective clothing for the rest of my fucking life! Not if I don't want to—

Mom: That's not the same thing.

Me: It *is* the same thing! It's exactly the same fucking thing! He's gonna have to make concessions. He may not like it. It sucks, I know, but it's how it is—and don't make it worse. You've gotta stand up to him and tell him to stop acting like a petulant child.

Mom:

Me: I'm going to Koo Koo Roo. I'm gonna pick up sandwiches. You want something?

Mom: Your father said he's not hungry.

Me: That's fine. I'll get him something and it can shrivel up and rot in my car, for all I care . . . he's gotta eat sometime.

And Then There Was Light

A week without the bottle! A whole, entire seven days of hell, but I did it. Parents in town and all. I planned on celebrating my achievement with a big, fat drink but then thought better of it and decided a new lip gloss would be sufficient. Adam wasn't convinced a week on the wagon was enough to merit much of anything, considering how many years I've been sucking down the sauce. It wasn't until I suggested he give up red meat (*his* lifeblood) for a week that he changed his tune, cocked his head, raised his arms to the heavens, and shouted, "Praise the lord, you did it!"

No sign of reindeer slippers. Seems her therapy slot has been filled by a gangly teenage boy. He sprinted past me a few moments ago—complete disgust emanating from his every pore. He was muttering something under his breath that sounded remarkably similar to "fuck her," which I assume referred to the woman who whizzed by only seconds later, shouting something about "next week's meeting," "washing his mouth out," and "not my fault."

Dr. Lesaux: You ready?
Me: Yep.

Dr. Lesaux: Here . . . let me rearrange these chairs for you . . .

Me: It's so bright in here.

Dr. Lesaux: My last client likes a lot of light.

Me: I love it. My pupils thank you.

Dr. Lesaux: So . . .

Me: So, I quit drinking for a week.

Dr. Lesaux: Congratulations.

Me: Thank you, thank you.

Dr. Lesaux: What prompted this?

Me: I just had been thinking a lot about how I've been feeling lately—kinda out of control and stuff—and, I don't know, it just seemed like the right thing to do. Plus, Adam didn't think I could do it, so of course I had to prove him wrong. I'd do almost anything to prove him wrong. He's not wrong a lot.

Dr. Lesaux: And did you notice any changes in your mood or your behavior when you weren't drinking?

Me: Yeah, I mean, the first few days were pretty rough. I actually thought I had the stomach flu or something. I had diarrhea and I was nauseous and shaky, but then, like, by the third day, my stomach calmed down, and I guess I was just more irritable. But my parents were in town, so, I don't know, they could have had a lot to do with my level of irritability.

Dr. Lesaux: And how did your parents' presence affect you?

Me: They made it harder to stay sober. My parents drink like fucking fishes, no question about it. I mean, we all do. My whole family. But it's like . . . it's like . . . *tradition*. Like, Adam's family, when they all get together, they eat. When my family gets together, we drink. Maybe it's a Christian thing . . . not that we're religious. It's definitely an Irish thing.

Dr. Lesaux: And what about your mom? Last session you were particularly concerned about her drinking.

Me: I had this realization last week, before I stopped drinking. I had just talked to my mom on the phone, and she was having a g and t, and I was about to make a g and t, and I started thinking that maybe it wasn't *her* drinking that was bothering me so much, but my own. Almost like I recognized myself in her or something.

Dr. Lesaux:

Me: It was like what we talked about a while ago when we were dealing with my dad. I remember you basically told me that I had to accept his way of dealing with his cancer. You kept emphasizing that we are different people and so we each have our own way of coping. What I realized with my mom is that we cope in the same way. When we get stressed, we drink more. So . . .

Dr. Lesaux: So . . .

Me: So . . . I don't know. So that's why I decided to stop drinking.

Dr. Lesaux: But are you still worried that your mother drinks too much?

Me: Yes, except I'm not *as* worried. Maybe she drinks too much, maybe she doesn't. What I really need to focus on is how I feel about how much *I* drink. I think I was, like, totally projecting my shit onto her. I mean, yes, I wish she drank less or quit for a while or something, but I also wish my dad wanted to talk about his cancer and I wish I had bigger boobs and I wish Adam didn't have to work so much. I wish that a lot of fucking things were different. I wish I didn't have to be here talking to you. I wish I had never gotten melanoma . . . but most of those things are things I have no control over. My drinking—that, I can change. I'm not saying I'm gonna stop drinking or anything. I just think I'm gonna be more aware. I'm gonna *try* to be more aware. I'm gonna try and catch myself if I notice I'm drinking, like, four drinks a night or something. I don't think I'm an alcoholic. Of course my mother, at this point, might disagree, but I just think I need to take control a little more.

Dr. Lesaux: This is a big step.

Me: I don't know about that. It's progress, though, right? Progress is good. Progress is always good.

Just the Two of Us

Okay, so, it's a little awkward. I admit it. My dad and me in a car together. Together and alone . . . *please, God, don't let there be silence.* Silence hurts worst of all. Radio. No radio. Windows up. Windows down. Cancer. No cancer. It all feels wrong.

My dad and I are on our way to a healthy, apple-a-day-keeps-the-doctor-away breakfast and then on to the hospital for a round of cancer cell Pac-Man. The car ride has been . . . trying, to say the least. We've covered rising temperatures in the Midwest and debated the implications of aerosol use on future weather patterns. We've considered Adam's movie release schedule for the next twelve months and determined that Universal's string of hits is due solely to the unique vision and creative insight of its marketing department. We've marveled at how, despite years of drug abuse, Stevie Nicks's voice really *has* improved with age.

And so now, twenty-five minutes into this torturous commute, with all "safe" topics far, far behind, I find myself hanging on by the short and curlies. I've spent the last three minutes milking "ol' reliable": asking an endless string of remodeling/home-improvement questions in a desperate attempt to fill the air with *something* other than the occasional traffic-related sigh and/or throat clearing.

Me: . . . and even though I *know* the slate would *look* better, I don't think our balcony can support the weight. What would you guess the weight limit is? Per square foot?

Dad: I'd have to look at your balcony again.

Me: Sam, our contractor, mentioned something about floating the tiles. Do you know anything about how they, you know, do that?

Dad: They create a foundation with some "give," which allows the tiles to move without cracking. Because the balcony is exposed to direct sun and rain, the tiles will change size. They'll shrink or expand, depending on the weather, so you want them to have the ability to move without worrying about anything separating or splitting.

Me: Are the labor costs a lot more expensive with "floating"?

Dad: Labor will be more, because of the extra time involved, but material costs will be minimal.

Me: Maybe next time you're out here we'll have a new balcony . . . well, not next time, since you'll be here next week. But maybe the time after that. We should figure out where we're gonna eat breakfast. Do you know where you wanna go?

Dad: I'll leave that up to you.

Me: Well, we've got several options. There's Babalu. It's a Cajun-y, southwestern kinda place. It's got great blue-corn muffins and eggs and hash and stuff. Maybe it's Jamaican. Yeah, it's definitely not Cajun, now that I think about it. Adam and I used to go there all the time when we lived in Santa Monica . . . um . . . there's an Au Bon Pain. They have bagels and chocolate croissants—

Dad: Wherever you want.

Me: There's also an IHOP . . .

Dad: Let's do that. Is it close to the hospital?

Me: Yeah. Well, they're all close, so . . . whichever.

Dad: IHOP. That's easy.

Me: It's right across from the hospital, so we might be able to leave the car in their lot and just walk over to your appointment.

Dad: I don't want you to do that. You don't need to go with me.

Me: I know, but I might as well go with you, since I'm driving you to the airport.

Dad: Oh, no no no.

Me: Yeah, we already discussed this.

Dad: No, we didn't.

Me: I told Mom I was taking you.

Dad: No. That's absolutely crazy. The airport will be a madhouse, and it'll take you all day to get home.

Me: No, it won't. It'll take me probably half an hour at the most.

Dad: You can't go in with me when they give me the shot.

Me: That's fine. I'll just wait in the lobby area. Maybe I'll go say hi to Amy in the Positive Appearance Center.

Dad: You're going to waste your whole day—

Me: Dad. This way, we'll have a little more time together. I'm taking you to the airport.

FIFTEEN MINUTES LATER:

Me: I'll have two egg whites scrambled and a side of wheat toast.

IHOP Server Extraordinaire: That it?

Me: Actually, could I also get a side of tomatoes?

I.S.E.: Garlic or rosemary?

Me: No, *tomatoes.* Just a couple of slices.

I.S.E.: I'll have to ask. I'm not sure we have tomatoes—and you?

Dad: I'll have the blueberry pancakes with a side of bacon, and more coffee when you get a chance.

Me: Dad, don't you think you should lay off the coffee until after your appointment? The caffeine, your veins . . . remember?

I.S.E.: You want more coffee or not?

Dad: Make it decaf.

Me: Oh, and what kind of decaffeinated tea do you have?

I.S.E.: Chamomile.

Me: I'll have that, then.

I.S.E.: It's gonna be a couple minutes for the tea.

Me: That's fine. God, I haven't been to IHOP in so long. It reminds me of when we lived in Atlanta and I used to go to Bob's Big Boy with Nina after soccer games.

Dad: I wonder whatever happened to her . . .

Me: Nina's family went to Bob's all the time. Remember, Nina's mom never cooked. They ate there, like, twice a day . . . yeah . . . I always liked the breakfast buffet. I remember they had really good mini–blueberry muffins.

Dad:

Me: They don't have Bob's out here . . . I remember that place always had a hard time hanging on to their Big Boy. It became a really popular thing to steal.

Dad: I bet most kids stole it on a dare.

Me: Definitely. So, how's work going?

Dad: Good.

Me: Has it been busy?

Dad: Not too bad.

Me: Been doing a lot of traveling?

Dad: A lot of day trips. New York, Chicago, Cincinnati . . .

Me: I'm sure those are the worst kind. The day trips probably really mess with your body clock.

Dad: They can.

Me: . . . yeah . . .

Dad:

Me: *That's it. I can't do this anymore. I'm wiped out. Too much effort for too little reward.*

I need some new material, but my mind's blank. I am completely tapped out. Zip, zero, nada. I am speechless and taskless. I've shredded all the napkins within two feet of my limbs, with the exception of the one draped across my father's multiweather/multitask Orvis corduroy cargo pants. I have checked and rechecked the salt and pepper shaker tops for signs of tampering by some rebel teenager. I have even created miniature origami swans out of emptied Sweet'N Low packets. Any psychologist worth her salt would have a field day with the evidence on this table. I need something—anything—to keep my hands busy. My mind is racing . . .

Me: *I'm in real trouble here . . . the silence is deafening . . . for the love of all things holy—*

I.S.E.: Here you are. Pancakes for you . . .

Me: Those go over there. I had the eggs.

I.S.E.: Who had the wheat bread?

Me: I did. And I never got my tea.

I.S.E.: Oh. No one brought it?

Me: Nope.

I.S.E.: Anything else you need besides the tea?

Me: Not for me.

Dad: You want some coffee?

Me: No, I'm fine. I'm off coffee for a while. I've been drinking mostly green tea. It's really good for the immune system. I've been getting this loose tea from Chinatown. It's got, like, corn kernels in it. It's really good. I'll send you some. It almost tastes like liquid popcorn. Mom would probably love it.

Dad: Your mother's starving me to death.

Me: She's just trying to get you to eat healthier.

Dad: We should probably head out in a couple minutes.

Me: We just got our food. What time is it? We've got, like, twenty-five minutes. It'll only take five minutes to walk across the street.

Dad: Okay.

Me:

Dad:

Me:

Dad:

Me: . . . mum.

Dad:

Me:

Dad:

Me: . . . yum.

Dad:

Me: You want my other piece of toast?

Dad: You sure you're not going to eat it?

Me: Positive.

Dad:

Me:

Dad: Bite of pancake?

Me: No, thanks.

Dad:

Me: Could you hand me the salt?

Dad:

Me: Thanks.

Dad:

Me:

Dad:

Me:

Dad: Miss . . . could we get some more napkins over here?

Me:

Dad:

Me:

Dad:

Me: Wow, I'm stuffed.

Me: That was good. They make good eggs. It's all the butter, I guess.

Dad: You sure you don't need anything else?

Me: No, I'm good. You get enough?

Dad: It was the perfect amount.

Me: Miss . . . check.

We walk across the street to the hospital, and I finally give in to the silence, the quiet I've been battling since daybreak. I take a deep breath, a breeze lifts my hair off my forehead, and I am reminded of long drives home after hard soccer games. My dad and me. Alone. With the top down on my father's lime green convertible Bug, we'd ride home quietly, each in our own world, the stereo playing softly in the background, usually an old tape of the Beatles or Neil Young, the volume turned down so low it was hard to tell if it was playing at all. The wind drying the sweat on my face until my skin felt caked and tight. I'd watch the kudzu whip by as I wove my arm up and down like a roller coaster, feeling the force of the wind against the palm of my hand. I'd replay the game in my head, reminding myself of things I'd done wrong. Reassuring myself of all I'd done right. My mouth sweet from the Gatorade. My fingers sticky from the orange quarters.

I'd occasionally glance at my father, his right arm resting on top of the steering wheel, his left dangling over the car door. I remember I always thought he was gonna get it cut off someday, hanging it from the car like he did, but he never seemed to worry. His coach's whistle still around his neck, whistling when the wind caught it just right. It was some of the only time I ever spent alone with my father. Just the two of us. The coach and the player.

As my father made the final turn onto our street, the sun would come glaring through the dusty windshield. We'd raise our hands to our brows, blocking the sun from our eyes, squinting the same squint, our noses uniformly crinkled and upper lips raised to expose our front teeth. We were together on those Saturdays. Quiet and apart, but together . . . and the silence was comfortable back then.

Tom: Hey there, you two.

Dad: Hey, Tom.

Tom: Jon, you can head on back. Howard's ready for you.

Me: Dad, I'll wait out here. Good luck.

Tom: You two look a lot alike. I just noticed that.

Me: Yeah.

Tom: You can go back with him if ya want. Sit with him.

Me: Oh . . . I didn't think I was allowed back.

Tom: Go on back if you like. He's just in the lab.

Me: Oh . . . um . . . okay. Actually, maybe I'll just wait out here, give him his privacy. Thanks, though. Maybe . . . maybe next time.

A Rose by Any Other Name

Rose: Hey, you.

Me: Hey. It's so good to see you. How are you?

Rose: Great. Really good. This is the beginning of my third week of treatment. Can you believe it? It's really flown by.

Me: How do you feel?

Rose: Fine. I really do. I'm still at work. I've been able to keep a full schedule. I haven't slowed down a bit.

Me: And you haven't noticed any change in your energy level?

Rose: Maybe slightly, but then I think it's just my imagination. And—as you can see—I still have all of my hair. I noticed a little hair on my pillow yesterday when I woke up, and then a little more this morning, but for the most part, it seems to be holding steady. Where's Amy? Is she around? I wanted to show her my full head of hair . . . and you said I'd need a wig.

Me: She went across the street to drop some stuff off. She should be back in a few minutes. You might run into her on your way down to the parking lot.

Rose: I'd wait for her to get back, but I've got a meeting in Hollywood and I just *know* the traffic's going to be *hor*-rendous. Tell Amy I stopped by, will you?

Me: I will, definitely. I . . . um . . . wanted to tell you that actually, most women don't usually start losing their hair until their third week of treatment.

Rose: My oncologist mentioned that, but I think I'd have noticed more of a change by now. I mean, it's still *so* thick. See, I mean, if I pull on it, it really doesn't come out—oh . . . well . . . wow . . . well, this is the most that's come out so far. I mean . . . up until today . . .

Me: *Judging from the look on her face, I think I just witnessed one of the most significantly horrifying moments in Rose's life. The tan-colored Dooney & Bourke purse dangling from the index finger of her right hand seems to only slightly outweigh the fistful of "healthy, thick" hair in her left hand. I'm sure Amy would know the right thing to say to a woman who's just realized her helmet of "healthy, thick" hair is on its way out, but, of course, Amy's not around, so instead I must come up with some casually comforting words of wisdom to counteract the effects of the "healthy, thick" hair that's staring back at me like a disturbingly "healthy, thick" rodent.*

It's . . . not that bad. You do have a lot of hair, so . . . I bet it will take you longer to . . . ah . . . lose all of it.

Rose:

Me: Would you like me to shave your head?

Rose: What? No! Why would I want you to shave my head?

Me: A lot of women find it less traumatic to wake up in the morning with short hairs on their pillow, as opposed to long.

Rose: Well, I'm *not* shaving my head. I might get a shorter cut or something, but I'm definitely not going to shave my head. You know what . . . I know what I'll do. I'll get my hair trimmed, and then in a couple of weeks—

Me: Rose, in a couple of weeks you won't have any hair.

Rose:

Me:

Rose:

Me: I just want you to be prepared. I really have to say that shaving your head will make this process a lot easier.

Rose: I appreciate your opinion, but I think I'll wait and see what happens.

Me:

Rose: I've gotta run.

Me: I'll tell Amy you stopped by. It was good to see you.

Maybe she won't lose any more of her hair. Maybe she'll hold steady with the one bald spot. Maybe her unshakable determination is enough to keep her "healthy, thick" mane mostly in place. Maybe *I'm* wrong and *she's* right and maybe she'll become a miracle of science, write *The Modern Woman's Guide to Keeping Your Hair,* go on tour, and get paid thousands upon thousands of dollars to tell her miraculous story of courage and fortitude to hordes of wide-eyed chemo patients. Maybe she'll host "Good Hair Day L.A." parties or start her own line of luxury shampoos, conditioners, and hair clips. Maybe she'll march in anti–shaved head parades and chant things like, "My hair is here to stay," and, "Long is strong," while thrusting into the air a picture of a shaved head with a red line slashed diagonally across it.

But maybe—just maybe—her public-speaking career will end before it even begins. Because maybe Rose will wake up tomorrow morning to find a significant pile of hair lying in bed next to her, the dark stringy mass looking back at her as she fumbles for her alarm. And maybe, as she showers, washing her hair as usual, she'll realize that the majority of the hair she thinks she is scrubbing clean is, in fact, no longer attached to her head and is instead tangled up in a sudsy ball, dangling from her wet, soapy fingers.

I think I'll probably run into Rose again, though I doubt very seriously she'll show her face in the Positive Appearance Center. I'll most likely bump into her in the halls of the cancer floor or come across her and her tan Dooney & Bourke purse on my way down to the parking lot. It will be difficult to see her. No doubt it will break my heart. I won't know what to say, and probably neither will she, but there will most certainly be an unspoken acknowledgment of her lack of hair. As much as she and/or I would like to believe in the contrary, by the end of this week, Rose will be mostly bald. She just doesn't seem to want to know it yet.

Nothing Left to Stand On

Adam: How was work?

Me: It was good.

Adam: Everyone have both their ears today?

Me: As far as I could tell. I saw Rose again. I did meet a man without a shin, though.

Adam: What do you mean? How do you know he didn't have a shin?

Me: Well, this guy came in looking for a skin graft kit, and we got talking, and it turned out he had a melanoma on his shin, like, nine years ago. He's had six localized recurrences since then. He just had his seventh surgery. I asked to see his shin so I would know what size kit to give him. And when he lifted his pant—

Adam: I don't want to hear this.

Me: It wasn't bloody or anything. It was all bandaged—

Adam: Okay, okay, okay.

Me: It was pretty unbelievable. When he lifted his pant leg it looked like he had only bone below his knee. Like all the tissue had been—

Adam: I really, really don't want to hear this.

Me: I know, but it wasn't gross. I mean, it didn't even look like a leg if you—

Adam: Ooo-kay. I'm good.

Me: You asked how my day was, so I'm telling you about my day. *That* was my day: talking to a man who is crippled because of a fucking mole. That was the day.

Adam: Well, don't *go* if it depresses you. No one's forcing you to go.

Me: What are you talking about? I like it. I like being there. I like talking to the people that come in. I'm meeting the most amazing people. I mean, with this guy today, we talked about Gregory and the vaccine and all his recent surgeries. And he told me about how he's been able to deal with his life without the use of one of his legs. And it wasn't gross or scary or anything. It was nice to be able to talk about that kind of stuff and not feel like I have to censor myself.

Adam: You feel like you have to censor yourself with me?

Me: Well, yeah, kinda. Yeah, because you never seem to want to hear the whole story. You always get grossed out.

Adam: Well, get better stories.

Me: I don't have any. These are the stories I have.

Adam: Fine. I'm sorry. I didn't realize I was upsetting you. Why didn't you tell me it was bothering you, the fact that I allegedly never let you finish a story? Finish your story.

Me: No. You ruined it.

Adam: Come on. I'm listening. Finish it.

Me: I don't want to.

Adam: Finish it. I want to hear it. I do. Seriously. Finish.

Me: I already did.

It may seem morbid that I like going and hearing patients' stories. But as horribly shocking and painfully sad as most of the stories are, I still enjoy hearing the patients talk about their illness: their cancer, their side effects, their recovery, and sometimes even their death. I'm meeting people in the most vulnerable time of their lives. Many of them are confronting their own mortality—a few are still trying to accept their illness, some are struggling to make peace with it, others are looking to make peace with themselves, but all of them are willing to share. Share all of it with me. And it's truly amazing. It's inspiring. These people! I can't believe these goddamned sick people! I am constantly amazed at their strength. They are so strong, so powerful. They've dealt with more pain and hurt and fear than they probably ever imagined they could.

And watching them tell me their stories, I experience something that can't be explained to Adam. I'm connecting with them on a level deeper than an ordinary exchange between two strangers allows. And it's *that* connection that Adam will never understand. And that connection is why I go. Maybe it's selfish. Maybe they're healing me more than I'm healing them. But then again, maybe not. And then again, does it really matter?

Pen and Ink

I'm getting a tattoo. A sudden decision twelve years in the making. I've wanted a little somethin'-somethin' since high school, but back in the day, the threat of disinheritance and possibly death at the hands of my father was enough to convince me otherwise. I'll never forget the dinner at which my sister decided to play a joke on my dad and *accidentally* reveal a tattoo in the shape of a rose placed oh so discreetly on the upper part of her left breast. I have yet to see a person come so close to levitation as when my father spotted the monstrosity. He was on his feet in seconds flat, face boiling rose-red. To this day I'm fairly sure he would have strangled the last dying breath out of her had it not been for my mother screeching in abject terror, "It's fake, Jon! For the love of God, it's fake!"

So, since tenth grade, I've been biding my time. Waiting for that perfect moment when all is right with the world. The moment when the planets are aligned and my parents no longer pay my rent. The moment when the threat of disinheritance no longer carries the immeasurable weight or immense interest it used to. The only person I have to contend with now is Adam. Not that he objects to the idea; it's just outside his comfort zone. Of course, nearly everything is outside his comfort zone, since that zone is basically 2.5 inches square, "To the left of the erasers and anything below the pencil sharpeners." But deep down, in the darkest recesses of his melon (in a place he rarely admits exists), I think he kinda likes the idea of being married to a bad girl, a girl with a tattoo . . . or so I've convinced myself.

The big question now is, what design should I get? It needs to be something significant. Something that represents me. The new, older, wiser me. A picture or symbol that reflects not only who I am, but who I hope to become. Something I can look at for years to come and not get sick of. Something of the moment, but not *too* of the moment. Timeless and yet specific.

I have come to get a tattoo on this day, in this year, for a specific reason . . . why? What about me, in this particular moment, is different enough to push me to such a level of tattoo commitment? Why am I here? . . . okay, now I'm really freaking myself out.

Tattoo Guy: Uh, a flag's good.

Me: Um, yeah . . . I don't think a flag's really me.

T.G.: Since 9/11 and all the fucking shit that's gone down, seems like everyone wants a fucking flag—gotta be patriotic, man.

Me: Yeah . . . do you have any more samples of dragonflies?

T.G.: Nay. I can design something for you. What are you thinking, like, a dragonfly with flames on the wings or something?

Me: Um, no, probably not with flames . . . I'm looking for something small.

T.G.: Like, how small? The smaller you go, the less detail you're gonna get.

Me: Oh.

T.G.: Where you think you want it?

Me: I was thinking about on my foot somewhere. I'm an actor, so I don't want it anywhere too conspicuous.

T.G.: Foot's not good. Tattoo won't hold up. It's gonna fade and look like shit.

Me: Oh.

T.G.: Upper arm is good.

Me: Yeah, no, I don't think that would be a good idea . . . *what to get, what to get? God, my hands are really sweating. Be brave. Be brave. If you chicken out now, you're never coming back. Okay, focus.* What about symbols? You have anything else I could look at?

T.G.: I got some Chinese and Japanese shit . . . here, look through this. You seen a cat around here?

Me: No, I don't think so.

T.G.: You'd know it if you saw her. She's got thumbs.

Me: What? What do you mean?

T.G.: Thumbs. You know, like, she's got like regular paws and shit, but then she's got thumbs.

Me: *I may throw up. Just be brave. Be brave.* Like human looking thumbs or . . .

T.G.: Nay, nay. Like cat thumbs. They're all furry. You gotta see it. She grabs shit and everything.

Me: Opposable thumbs.

T.G.: You see anything you like?

Me: Oh . . . um . . . actually, I do like some of these Japanese characters. Could you do something in brown ink to make it look like henna?

T.G.: Yeah, it's just gonna cost a little more 'cause I gotta custom-blend the color.

Me: That's fine.

T.G.: It should prob'ly be, like, a brownish purple, 'cause you don't want, like, a shit-brown color. Let me start mixing something up. You can see if you like it.

Me: Okay . . . and you're sure these characters all mean what they say they mean?

T.G.: Oh, yeah. The page you're lookin' at is from Japan, so it should be pretty fucking right on.

Me: *A word. One word that's going to be with me, on me, for the rest of my life. Most of these characters, I can eliminate right off the bat. I'm sure as shit not gonna walk around for the rest of eternity with a diarrhea-brown tattoo meaning "Sexuality," "Masculinity," "Goddess," or "Home." "Friend," "Foe," "Fight," and "Freedom" are also out. "Sun," "Moon," "Water," and "Rain" do nothing for me. It's gotta be something great. Something with more than one meaning . . . or . . . or something that could be interpreted in more than one way . . . oh my God, I've found it.* Hey, yeah, I think I know what I want. This one. Seems fitting.

T.G.: Cool.

Me: Cool.

Positive Appearance Center: Free at Last

Me: Let me know if I can help you with—

Customer: Yes, please. I desperately need a comfortable bra. Do you sell cotton ones with no underwire?

Me: Are you talking about a mastectomy bra?

Customer: No. Well, yes, I guess. I don't know. I need something that is as comfortable as humanly possible. See, I'm in the melanoma vaccine trial—

Me: My father's in that trial.

Customer: Oh, so you know. I have all these ulcerations under my arms from the BCG. I'm sure your father has the same ones. And my bras rub the scabs off, so the ulcers never seem to get a chance to heal. These places are killing me, and I've already ruined a bunch of my bras trying to pull out the underwire, which you really can't do, as it turns out. I haven't been able to wear a bra for the last week—I kept meaning to come up here; I can't believe it has taken me so long to get up here—and I need something for support. My breasts are too big to be unsupported. Look at these things. They're awful. I'd go braless if I could, but they're just so big. I really hate to do that.

Me: We definitely have something that will help you. Almost all of our bras are cotton, and you know what would be good? We have these super-super-soft sports bras. All cotton, no thick elastic bands or anything. I'll pull a couple off the racks and you can try them on. I think you'll really like them. Our breast cancer patients love them.

Me: Okay, here you go. Try these on. See what you think. Yell if you need help with anything.

Customer: Actually . . . I still don't have full mobility in my arm from when they removed lymph nodes. I hate to ask, but could you help me take off my shirt? I haven't quite mastered the one-armed thing yet. Also, you're going to have to help keep me from oozing on the bras. Most of my places are scabbed over, but I'm afraid if one of the bras rubs them the wrong way, they might start—

Me: Here, let me help you. That's what I'm here for . . . let's make this as easy on ourselves as possible. Let me unbutton your shirt for you . . . all righty, then. O-kay, one arm out . . . one to go . . . okay . . . good. You're doing great . . . *stay calm, stay calm. Don't let her see you flinch. Oh, God, something's oozing. Okay, focus. Breathe. It looks like someone took a lit cigarette and had a field day on her torso. Torture. It looks like some horrible form of antiquated torture.* Oh, wait, one . . . let me get some gauze. And . . . here . . . you hold the gauze; one of your places is bleeding, and I'd hate for you to get blood on your shirt . . . okay . . . we're making progress here . . .

Customer: I'm sorry for asking you to do this. I just hate that I can't do it myself.

Me: No, no, don't be silly. Not a problem . . . your . . . ulcers look pretty sore.

Customer: Well, it's the bras that really make them hurt. At least your father doesn't have to worry about that.

Me: Yeah . . . actually, he hasn't gotten any ulcerations from the vaccine.

Customer: Oh. Really? Gosh, I just assumed everybody got them. They told me everyone gets them. Wow, he's really lucky, then.

Me: Yeah. No, he's had very few side effects. Which is fortunate since he commutes from Ohio.

Customer: I live in Michigan, but my husband and I decided to move out here temporarily until I finish the vaccine. I can't believe your father has been able to do so much flying. I always feel really crappy after my shots.

Me: I guess . . . he's . . . really lucky. Okay, now the hard part. Once we get this bra on, you may never want to take it off. If you could just put one arm in the air and I can . . . wait, oh, shoot, the gauze . . . hold on . . . okay, almost there . . . and . . . we . . . did it. Wow. I hope you like it, because I'm not sure we'll be able to get it off.

Customer: Ahhh. This feels *sooo* good. I can't even tell you. This is soooo much better than my regular bras. You are a lifesaver.

Me: I'm so glad it works for you. Yeah, I'd stay away from anything with an underwire. That sounds just awful. I can't imagine how uncomfortable that must have been.

Customer: I feel like a new woman . . . I tell you, I really haven't felt like doing much of anything since I started the shots, but with this bra and everything, I think I might just want to go out to dinner tonight.

Me: How many of these do you want?

Customer: How many do you have? I might want to wear these all the time. My breasts feel wonderful!

Me: I'm . . . so glad.

Customer: How 'bout I start with four, and I can always come back and get more.

Me: Okay. I'll get these others wrapped up.

Customer: Thank you. You . . . you really made my day.

Me: Okay, you're all set.

Customer: What does your dad look like? In case I run into him . . .

Me: He's about five foot ten, blond hair, blue eyes, glasses, very round head. A male version of me, basically.

Customer: Well, I'm sure I'll see him at some point. I feel like I practically live here.

Me: My dad feels the same way. Good luck with everything. And come back if you need any more of those bras.

Customer: You bet. Tell your father I'll be praying for him.

Me: . . . oh . . . yeah . . . okay. Thanks.

LATER
Ring, ring.

Mom: Hello?

Me: Hey, Mom, it's me.

Mom: Hey there, chickadee.

Me: What are you up to?

Mom: Oh, just dusting. Everything's got about three inches of dust on it.

Me: I doubt it.

Mom: No, really, I don't dust anymore. Especially with all the traveling we've been doing. What's up?

Me: Well, it's really weird, I met this woman today and—is Dad around?

Mom: He's down on the computer.

Me: I met this woman who's doing the vaccine trial, and she has all these ulcers. She said it was from the BCG. Something about the injection sites. She came in looking for bras. Dad doesn't have anything like that, right?

Mom: Well, they're getting . . . better.

Me: Where does he have them? He never talks about them.

Mom: Oh, you know your father. He would never talk about something like that. He's got too much pride.

Me:

Mom: They look really sore. He'd kill me if he knew I was talking to you about this. The ones under his arms are the worst.

Me: The woman I helped at the store, hers looked terrible. They were oozing and really raw.

Mom: I can't imagine having to wear a bra.

Me: No kidding.

Mom: I don't think I'd wear one.

Me: I sure as hell wouldn't. She didn't have a choice, though. She was, like, a D. Will you see if Dad can pick up the phone?

Mom: You're not going to say anything to him?

Me: Yeah, why?

Mom: No, you can't. He'd never forgive me.

Me: What are you talking about?

Mom: Hillary, don't say anything. Promise me—you have to promise me—you won't say anything.

Me: Fine, fine.

Mom: You have to respect his priva—

Me: Fine! I won't say anything. Jesus. You wanna see if he can talk? I just wanna say hi.

Mom: Jon! Jon, pick up. Hillary's on the phone . . .

Dad: Hello there.

Mom: I'm hanging up.

Me: So, what's up?

Dad: Not much. Just doing some work on the computer.

Me: And you're feeling good?

Dad: Yep. Doing good. How are you feeling?

Me: Good. Really good. I've been working at the hospital a lot lately. You know . . . keeping busy. I met a woman today who's doing the vaccine trial. I told her to look out for you.

Dad: Do you remember her name?

Me: No, but I told her what you look like, so I bet she'll introduce herself. She was having some, um, irritation from the vaccine, so she needed bras without underwire. She was *so* appreciative. She left a new woman.

Dad: Good.

Me: Yeah, I'm really enjoying working there. I feel like I'm actually *doing* something. It's a nice feeling.

Dad: Well, I should get back to work. We'll be seeing you soon.

Me: Yeah. Okay, well, don't do too much.

Dad: You too.

Me: Love you.

Dad: Love you too.

Click.

He's so interesting. People are so interesting. So consistently inconsistent. Here's a man who will protest against wearing sunscreen but not make a peep about oozing, bleeding blisters. A greasy face from a waterproof SPF—that, we hear about. His eyes burning because he insists on wearing body sunscreen on his face—on that, we get an earful. But ulcers—red, bleeding, scabby, scaly ulcers—not a peep. Nary a whisper.

Being "Brave"

Thirteen steps from the elevator to the front desk. Ten steps from the front desk to the lab, three to the scale, and another two to the blood pressure cart. Eight steps to room number 4, which contains two fluorescent lights, one laminated coffee table, two oversize chairs, and one examination table with two bottom drawers each filled with five hospital gowns. On the wall hangs one pain-management Xerox with ten faces, each one representing a single unit of pain, one magazine rack containing half a *Self* magazine, and two faded posters promoting two hospital support groups (one for breast cancer and one for everything else). On the floor sits one basket filled with two informative, self-help cassettes and zero cassette players. It's the same. Always the same.

I know this room better than I know most rooms in my own house. I've spent time in this room. Real, quality time. The kind of time parents always talk about in the abstract—quiet time. I have spent countless hours in semideep contemplation, pondering all the great questions about life and death and the hereafter. I have broken down my predicament into categories and subcategories: the good, the bad, and the ugly of it all. I have cried in this room many times, for many different reasons. I have prayed in here. I have cursed the godforsaken crucifix and taken the Lord's name in vain many, many times in here. I have lived a full life, all confined within these four hospital walls.

Knock, knock.

Me: Come in.

Gregory: Well, hello.

Me: You cut your hair.

Gregory: Yeah, well . . .

Me: It looks good. You look so . . . doctorly.

Gregory: Shall we have a look? . . . Any complaints?

Me: Not really. I was just in to see Dr. Bach a few weeks ago. She said everything looked good. I actually got out of her office without an excision, if you can believe it.

Gregory: Your arms look good . . . I have to say, she's done a great job of removing everything that looked suspicious . . . I mean, as I look you over, you really don't have any moles of substantial size . . . left.

Me: I'm practically mole-less.

Gregory: Lymph nodes feel normal . . . legs, good . . . a tattoo, always good.

Me: Yeah, I got it a few weeks ago.

Gregory: What does it mean?

Me: It means "brave." Not that I really *am* or anything. It's more of a reminder, you know, that I should try to be . . . it was between this and a tattoo in the shape of a mole, but then I figured it would be just my luck to get a real mole under the tattooed one.

Gregory: A tattoo in the shape of a mole. Now, *that's* something I'd like to see.

Me: Yeah, I thought it would be pretty fucking funny. Adam didn't see the humor in it.

Gregory: Well . . . everything looks good. You can get dressed. All the moles you have left are all really tiny. It's great because if anything *does* start to change or you get anything new, you'll notice it right away.

Me: What about the one in my crack? How's that one?

Gregory: Looks fine.

Me: It's a tough one to watch.

Gregory: Yeah, everything looks good.

Me: Great. That was easy.

Gregory: You have any questions for me?

Me: Um, actually, I just want to talk about the pregnancy thing for a second. I'm coming up on my year mark in a few months, and I've been talking to a lot of people about pregnancy and stuff, and Adam and I have been discussing it a lot, and you know it's really something I want to do . . . so . . . I don't know . . . I was just wondering if you're still thinking I need to wait five years or . . . or what.

Gregory: I think it's a little premature to be having this conversation—

Me: No, I know, it's just—

Gregory: —but I will say that you're looking really good. You've been vigilant with your checkups, and it's paying off. You have very few moles, if any, that I'm concerned about.

Me: I really trust Dr. Bach, and when she says something needs to come off, I get it taken off. I've done a lot of research on melanoma and pregnancy, I've talked to a lot of different people, and I really think that at some point I'm going to be willing to take the risk and try to get pregnant. I've researched surrogacy, and for a while I thought maybe that was an option for me, but I don't know . . . I . . . I . . . I want to be pregnant.

Gregory: I understand.

Me: And I don't think—based on all the reading I've done—I would be taking an enormous risk, by the way.

Gregory: Well, like I said, I think it's a little early to be having this conversation, but I will say that I'm really happy with where you are. Now, I'm not making any promises, but *if* things keep looking good and *if* you continue to be as vigilant with your checkups and in another year you haven't gotten another melanoma, then I might feel okay with you getting pregnant.

Me: Really? You would give me the okay? I mean, assuming I don't get another melanoma and all that . . .

Gregory: I would probably give you the okay.

Me: Okay. Great. I . . . that's all I wanted to hear. I know you can't know what's going to happen and all that, but, you know, I really feel like it's going to be okay. I really think I'm going to get pregnant and not have a problem. I don't know why. Maybe every woman who's had melanoma feels that way, but . . . I really think I'm going to be okay. And it's worth it to me to take the chance. That's what I've really come to in all this.

Gregory: I completely understand. My wife and I have six kids.

Me: Six! Actually, I can totally picture you with six.

Gregory: It's wild.

Me: Six . . . God, the sixth one must have practically dropped out of your wife.

Gregory: Practically. So, I'm going to head off. It's a madhouse out there today.

Me: Yeah, sorry for holding you up.

Gregory: See you in a couple months?

Me: You know it. Thank you.

Gregory: You are very welcome. Be good.

Me: Always.

Gregory: Yeah, right.

Enough Said

Me: Ad? Are you awake?

Adam: Yeah.

Me: Do you know what today is?

Adam: Um . . .

Me: A year.

Adam:

Me: Do you want to wish me a happy anniversary?

Adam: I don't know. Is that what one does?

Me: I don't know. But it's a year of me being cancer free. So . . . that's good.

Adam: Yeah, I guess it is.

Me: I think it's strange that my dad is flying in today.

Adam:

Me: When he called last night, he couldn't stop talking about this Cuban restaurant he heard about. It's supposed to be in Hollywood. Some place close by. The last time he was here, a salesman at Nordstrom recommended it.

Adam: Of course. Where all great restaurant recommendations come from.

Me: It's supposed to be authentic Cuban food. My dad said that certain nights of the week they have jazz music. I thought maybe we could go there tonight for dinner. A celebration of sorts.

Adam: Whatever you want.

Me: I'm gonna have to try to find it online. My dad can't remember the name or exactly where it is. He thought the name started with an *F*, though . . . I'm surprised he wants to eat Cuban. He hates garlic.

Adam: Has your father ever *had* Cuban food?

Me: Fuck knows . . . hope he realizes how much garlic they use.

Adam: You might want to mention that to him.

Me: Yeah.

Adam: Hey, bub?

Me: Yeah?

Adam: I love you.

Me: I love you too.

Adam: Bub?

Me: Yeah?

Adam: Happy anniversary.

Ring, ring.

Adam: Hello? She's right here. You want to talk to her?—It's Tess . . .

Me: Hey.

Tess: Happy anniversary! It's okay for me to be excited, right?

Me: Of course. Adam didn't even remember.

Adam: Now, that's not fair. I'm just not in any hurry to celebrate the anniversary of the worst day of my life.

Me: Tess, did you hear that?

Tess: Tell him I understand.

Me: She says she understands.

Tess: So, I wanted to find out your schedule for today. I have something I want to drop off.

Me: Oh. Um . . . well, I have a lot of cleaning to do, so I'll be home most of the morning. I think my dad gets in around three. And then I'm gonna go with him to his appointment with Gregory. So, anytime before two is fine.

Tess: I see my last client at noon, so maybe I'll drop by around one o'clock.

Me: Sounds good.

Tess: I've gotta run. I've gotta drop the cat off at the vet, finish making these cupcakes for a client of mine, and find an alternate copy of my dissertation that I *know* I have somewhere in my car.

Me: What time do you need to be at school?

Tess: Well, technically? Now.

Me: Good luck. I'll see you around one.

Tess: Bye. Love ya.

Me: Love ya.

Click.

ALL'S WELL THAT ENDS WELL:

Ring.

Me: Hello?

Mom: What are you up to?

Me: Hey, Ma. Oh, not much. Just cleaning up the guest room for Dad. I think I found that Cuban place he's been talking about. Does El Floridita sound familiar?

Mom: Not really, but I can't remember what day it is, so—

Me: I figured it would be a nice place to celebrate. I made a reservation for eight o'clock. I hope he's not too tired. I just don't think Adam can make it any earli—

Mom: Don't worry about the cleaning. I'm sure the guest room is spotless. You do too much. You never give yourself a chance to rest.

Me: What are you talking about? I just want to put clean sheets on the bed, do a couple little things in the guest bath—

Mom: What celebration?

Me: What?

Mom: Did you say something about a celebration?

Me: Yeah . . . today is my year.

Mom: Wait, what's the date?

Me: June twentieth.

Mom: I thought your anniversary was next week. I even had it marked in my calendar. Are you sure it's today?

Me: It's today. Trust me. Remember? It was a Wednesday? You got in that morn—

Mom: I will never forget when you told me. I was sitting on the bed at the . . . what's the name of that hotel down the hill from you?

Me: The Standard?

Mom: No, no, no. The one with the . . . you know . . . that . . . the blue around the pool—

Me: That's The Standard.

Mom: Well, it wasn't The Standard. I *know* The Standard. It's the one where we ate outside one time. Remember? You know which one I'm talking about . . . I think it was—

Me: The Argyle?

Mom: Is that the name of it?

Me: Well, it's the only other hotel you've stayed at on Sunset—

Mom: That must be the one, then. I'll never forget sitting on the bed, and you called from the car and said—

Me: I was in the car?

Mom: You were in the car when you told me the news.

Me: No. I was home. Trust me, I remember.

Mom: And Adam was with you.

Me: Adam, at home during a workday.

Mom: I'll never forget it. You don't forget moments like that.

Me:

Mom: You still there?

Me: Yeah, I was just thinking. A lot's happened in the last year.

Mom: Yes, it has. I wish you hadn't had to go through all of it.

Me: I don't.

Mom: What do you mean?

Me: I mean, I don't wish that it didn't happen.

Mom: How can you say that?

Me: If it hadn't happened to me, then who knows if Dad would have gone to the dermatologist, and then maybe . . . I don't know. I don't know what would have happened. Things happen for a reason. I really believe that. There's always a plan; we just can't know exactly what it is. We don't get to know it in advance. But there's a plan. It's hard to accept that sometimes. But just think, if we hadn't moved to California, and we hadn't lived up the street from the Müllers and met Janice—who introduced us to Dr. Bach in the first place—then I never would have been going to see a dermatologist, and Dr. Bach wouldn't have found my melanoma. Which means . . . which means a lot of things, most of which are bad. I wouldn't take back any of what's happened to me because I feel like it had to happen in order for Dad to be where he is, getting the vaccine and all that . . . it's all part of the plan.

Mom: Do you think you would have gotten melanoma if we hadn't moved to California?

Me: Yes. Maybe. I don't know. I think about that sometimes. I try not to think about that, sometimes.

Mom: Do you think the whole beach culture in California had anything to do with it? Would you have gone to the beach as much if we hadn't lived in California?

Me: Well, um, no, considering Georgia doesn't *have* a beach. But I don't think moving here gave me melanoma. I think I would have gotten it anyway . . . it's so weird to think about a choice, a certain decision, that seems insignificant at the time, but then you look back and see how it changed the course of an entire life. An entire family. I mean, even if we *had* moved to California, and we had lived on the same street, in the same house, everything the same, what if Janice had never mentioned Dr. Bach to you? I mean, how did it even come up in the first place? It's so weird.

Mom:

Me: I think if we had stayed in Georgia, I never would have gone to a dermatologist. No one in Georgia goes to a dermatologist. I think if we had stayed . . . I think if we had stayed, I would have died from melanoma. That's what I think. Me and Dad both.

Mom:

Me: But we *did* move, and look how well *that* turned out. Look at all the fun we've had.

Mom:

Me: I love you. None of this is your fault. You know that, right?

Mom:

Me: Mom?

Mom: Sometimes I just think—

Me: It's not your fault. You put sunscreen on me when I was a kid. That's all you could do. It was in the cards. I've gotta go. I've gotta finish this bathroom before the Tilex eats away the actual tile. I'll talk to you later.

Mom: I love you, sweetie.

Me: I love you too.

Click.

1:23 PM:

Knock, knock.

Me: Coming.

Knock, knock.

Me: I'm coming.

Knock, knock.

Me: Tess? *Tess?* Can you hear me?

Tess: Hilly? Sorry I'm late.

Me: I just put lotion on my hands and I can't turn the door kno—

I'm taking a mental picture of this moment because I don't want to ever forget it. When I'm one hundred years old, celebrating seventy-five years of being cancer free, I want to remember my best friend standing on the threshold of my front door, holding a bag of honey-nut Chex Mix in one hand and a cup of coconut sorbet in the other. Oh, and the candles. She has put these beautiful, tall, skinny red candles in the sorbet. And the candles are lit. And they are dripping. Making teeny, tiny red dots all over my sorbet, my beloved sorbet. And I don't even care because—

Tess: Happy year anniversary to you. Happy year anniversary to you. Happy year anniversary to *Hillllllllllllllyyyyyyy.* Happy year anniversary to you.

Me: Oh my God! I can't believe you!

Tess: I got the sorbet from the diner at The Standard. I know it's your favorite.

Me: I can't believe you did that. Thank you so much. I'm totally crying right now.

Tess: Yeah, me too, me too. Make a wish.

Me:

Tess: You make one?

Me: Yep.

Tess: Will you tell me what it is?

Me: Nope.

Tess: Can I guess?

Me: Nope.

AFTER THE SORBET . . . AND THE CHEX MIX:

Tess: What did your mom say? Did she wish you a happy anniversary?

Me: No. Well, after I told her it was today, she did. No, actually—technically—she didn't. She had the date wrong. She said she thought it was next week . . . she had the whole entire thing mixed up. She started telling me how she'd never forget when I told her the news, but then she went on to describe a totally wrong version of what happened. She couldn't have *been* more wrong. She combined, like, three different trips together. Whatever. I didn't have the heart to tell her. It's really not important.

Tess: How does it make you feel that your mother and husband forgot your anniversary?

Me: You are *such* a therapist right now. First of all, my mother didn't forget; she just got . . . confused. And, well, it doesn't make me feel *bad,* strangely enough. I don't know.

Tess: And what about your dad? Does he know what today is?

Me: I don't think so. I doubt it. But that's fine. It's better that way, actually . . . I don't really know how to explain it. It's like, I don't need other people to be excited for me, because *I'm* excited for me. And it's too hard for my mom to get worked up about *my* year, with all that's going on with my dad. She needs to focus her energies on him. And Adam, he didn't really forget. When I woke up this morning, I rolled over to see if he was awake, and he was lying on his back, eyes plastered to the ceiling, pulling out his chest hairs, making them into little chest-hair brushes, like mini-broomsticks. He does that when he's nervous. He knew exactly what today was; he just couldn't figure out what he was supposed to say. Actually, that was a brilliant moment. Adam, speechless. Rare.

3:45 PM:

Knock, knock, knock.

Me: Coming . . .

Ring.

Me: Shit. Hello?

Mom: Hillary?

Me: Hey, Mom.

Mom: I didn't recognize your voice. You sound out of breath.

Me: I was running to get the door. Hold on one sec. Dad just got here. *Coming!* . . . hey, welcome.

Dad: The house smells so good.

Me: Thanks. You can put your bags in the guest room. We should leave for your appointment in a couple of minutes. Traffic will be pretty bad at this hour.

Dad: You don't need to—

Me: Dad, hold on a second. I've got Mom on the phone. Mom? Hello?

Mom: I'm still here.

Me: Sorry. You called just as Dad came to the door.

Mom: Oh, I'll let you get back to your father. I just wanted to wish you a happy anniversary.

Me: Oh.

Mom: I don't think I said it when I talked to you before. Have a wonderful dinner with your father. You two deserve a celebration.

Me: Yeah, it should be nice. I hope the restaurant is good.

Mom: I'll let you go. Have fun tonight. And tell your father to call me after his appointment.

Me: Okay. I'll talk to you later.

Mom: I love you, sweetie.

Me: I love you too.

Click.

Dad: What was that about?

Me: Oh . . . um, Mom just wanted to make sure you landed safely. And she wants you to call her after your appointment. We should probably go. Traffic gets heavy right about now.

Dad: You don't need to go with me.

Me: I know. I want to.

Dad: But I'd . . . okay.

Me: Good. I'll drive.

A FINAL STOP:

Silence. My dad and I are riding a bumpy St. John's elevator to the
third floor (*our* floor) in complete silence. And even though I'm staring
up at a brown streak smeared across the top of the elevator door, and
despite the fact that my father seems to be examining a scuff on his all-
purpose/all-weather/all-season boots, it's not an awkward silence linger-
ing between the two of us. Not like so many we've shared over so many
years, so many times before. This particular silence is almost peaceful.
It's unifying. The quiet seems to be saying so much—so much about our
relationship. Our *new* relationship. It feels like it has taken so long and so
much out of both of us to create something so simple. Like it has taken an
endless stream of events to create this simple moment of peace between
my father and me.

Silence. I am comfortable with the silence. Comfortable with the
full quiet of the moment—the moment I've been waiting for for a very
long time.

Ding.

Tom: So, we've got both of you today, I see.

Me: No, I'm just here to hang out. I'm the driver.

Tom: Jon, if you're ready, you can head on back to room 4. Dr. Gregory
should be with you soon. He's not running too behind today.

Me: I'll just wait out here.

Dad: You can come back with me if you want.

Me: Oh. Okay. Yeah. If you don't mind. I don't know if I told you, I
made a reservation at that Cuban place you were talking about last night.
At least I think it's the right place. El Floridita. Does that sound right?

Dad: That's it. How did you find it?

Me: Online. It wasn't easy, though. I only found one site that had it listed under "Hollywood Cuban restaurants." It must be a local secret or something.

Dad: Did they say anything about having music?

Me: Yeah, but the band isn't playing tonight. I didn't know you were a fan of Cuban food. Wow, this room is freezing.

Dad: I usually have to leave my pants on under my hospital gown.

Me: Me too. Or I put my gown on and then put my shirt on over it.

Dad: Yeah. And I also try to remember to wear warm socks when I have an appointment.

Me: I do the same thing. I always wear my wool Eddie Bauer ski socks. The ones you got me. They are so warm. They're the best hospital socks. Do you want to put your gown on? I can go wait out—

Dad: No, no, you're fine. I'm just going to take my shirt off.

Me: Does your scar still—*oh my God.* Dad, those . . . things . . . under your arms. From the vaccine.

Dad: Where they injected me. I got ulcers at all the injection sites. They're almost healed, though.

Me: The women I met at the Positive Appearance Center had them. Do they hurt you?

Dad: In the beginning they hurt like a son of a gun. They're much better now.

Me: *This is better . . . ?*

Dad: I'm a fast healer.

Me: Yeah, I guess you are. *I guess you are.*

Knock, knock.

Dad: Come in.

Me: *Please.*

Dr. Gregory: So, it's a family affair.

Me: You know me. I just can't stay away.

Dr. Gregory: Shall we have a loo—

Me: I think I'm gonna wait outside. I'll be in the waiting room, reading my book.

I am casually walking down the hall. An up-tempo kinda casual. Okay, it's a brisk walk. *Very* brisk. All right, *fine*—it's more of a skip. A fast-paced, huge-strided skip. Like what you do when you need to get out of a situation as fast as humanly possible but don't want nurses to look at you funny. I'm sure you've been in the same situation dozens of times. You know the one I mean—the one where you discover something that literally shakes you to your core. When you finally see something that's been right in front of you all along and you can't for the life of you figure out why you didn't see it sooner. The kinda thing that forces you to jump up, move around, take a deep breath, and regroup . . .

I just saw my father as a person. Just now, right in front of me, he was flesh and blood. For the first time ever, he seemed really human. Not like a parent or an elder or even a friend. Just a person. A person not all that unlike me. Watching my dad slowly slip a hospital gown over his shoulders while carefully trying to avoid rubbing the scars that are sprinkled along the sides of his torso, I related to him on a level deeper than father-daughter. Much deeper than parent-child. I saw him as a man. As a man who wanted me to see his battle scars. As a man who wears a shirt over his hospital gown. As a man whose toes get cold—just like mine. It's *that* realization that's racing through my head as I'm fast-skipping toward the waiting room.

Dad: All right. I'm all done.

Me: That was fast. Everything looked good?

Dad: Yep.

Me: You ready to go?

Dad: You bet. Why don't you let me drive?

Me: No, you don't need to . . . okay. That would be nice.

6:25 PM:

As we drive to dinner, I'm far away. I know Adam is saying something about the traffic and my dad something about garlic, but it all seems very far away. I'm so far. A million thoughts are running through my head: images, feelings, sounds, smells. It's all twirling around, swirling, getting stirred up in the big pot that sits atop my shoulders. I'm dizzy with memories. A year's worth of memories are drowning out everything around me . . . I can't hear Adam or my father anymore. Instead I'm hearing Dr. Bach and Gregory and Lesaux and I'm smelling the hospital room where I wanted to circle the place on my stomach and I can see the crazy lady with her reindeer slippers and I can smell the aftershave on Adam's cheek as he hugged me goodbye before my surgery. The hairs on my arms are standing up, waiting at attention for the next set of sensations: my mother waving goodbye, movie theater carpet, a hanky-size hospital blanket, a dressed-up test tube, a whiff of Chanel no. 5, red candles . . . it's all washing over me. A million thoughts a second. Cold toes, an elevator ceiling, IUD string, sunscreen between my fingers, sweat on my palms, the smell of iodine, the woman without an ear, my dad's scar, the cold liquid being pumped into my vein before surgery, an army of blue dots, the weight of my volunteer badge dangling from my pocket . . .

BUT AT THE VERY, VERY END:

Me: Goodnight, dad.

Dad: 'Night. Today was a big day.

Me: It was a little hectic, I guess.

Dad: No, I mean it was an important day for you.

Me: Oh. Yeah. It was a big day.

Dad: Congratulations. On your "year."

Me: Thanks.

Dad: I like it.

Me: What?

Dad: Your ankle. Your tattoo.

Me: Ah, Mom told you. Yeah, I told Gregory it was between "brave" and a tattoo of a mole. He laughed. Sleep good.

Dad: You too.

Me: I will. Love you.

It's all here. Inside. My year. Stored up for me to play and replay, over and over whenever I want . . . even if I don't want. 'Cause even if I don't want, it will continue to play. Play and play out. And it all *means* something. Something different. It all means something to me, anyway. It all *did* something to me. I can feel it moving through me. All of it. The last year. Filling me up. I feel all . . . puffed up.

I feel full. Full of life. I feel alive.

2010

I drive. I'm a driver. That's what I do—of late. My days are spent bob-
bing and weaving through the eastside, Florence and the Machine puls-
ing in the background, the HOLLYWOOD sign just out of reach. Griffith
observatory teasing me to my right, I daydream I am up there, looking
down . . . to school and back again, ballet class, swimming, piano, gym-
nastics, art class, music class, class about how to register for the next,
best . . . class.

These are the places I can be found. And all for what? For who?
For whom?

For two of the most wildly fan-fucking-tastic kids who have ever
lived. Not that I am biased. This is truth. My older one eased her way
into this world wide-eyed and comfortable, despite an unfortunate forehead that swooped back like an eggplant from endless hours in my birth
canal—a forehead with nearly two lobes from all the pressure, and yet
she didn't seem to mind. She's never been in a big hurry. And the world
waits for her. That's Willa. She's an old soul. Been around the block a
time or two. She can look you in the eyes and know what you need,
what you need to hear, and then she'll tell it to you . . . and keep telling

it to you, and keep telling it to you—an endless diatribe of observations, advice, and predictions.

A big head with an even bigger brain. She's smart. Like, *real* smart. The good kind. The *hard* kind. The kind of smart that keeps her up at night pondering life and death, questioning why we're all here and what's the point, anyway? The kind of smart that makes a parent thrilled and terrified all at the same time. I live in constant fear of the next question. I start sweating when I hear her start slow with, "Mom, I've been wondering about something . . . " She's that rare combination of heart, soul, brains, and motormouth. That's Willa.

And then there's my second child. A child who put me on bed rest for thirty weeks. A child I bled for, a child who wasn't supposed to make it and yet practically crawled her way out of me at exactly forty weeks with little more than a grunt from my end. That's Harper. She's my warrior, a war buddy—we've been to hell and back, and so we share this unspoken bond . . . but she ages me. My eyebrows have all but turned white, and as I pencil them in each morning I catch myself whispering her name under my breath. She can be tough as nails, a real bona fide bitch, but not to me. Never to me. To me she's an angel . . . with devil horns and a weakness for all things gelatin. She's quick-witted, a Montessori workhorse, determined, imaginative, and, of course, the youngest. A second child through and through. Always plotting and planning how she can stand out, get my attention, get there first, get the last marshmallow, the last kiss, more, better, bigger, anything to beat . . . Willa.

They are my life, and so I drive. Willingly. I'm a mother now.

Me: So, girls, tell me about your day. Harper, did you talk about cornucopias?

Harper: We did a song!

Me: Great, let me hear it.

Harper: I am thankful for my fami-*lee* and for my diarrhea, poo-poo buuuuutt, butt face, pee in your mouuuth—

Willa: Harper, that's gross.

Harper: Poot.

Me: Okay, Harper, that's enough.

Harper: Penis.

Me: Seriously, Harper, I'm going to take away your allowance. What did you guys do today? Did you . . . talk about what you're thankful for? Oh, that reminds me. Willa, I doubt you remember this, but when you were in preschool, you made this place mat that said what you were thankful for. You remember what you wrote?

Willa: Something about the Earth?

Me: No, nothing about the Earth.

Willa: I know. I remember. It was about my family.

Me: No. Everyone else in your class was thankful for their family . . . movies. You said you were thankful for movies.

Willa: I did!

Harper: Well, you *do* like movies. Right, Mom, right? Willa and Dad are the same, and you and me are the same. Willa and Dad are lazy and like to watch TV, and me and you are good at putting our clothes away and don't really watch TV that much. Right?

Me: Harper, you know I don't like it when you say Willa is lazy.

Willa: But I *am* lazy!

Harper: Ask me what I'm thankful for! Ask me!

Me: You're not going to say diarrhea, are you?

Harper: I'm thankful for my best mommy in the whole wide world.

Willa: Harper, everyone says they're thankful for their mother. That's, like, what every single person in my entire class said. They were thankful for their family, their dog, blah, blah, blah . . .

Me: So, what did you say?

Willa: You're going to like this one, Mom. This is a good one.

Me: What?

Willa: Well, Alison first asked us to think about the most important thing in our life, so I said love—

Harper: Gummies! Or avocados. Can avocados be the most important thing in my life?

Me: Yeah, I . . . guess. You think avocados are more important than your family? Than me or Dad or Willa?

Harper: Well . . . I love you and Willa more than avocados, but I'm not so sure about Dad—

Me: Harper, that's a terrible thing to say—

Willa: *Can I finish what I was saying!* I said "love" and—

Me: That's very sweet. I think you're right. Love *is* one of the most important things in life.

Willa: No, no, that's not the part I wanted to tell you! Don't interrupt me! I *said* the most important thing in life is love and . . . sunscreen.

Me:

Harper: Like, for Mom.

Me:

Willa: Yeah. Like, for Mom.

Author's Note

As I write these final pages, some decade after the shock of my initial diagnosis, I realize how far I've come. In 2001, everything about my life was in question: my health, the possibly of not having children, my . . . future. I remember feeling lost, not really knowing what to do next, and yet filled with a nagging determination to beat this "thing" I was up against. To conquer and move past it—that was the mission at hand.

I can now say, with time and age and hundreds of ounces of sunscreen behind me, there is no real way to move *past* a cancer diagnosis. To move past something evokes a sense of finality, and unfortunately, with cancer, there is no actual endgame . . . except the inevitable. Staying proactive about one's health requires awareness and constant vigilance, particularly when it comes to such a worthy opponent. Fighting cancer, whether it is breast or prostate, colon or lung, is a continuous battle. The battle may not be raging every moment or in the forefront of one's mind every hour of every day, but it's never far behind. It's there, kinda wandering around, poking its ugly head into and out of the action. Yes, melanoma is a part of my history, but it is also my present and my future, and *that* I have come to accept.

In 2003, after two years of "no evidence of disease," my oncologist gave me the green light to get pregnant. I was monitored and checked and scanned and counseled, and I was grateful through it all. I was grateful for the opportunity. I never knew how much I wanted to have children as I did the moment that option was nearly taken from me.

My second melanoma was diagnosed in 2005 and again caught early. My third melanoma, well, was removed just days ago, along with a lymph node in my neck. After eight days of endless waiting, I received the "all okay" from my oncologist that the node had tested negative for melanoma—early detection continues to save my life.

My father, as he approaches his ten-year anniversary, has had no recurrence of his original tumor, nor has he had other new primaries. While I can't know for sure, I feel very strongly that the vaccine trial that he (reluctantly) participated in saved his life. A version of his treatment is still used today.

I continue to have moles removed, most of which are abnormal, precancerous, or premelanoma. This is my cross to bear. I'm done questioning or blaming. Rather, I focus my energy on protecting my girls and educating whomever will listen. Decked out in my all-black, full-body rash guard (armed with sunglasses, a hat, and a tube of water-resistant SPF), I have been called the Sunscreen Guru, the Shady Lady, the Swimming Ninja. These titles I wear willingly and proudly, because I have earned them—the hard way. And I know I am finally *doing* something . . . something important.

As for my hospital "family," I have lost touch with most all of the wonderful people I was fortunate enough to cross paths with during my time there. Ultimately, though, this story is for them. I think about them. I imagine them all living their lives—cancer free—with flowing manes of wonderfully thick hair. I know this is a fantasy; I know most of my friends lost their battle. There are few miracles, but still . . .

I like to imagine.

I hope.

I sometimes even pray.

Acknowledgments

Special thanks to Norm Aladjem for starting me on this crazy adventure, to my incredible agent, Laura Nolan, for her enthusiasm, persistence, and continued belief in me and "the cause," to my editor Brooke Warner for embracing my book's eccentricities and saying yes, to Kori Bernards for her tireless determination, to Dr. Leland Foshag for his steady hand and generous spirit, and to my team of friends and misfits, who have specifically encouraged, inspired, and supported this wild ride: Emily Ain, Julie Berk, Maya Brenner, Jill Greenberg, Kelly and Ron Meyer, Jennifer and Fred Savage, Jim and Barbra, Tim Turnham, Audrey Prins-Trachtenberg, and Patricia Weitz. Each of you, in your own way, has made this journey possible . . . and bearable.

My girls, Willa and Harper, who make me want to make them proud. Willa, you are my heart. Harper, you are my strength. Mom and Dad, I love and appreciate you both more than words. Mom, I officially forgive you for telling me I have a big forehead . . . mostly because I finally realize I *do* have a big forehead. You have always believed in my writing, even before I had anything to say. Dad, thank you for trusting me to share our story. I am inspired by your work ethic and by how you still try to buy Mom shoes every Christmas, even though she hasn't kept a single pair.

Lee and Noel, I decided early on to spare you from my crazy musings. Lee, we both know you are the writer. I hope one day you'll decide to share your writing with the rest of the world. Noel, to me, you'll always be six, have a bowl cut, and be moments away from stripping off your clothes and doing your "naked dance" in my bedroom.

Lex, you were, and always will be, my best friend. No matter how different (you think) our lives have become, you remain a constant symbol of unconditional friendship. Thank you for your love, support, and counsel. And Susan and Andrew, thank you for always being interested and listening and pushing me to finally *finish!*

Most important, my amazing husband, Adam, who has been with me since long before I could legally drink. You are my rock. You give me perspective and encouragement, always. You've taught me how to hug (tighter is better), how to cook, and how to be a wife, and you've made me a mother. Your faith in me gives me the courage to keep keepin' on. Thank you . . . for everything. I love you.

© Jill Greenberg

About the Author

Hillary Fogelson is a writer, blogger, tweeter, melanoma survivor, sun protection activist, and sunscreen guru. A graduate of NYU, she lives in the shadows of the Hollywood sign with her husband, two daughters, and Alvin the dog.

Selected Titles from Seal Press

For more than thirty years, Seal Press has published groundbreaking books. By women. For women.

Kissing Outside the Lines: A True Story of Love and Race and Happily Ever After, by Diane Farr. $16.00, 978-1-58005-396-9. Actress and columnist Diane Farr's unapologetic, and often hilarious, look at the complexities of interracial/ethnic/religious/what-have-you love.

Rocking the Pink: Finding Myself on the Other Side of Cancer, by Laura Roppé. $17.00, 978-1-58005-417-1. The funny, poignant, and inspirational memoir of a woman who took on breast cancer by channeling her inner rock star.

We Hope You Like This Song: An Overly Honest Story about Friendship, Death, and Mix Tapes, by Bree Housley. $16.00, 978-1-58005-431-7. Bree Housley's sweet, quirky, and hilarious tribute to her lifelong friend, and her chronicle of how she honored her after her premature death.

Fast Girl: Don't Brake Until You See the Face of God and Other Good Advice from the Racetrack, by Ingrid Steffensen. $16.00, 978-1-58005-412-6. The quirky, real-life chronicle of how one woman stepped outside her comfort zone, shrugged off the shackles of suburban conformity, and changed her entire perspective on life through the unlikeliest of means: racecar driving.

Dancing at the Shame Prom: Sharing the Stories That Kept Us Small, edited by Amy Ferris and Hollye Dexter. $15.00, 978-1-58005-416-4. A collection of funny, sad, poignant, miraculous, life-changing, and jaw-dropping secrets for readers to gawk at, empathize with, and laugh about—in the hopes that they will be inspired to share their secret burdens as well.

How to Die in Paris: A Memoir, by Naturi Thomas. $17.00, 978-1-58005-364-8. The edgy, poetic memoir of a young middle-class black woman who escapes a tortured past in New York to pursue a new life in Europe—only to find herself broke, desperate, and contemplating suicide on the streets of Paris.

Find Seal Press Online
www.SealPress.com
www.Facebook.com/SealPress
Twitter: @SealPress